LOVE OF BLOOD

ABOUT THE AUTHOR:

Born in Winchester, Hampshire; in1948, **Christopher Berry-Dee** is a direct descendant of Dr John Dee, Court Astrologer to Queen Elizabeth I. He served as a Royal Marines 'Green Beret' Commando, and is the former founder and Director of The Criminology Research Institute (CRI), as well as the former publisher and Editor-in-Chief of *The Criminologist* – the world's oldest and most respected journal on matters concerning law enforcement, penology, forensic psychiatry/psychology, penal reform, the judiciary, and all criminology subjects.

Christopher has interviewed and interrogated over thirty of the world's most notorious serial killers and mass murderers, and has appeared on TV as a consultant on serial homicide. He was co-producer/interviewer for the acclaimed twelve-part documentary series *The Serial Killers*, and has consulted on the cases of Fred and Rose West, Ian Brady and Myra Hindley, and Dr Harold Shipman in the TwoFour-produced TV series *Born to Kill.*

Notable book successes include: *Monster* – the book that formatted the movie about the US serial killer, Aileen 'Lee' Carol Wuornos; *Dad Help Me Please* – concerning the tragic case of Derek Bentley, who was hanged for a murder he did not commit (subsequently detailed in the film *Let Him Have It* starring Christopher Ecclestone); and *Talking with Serial Killers* – his 2003 bestselling true-crime book, and its successor volume, *Talking With Serial Killers 2.*

LOVE OF BLOOD

THE TRUE STORY OF NOTORIOUS SERIAL KILLER JOANNE DENNEHY

CHRISTOPHER BERRY-DEE

JOHN BLAKE

Published by
John Blake Publishing Limited
3 Bramber Court, 2 Bramber Road
London W14 9PB

www.johnblakepublishing.co.uk

www.facebook.com/johnblakebooks ⬛
twitter.com/jblakebooks ⬛

First published in paperback in 2015

ISBN: 978-1-78418-262-5

British Library Cataloguing-in-Publication Data:

A catalogue record for this book is available from the British Library.

Design by www.envydesign.co.uk

Printed in Great Britain by CPI Group (UK) Ltd

1 3 5 7 9 10 8 6 4 2

Papers used by John Blake Publishing are natural, recyclable products made
from wood grown in sustainable forests. The manufacturing processes conform
to the environmental regulations of the country of origin.

Every attempt has been made to contact the relevant copyright-holders,
but some were unobtainable. We would be grateful if the
appropriate people could contact us.

CONTENTS

ACKNOWLEDGEMENTS

Christopher, you are certainly pushing her [Dennehy's] *buttons.*
DCI MARTIN BRUNNING. BEDFORDSHIRE,
CAMBRIDGESHIRE AND HERTFORDSHIRE MAJOR
CRIME UNIT – EMAIL TO THE AUTHOR, 2014

Joanne Christine Dennehy is a sadistic serial murderer who claims to have killed three Peterborough men on her own. However, this book exclusively asks a shocking question; despite a massive police investigation and Crown Court trial, could two killers have actually worked hand-in-hand to commit multiple homicide? I ask whether Dennehy's accomplice could have been Gary 'Gaz' John Stretch. Never charged with any of the killings, he was only charged with two counts of attempted murder in Hereford, and three counts of preventing the lawful and decent burial of a human body. Nevertheless, had police not apprehended the pair as quickly as they did they might easily have become an even more notorious killing team than Fred and Rose West or Ian Brady and Myra Hindley.

For the most part Joanne Dennehy and Gary Stretch have

preferred to keep their mouths shut, not just to me but also the police, psychiatrists and psychologists, even their own kith and kin. But in doing so, using offender profiling skills we will try to get right inside their heads and come to learn more about what makes them tick than they themselves know.

Love of Blood is dedicated to DCI Martin Brunning, DS Andy Crocker and the officers of the Bedfordshire, Cambridgeshire and Hertfordshire Major Crime Unit, who worked the Joanne Dennehy murders. Moreover, on behalf of my publishers and myself, I extend a very special thanks to David Old of the Cambridgeshire Constabulary, who handled media enquiries during 'Operation Darcy', giving 'The Boss' blue sky to carry out his job, unhindered. David, I know you are a busy guy and I did pester you a bit, yet every time you came up trumps. And I will add to this West Mercia Police, especially DS Mark Jinks (Hereford Criminal Investigation Department). I finally got around to speaking with Mark a bit late in the day – my fault entirely – and he is yet another very busy law enforcement officer, too. Nevertheless, he came up trumps with any information I required. Thank you, Mark, and well done to your colleagues who arrested Dennehy and Stretch. Also, to Chris Ammonds (former PR Manager, Corporate Communications, Warwickshire & West Mercia Police). We should take our hats off to the West Mercia police officers who acted instantly in response to a 'Wanted for Murder' circular issued by the Cambridgeshire Constabulary for they gave it their highest response priority, most certainly stopping Dennehy and Stretch from killing again although they had tried hard enough – as in twice.

ACKNOWLEDGEMENTS

Throughout this book I have given appropriate credit to those who, in their professional capacity, assisted me as best they could. These include: Sarah Murnane –High Court Judges Clerk to sentencing judge Mr Justice Robin Godfrey Spencer. To Mr Justice Sweeney for conducting such a fair trial. Roger Davis (The Ministry of Justice, Clive Petty House, London). Governor Ms Pattison-Rideout and Deputy Director Chris Purkess (HMP & YOI Bronzefield) – you assisted me within your remit and where you possibly could. Your responses were always professional and well received by me.

Now to my colleagues, beginning with my dearest friend, investigative journalist Andy Stone, who has stuck by me through thick and thin and helped enormously with this book. Stephen Briggs – reporter for Peterborough's *The Evening Telegraph*; Louie Smith of the *Daily Mirror*; Arthur Martin, Guy Adams and Andy Dolan of the *Daily Mail* and Rob Pattinson of the *Sun*.

David Heming – Senior Coroner for Peterborough, and Mr J. R. Arnott on behalf of certified accountants Bulley Davey – Business Recovery and Insolvency Specialists. To Dr Bhatti – St Mary's Hospital, Portsmouth. Allison Stratford – NHS Trust HQ. Sue Atkins – (MAU) Queen Alexander Hospital, Portsmouth.

Most of the others I wrote to did not have the courtesy to reply to any of my letters, or they made subtle requests for a 'donation' of sorts for their cooperation – something they did *not* get.

John Treanor who lived with Dennehy, on and off, for twelve years, promised me an interview. He wasted my valuable time

– and a round trip of almost 500 miles – in spades. When I arrived at his house to talk to him, as previously arranged the day before, he was suddenly unavailable, offering an excuse one could not make up if one tried, or so it seemed to me.

I wrote to Gary Stretch. Through his lawyers, Richard Brown & Co., I was given polite, short shrift, saying their client thanked me for my letter but he had nothing more to say and didn't wish to take part in my 'project'. Then there are the parents of Joanne, Kevin and Kathleen Dennehy. Quite by getting an address wrong, I met with Kathleen for just a few minutes, during which time she was keen to say a big 'thank you' to DCI Martin Brunning. They felt unable to contribute to this book so we must respect their wishes and not intrude any further into their shattered lives, for their own heartbreak we cannot imagine. And this is echoed by a very senior medical professional, who said to me: 'Her parents must be... oh, dear me... I simply cannot imagine how they feel.'

When one picks up any book obviously the author's name can be seen on the cover, the publisher's corporate logo on the spine, but it is a massive team effort to go from a blank white page on my PC to getting the finished product into the stores or onto Amazon, or wherever else a book is advertised on the Internet.

All those at 'Team John Blake' and everyone else involved with the cover design, copy-editing, production and marketing of this book are true professionals. So, I thank my executive editor, Toby Buchan, for his skills, his patience and support, in converting my typescript into something readable. To my copy-editor Jane Donovan for going through the text with a fine-toothed comb. Also, my long-time dear friend and publisher John Blake and all of his colleagues, to include Rosie, for taking the brave move in commissioning *Love of Blood*. And bless you, Joanna, for getting the much-needed cheques out on time :).

I have not yet written a book without mentioning my writing mentor Robin Odell – undoubtedly one of the world's most authoritative crime historians – who supported me from the day I first picked up a pen and put it to paper so many years ago. Thank you so much, Robin. I have used some of your reference material in this book, giving credit where it is due. And I recall you saying to me, just as the fax machines gave way to the Internet age: 'God help us all now you have access to the Worldwide Web.'

Then there is Frazer Ashford, a first-rate TV documentary-maker and the guy who enabled me to make twelve programmes about serial killers throughout the US. He'll smile when I refer to 'The Two Minnies' on the beltway around Fort Worth, or the belly-expanding Indian breakfast someplace along US Highway 101. And, when I was once strapped down in an electric chair to experience the execution protocol, Frazer remarked: 'Something is wrong... the current is not switched on!'

On a personal level, always much love to my sister Lizzie, her husband Jim and all of 'Clan Stothard'. To my daughters, Joanna, Sasha and Zoe, and my son, Jack. Claire, Trevor and Carol, you have been very supportive of me in the writing of this book. To my long-time friend Wilf Cummings ('The Peoples' Memorial', Langstone Harbour, Portsmouth) and his partner Jan. Former Detective Sergeant Phil Swan – a former Royal Marines Commando like me, and a true all-weather friend. David 'I always bet on winners' Todd. Doctors Andy and Laura Preston for your Christian counseling and fab dinners. My co-writer on two books, Tony Brown, John Clayton. Mark, Kate, Lauren Oakley from the good ole US of A, and my Canadian friend, the award-winning actor and novelist, Alan Scarfe, author of the acclaimed *A Handbook for Attendants on the Insane: the autobiography of 'Jack the Ripper' as revealed to Clanash Farjeon*.

This has been a most difficult, oft times heartbreaking project, not only in the research but also to write up. The genesis for *Love of Blood* came with a news cutting, quickly followed by a letter from Joanne Dennehy herself, who indicated her full cooperation from the outset. Then she reneged. When we disagreed on something, like all sociopaths she rebelled in an effort to wrestle back control. Communication between us withered on the vine. However, what started as an exercise in studying the life and crimes of Joanne Dennehy became so much more. It turned into a journey along a 'Murder Road' that led to an abyss and that abyss looked back at me, as it will you, when you read through the pages that follow.

As this book illustrates one does not become a serial murderer overnight and the same applies to an investigative criminologist. It has taken decades of working with killers, law enforcement, penal reform, the judiciary, attorneys, victims' next-of-kin, psychologists, psychiatrists, general medical practitioners and everyone concerned with protecting society from these highly dangerous people to bring all of my knowledge and investigative skills to the pages you are about to read.

Therefore, historically, I thank all of my friends and colleagues in the US and in the UK. To list everyone's name would far exceed the allocated word count, however, the FBI, FDLE, US Marshals Service, the Metropolitan Police, Avon and Somerset Constabulary, and HM Customs & Excise 'Special Investigations', the St Petersburg (Russia) State Police and the Singapore Homicide Police are amongst them. Moving down from there, I thank the numerous state and county law enforcement jurisdictions I have worked with, and over the years I have been granted exclusive access to offenders held in 'Super-Max' correctional facilities throughout the US. These include Federal institutions as well. Indeed my old pal Russell J. Kruger, Chief Investigator, Minneapolis PD, who worked the Harvey Carignan serial homicide cases, once remarked to a journalist: 'I just don't understand Chris Berry-Dee. He's the only guy I know who is trying to get into prisons when everyone else is trying to get out. These Brits are not right in the head, ya know!'

Back in 2003, when I was director of the Criminology Research Institute (CRI), I submitted a book on killers to Virgin True Crime. Within a day the commissioning editor informed me this most certainly was *not* the sort of book that would appeal to their elderly readers. Two hours later I received a call back: 'Christopher, after some thought we think that all of our readers might enjoy it very much.' *Monsters of Death Row* is still published today.

With this in mind I stress that *Love of Blood* is not for the faint-hearted. Parts of it should carry a Government Health Warning because it might well damage your health. Writing it became not a nice place to be because it touches on extremely delicate matters that will shock the most loving parent to the core. That said, if one is inclined to study the motivations that compel people such as Joanne Dennehy to repeatedly kill, we are also obliged, however distasteful it might seem, to examine every aspect of her life and the lives of her associates. But along with Gary Stretch, Dennehy represents just two of the pieces in the jigsaw. We need all of the pieces to complete the story, and then ask, why?

Finally, I sincerely thank all of my readers, past and present, not only for buying my books but for your constructive letters and emails, too. Also to the booksellers for in this respect you are very much part of the team and, to echo these sentiments, let me lead you ever so gently by the hand to the edge of the abyss that is homicide at its most foul and then, without a moment's hesitation, I'll launch you in!

CHRISTOPHER BERRY-DEE

FOREWORD

*Joanne Dennehy despises weakness but she is
completely addicted to weakness and the experiencing
of her own power over men.*
CLAIRE HARRIS

As my regular readers already know, I speak as I find. Therefore, I make no apologies for the tone of this foreword since it will set you up for the remainder of the book. No fancy words, no cosy prose from Christopher, I can assure you of that because I'm about to take you on a journey along a 'Murder Road' and straight into a dysfunctional woman's mind, a place as black as the grave.

I'm not going to sugarcoat the text of this book with 'establishment lingo', or use fancy phrases to try and come across as some kind of expert in my field. Serial homicide is serial homicide whichever way you cut the cake. The individuals who commit such terrible deeds and those who associate and conspire with them are not worthy of the air decent people breathe.

At this point I need to clear something up. Despite numerous press articles who call her 'Joanna', her correct Christian name - the name used by her in her letters, in prison records, by police, the Crown Prosecution Service and at trial, is 'Joanne', and I am not going to sugarcoat Joanne Christine Dennehy, either. Middle-class, Home County English born and bred, she is, however, the first woman in UK, US indeed world criminal history to have stuck a knife deep into three men, killing them all. She is also the attempted murderer of two other men.

As for Joanne's former partner, the father of her two children? Over an intermittent period of twelve years John Treanor merely stood by, repeatedly cuckolded, verbally abused, punched by her and given black eyes, yet he loved, and wanted, Joanne even more.

Over a period of 25 years I have interviewed, face-to-face, more than thirty of the world's most notorious serial killers and mass murderers. I have entered into lengthy correspondence with many more. It is a matter of public record that I have cleared up cold-case homicides in the United States, and it is always the same: blood-spattered walls, carpets, soft furnishings, white goods, cars and sidewalks. Victims being police officers, the elderly or mentally retarded, men, women, children of all ages, unborn and newborn babies; their bodies dumped where they were killed, or placed in rapidly-dug holes in the ground, ditches and sewers.

I have sat with these human predators on death rows throughout the United States, where the reeking, sweet stench of cheap disinfectant, human sweat and evil personified permeates every brick of these correctional warehouses incarcerating those from the Legion of the Damned.

I have listened to their sickening, gut-wrenching tales of murder most foul; their boasts, intermingled with chuckles of glee, while they recounted how they caused so much suffering to their victims well beyond the comprehension of normal souls like you and me.

I have witnessed a good few executions: the hangman's halter in Singapore and Pakistan, the 'Goodnight Juice' (lethal injection in 'The Lone Star State') or a final sit down in 'Ole Sparky' in Florida, sending the condemned to perdition.

In the Washington State Penitentiary, at Walla Walla, I requested the entire Death Row tier population be unlocked. They sat around me in a circle, drinking Coke and eating the candy I had brought in, fascinated that an Englishman had decided to come to their home – their own 'Green Mile'. No threats to me at all because 'Dead Men Walking' are laid-back and, unless a stay of execution is granted, accepting of their fate; respectful, too. For two hours during this unique encounter they recalled their terrible crimes, with the strap board, the gallows, the noose, the long drop just a well-manacled, short stumbling walk away.

These murderous sociopaths/psychopaths – whatever label one would wish to tie around their necks – love to play mind games. Most often cunning as hyenas, they are control freaks who attempt to manipulate everyone with whom they come into contact, which prompts the chilling question: what chance did their vulnerable, often gullible, prey have against such twisted characters who can, at face value, appear as nice as the man or woman living next door?

These monsters have killed in every way imaginable: electrocution, running over using a vehicle, pushing over a precipice, throttling, drowning, manual strangulation, shooting, stabbing, flaying alive, bludgeoning, poisoning, hanging and burning.

One of my subjects superglued his helpless victim's lips and nostrils together, then sat by and watched while she died a terrible death. Suffocation by asphyxiation using a plastic bag is a common enough method but another pair of serial killers used a plastic bag into which they piped coal gas. One fugitive from the law even blew up a Tallahassee cop with a bomb placed inside a Sharpe microwave oven. How did he do that?

Think of any way of murdering a person and these people have already done it. I have met Phillip Carl Jablonski. He once ate a woman's eyeballs and cut off her nipples, carving his signature into her flesh before she expired.

Another monster, the aptly named Frederick Alan Gore, kidnapped schoolgirls and young women, raped and then spread-eagled them from a beam in his cellar, flaying them inch by inch at a time, gutting them like deer as they slowly died in agony, their entrails spilling onto a sawdust-covered floor. His exclusive confessions to me have been published in one of my books, helping fast-track his execution.

Tasked with caring for mentally retarded Louis 'Buddy' Musso, forty-four-year-old Suzanne Margaret Basso, and her son James O'Malley tortured and beat helpless Buddy for weeks while claiming his social benefits payments for themselves. In

1998, they bathed the hapless man in scalding hot water and scrubbed the blisters with a wire brush, poured cleaning fluid down his throat and then, when he eventually died, his body was dumped by the side of Main Street, Galena Park, Texas – and this wasn't Basso's first murder, either!

Then there was the now-executed Willie Seth Crain, a Florida lobster fisherman by calling, who, in 1998, kidnapped and raped seven-year-old Amanda Brown before placing her still-living body in one of his pots to let crabs finish off the work he had already started. But never before had I come into contact with a woman who was a sado, sexually driven homicidal maniac until I became involved with Joanne Christine Dennehy – a killer, whom, by the enormity of her crimes, the way she treated her victims leaves the notorious US serial killer Aileen Wuornos in the shade.

There is killing and there is killing. It is not the final body count that matters so much, more the manner in which all of her victims were slaughtered that makes Joanne Dennehy so evil.

During my frequent journeys along 'Murder Road' I am always desperately seeking some form of redeeming factor that might come from any of the cases I am investigating. As yet I have discovered not a single one, not even a snippet nor a micro-speck of decency anywhere to be found.

Aside from the principal character – self-confessed sexually sadistic, personality disordered sociopath Joanne Dennehy, whose body should now be rotting in a lime-filled grave behind prison walls, the entire supporting cast of her associates lack any decency whatsoever. So, please, *please* do not ask me if they are of the Anglican faith, or have a scrap of faith in *any* faith, in themselves, in anyone else to include their own friends and family, or in life's richly embroidered tapestry, because they haven't – full stop! The only time any of them may visit a church will be at their own funerals.

All of Joanne's accomplices in crime are pathological liars: bone-idle, money-grabbing social benefit scroungers who couldn't tell the time of day with an alarm clock hung around their necks. Weak-willed, sexual deviants, degenerate drug users, alcoholics and thieves; with what pickled brains Dennehy's male halfwit buddies have left snuggly tucked into their underpants, genitals ruling their heads – the etymology of 'dickheads', if you will.

Notwithstanding this, the more I searched for something good to say about any of them the worse it got. Desperately seeking a glimmer of hope, a light at the end of a tunnel if you will? It was downhill all the way.

Like peeling an onion, layer by layer the more the smell of this case made my eyes screw up. This book will make yours water, too. Here, you will find true accounts that will break your heart. Conversely, this book could make your blood boil incandescent with rage.

During the research for a work such as this on the face of it seems appropriate for the writer to focus on the murders and the killer's *modus operandi* (method of operating) and *modus vivendi* (literally, their way of living) because we all want to know the gory facts, don't we? Such crimes put bums on seats in cinemas, help TV ratings with no-holds-barred documentaries and offer up juicy, exclusive interviews for the press. Dig deeper, however, and one enters a sewer of human depravity – one we should not dare enter because the stench is just too great. Nevertheless, having wallowed around in the filth where these bottom feeders live, and having examined such characters under a forensic microscope, I promise you there will be a few laughs along this particularly heinous 'Murder Road', just to lighten your load.

I say this, while at once offering great respect to those lives lost and those left behind with their grief. Just like many of us, homicide police are normal people, with families and kids. In order to emotionally survive the grim work they undertake on *our* behalf – and these cops never take the horrors of their work home – they must become 'Brothers in Arms' and with this at times comes humour. It is the only way they can make it through just to lighten their load too. In the US, I have helped law enforcement locate buried bodies. I've been there when pathetic human remains have been exhumed from some marshy, mosquito-infested wood, or tugged out of a drain. Just as Cambridgeshire police reverentially treated the corpses of Dennehy and Stretch's victims found in ditches, cops do the same worldwide. Always solemn, yet highly professional occasions, with a cold beer afterwards just to lighten the load.

INTRODUCTION

In the letter you have written to me you say, in terms, that you do not feel any remorse for the murders, and to claim otherwise would be a lie. Within the space of ten days you murdered three men in cold blood. You are a cruel, calculated, selfish and manipulative serial killer.
MR JUSTICE SPENCER, A PRESIDING JUDGE OF THE SOUTH-EAST CIRCUIT, SENTENCING JOANNE DENNEHY, 28 FEBRUARY 2014

Do not choose a career in serial homicide without a love of blood, but blessed with a solid, middle-class upbringing, Joanne Dennehy was a teenager who had the ability to become anything she wanted.

Joanne was bubbly, highly intelligent, pretty and well spoken yet she later became obsessed, then overwhelmed by fantasies of committing abnormal sadomasochistic acts during which she would revel in the infliction of pain and humiliation on her victims before murdering them. She came to despise weak men, while at once addicted to seeking out their weakness and enjoying her power over them. Some say that she actually wanted to be a man. This is incorrect – she wanted to be better than a man, to do as she wished with them, and so she did.

1

Some of these types of deviants prefer to be the recipient of pain. Others like to inflict it. Dennehy is a sadomasochist, enjoying both. To her, every self-inflicted Stanley knife slash across her abdomen, every sharp needle she stuck into herself, every brutal killing was 'Value Added' to her warped psychopathology and varied psychoses. She didn't leave a light footprint, either.

Today, Dennehy sits in a cell at HMP Bronzefield, Ashford, Surrey. Alone with her inner demons to keep her company, she is now a bloated, shaven-headed shadow of the once pretty teenager she used to be. Because she was found to be legally sane, she can receive no meaningful treatment for her psychopathy. There will come a time when her condition deteriorates, her conduct becoming even more bizarre. Now in her thirties at least she has got something to live for – and that is dying.

> *I like to be beaten, sliced/stabbed amongst other things.*
> *I'm not sure I consider myself dangerous. I'd say im* [sic]
> *best kept happy. Killing you better is better for me.*
> Joanne Dennehy to a pen friend

When a personality changes from a Dr Jekyll to a Mrs Hyde the result can be one of extreme evil. Joanne Dennehy is unique in the black annals of British criminal history: she has become the first female offender to be sentenced to a natural life term by a sitting judge. Previously, successive Home Secretaries had endorsed full life tariffs upon serial killers Rosemary West, Myra Hindley and Beverley Allitt. Therefore, Joanne Dennehy is, unquestionably, one of the most malevolent sadistic alter egos within our prison system today.

Well done, Inmate A0616A DENNEHY Joanne. Congratulations, you win first prize! But with the notorious Rosemary West once living in the next prison cell, Joanne will be well fed and watered, receive first-rate medical attention, have her teeth filled when required, allowed all of the centrally-heated and air-con facilities afforded under her Human Rights till the end of her days. Indeed, shortly after her sentence was handed down in February 2014, we find her prancing about in her next-to-nothings as one of the cast of a performance titled *Sister Act*, all costing *circa*170,000 of the taxpayers' money to entertain hundreds of guests who paid up to 40 a ticket. Yet, the show must have made a serious financial loss.

Nevertheless, with any chance of Joanne obtaining a reduction in her natural life sentence then winning the sympathy of a misguided parole panel now kicked out of the window, any last-ditch sucking up to the Church with phoney claims of having 'Seen the Light' will fall upon deaf ears. The Almighty will not be at home if she rings His bell. So, I guarantee you this much, Joanne will not see Heaven. Let's count our blessings for she will never be a free woman again. She'll only be released back into society wearing a pine box – and not an ornate one with brass furniture at that.

Attempted murder and murder is nothing. It's like going down for a Sunday roast, easy!
Joanne Dennehy, statement to police April 2013

Prior to Dennehy's sentencing on Friday, 28 February 2014, in Court Two at the Central Criminal Court, Old Bailey, numerous other UK female killers had also served what are euphemistically called 'Natural Life' terms with their lives abruptly terminated by execution.

Aside from the three other UK female 'serial killers' referred to later in this book, as far as capital punishment is meted out perhaps the most notorious case was the hanging of peroxide blonde nightclub manageress twenty-eight-year-old Ruth Ellis for the shooting of her unfaithful lover, twenty-four-year-old racing driver David Blakely. The murder was committed as he left a North London public house on 10 April 1955 to walk to his car. Yes, he was a bit of a ladies' man, a 'Love Rat' at best, and today a jilter lover might resort to slashing his shirts and suits, significantly altering the bodywork of his Porsche with a liberal application of paint remover and then posting his indiscretions all over Facebook. Therefore, blowing holes in the cheater using a Smith & Wesson revolver would be considered extreme.

At her trial, in June 1955, Ellis, was asked what she intended when she fired the gun. She replied, 'I intended to kill him.' In fourteen minutes the jury found her guilty and she was executed on the gallows at Holloway Prison on 13 July 1955.

An earlier execution was the controversial 9 January 1923 hanging of twenty-eight-year-old Edith Thompson. A bookkeeper and manageress who worked for a City of London millinery firm, she, with her lover Frederick 'Freddie' Bywaters, a twenty-year-old ship's writer with the P&O line, provided a murder drama that has since inspired many books and plays. The hapless victim was Edith's husband, Percy. Four years her senior he was a shipping clerk, and the couple lived a humdrum life in Ilford, Essex.

On 3 October 1922, as the Thompsons were returning home together from a London theatre, Freddie stabbed Percy and disappeared into the night. Edith called for help for her dying husband. The following day she named her lover and both were charged with murder, the motive being established as getting rid of an obnoxious rival. Love-struck Edith was convicted solely on the evidence of sexually explicit love letters sent to Bywaters, all of which barely hinted at conspiracy to murder and little else.

Both accused were found guilty and sentenced to death. At the same hour on 9 January 1923, Bywaters was hanged at Pentonville Prison and Edith was hanged at HMP Holloway.

These days we live in more enlightened times. The death penalty has long been abolished. Any woman convicted of crimes such as those committed by Thompson and Ellis would face no more than a slap on the wrist in punishment terms.

Sado-sexual serial killers Myra Hindley, Rose West and Joanne Dennehy are another breed altogether for they didn't cross the line into a one-off homicide because of jealousy or getting rid of a rival; they killed because for them it was fun to kill. They glorified in murder and enjoyed the thrill of inflicting human suffering beyond the imagination of our worst Stephen King nightmares coming true.

Dennehy plunged her 3-inch lock knife [not the serrated dagger she holds in the notorious on-the-run from police photos] into her victims over and over again. The first man simply popped round to see her on the promise of something more than a peck on the cheek. Her second victim was fast asleep in his bed and drunk. A third dressed up in one of her black, sequined dresses in anticipation of kinky sex. The two men she attempted to kill in Hereford were simply walking their dogs in broad daylight. In several cases her knife dried black with their blood and it covered her clothes and bare skin. She reeked of it and she licked it off her fingers; while doing so she laughed and laughed.

In the West case, Rose participated throughout with her husband, Fred. The pair methodically trawled for most of their victims in their Ford Anglia car. Once back at their squalid home in Cromwell Street, Gloucester, their prey were taken down into the basement, stripped naked, raped, gagged and hung from a beam before some of them were slowly flayed alive, with necrophiliac acts being committed on the corpses.

Twenty-four-year-old Myra Hindley, along with wannabe Nazi, porn-driven Ian Brady, aged twenty-eight, participated in the most dreadful murders of three young children committed between 1963 and 1965, then buried the bodies on marshy Saddleworth Moor, north of Manchester. As trophies of their crimes this sick couple audiotaped the dying distress of one of their victims before snapping photos of each other posing at the burial sites.

I killed to see how I would feel, to see if I was as cold as I thought. Then it got moreish and I got a taste for it.
Joanne Dennehy to Dr Farnham during psychiatric examination, 26 October 2013

INTRODUCTION

Simply because she wanted to, Joanne Dennehy stabbed three men to death in Peterborough before attempting to kill two more in the City of Hereford. She loves the enormity of her crimes. The suffering she has caused is of no consequence to her. These are not matters that cause her loss of sleep for where there should be a conscience there is zero.

Yet this woman has the gall to profess that she would never hurt a woman, or a woman with a child, indeed ever harm a child, when she has achieved this in spades. And when you look into her eyes they resemble those of a Great White shark: unblinking, dead, devoid of feeling, emotion and conscience, so she is a scary woman, indeed.

> *Dennehy struck Robin Bereza like in the film* Pyscho, *thrusting and putting her whole weight behind it. The blade of the knife was as black as the handle with blood. She stank of blood. Afterwards, Gary drove off very, very calmly. It was as if they had just stopped for a McDonald's.*
> Mark Lloyd, giving evidence against Dennehy and Stretch at trial

Stabbing and hacking murders committed solely by women are *very* interpersonal, hands-on, extremely rare affairs, so infrequent that serial murderer Dennehy broke all the rules. Therefore, her case is completely unique. It is the first of its type in British and US criminal history, for here we have the first female serial killer who used a knife.

America's most notorious female serial murderess was bisexual Aileen 'Lee' Carol Wuornos, an interstate hooker

7

who had sex with at least 200 men, killing six of them using a .22-calibre revolver. But shooting a man in his body, or in the face at point-blank range, is a lot less personal than plunging a blade into a living person time and again during a fit of demonic rage. As any soldier will testify, shooting someone is one thing, sticking a bayonet in him entirely different. Killing with a firearm is 'disconnected', Thrusting cold steel into living flesh is something else.

Manual strangulation by ligature or using one's hands is another full-contact means of killing. It is a method avoided by women for the most obvious reasons. But don't believe what you see on TV because manual strangulation takes effort and time. Even the strongest male serial killers I have interviewed have admitted to me that their victims writhed around, kicked out and fought back; that their hands and fingers cramped up, only for them to release their stranglehold, massage their hands before reapplying their grip sometimes for as long as ten minutes before death supervened.

Knives are full contact weapons. Their wounds are classified either as 'incised wounds' – where the edge of the blade makes cutting gashes to the body, often during a struggle and frequently on the hands and arms of a victim trying to protect himself – known as 'defensive wounds', or there are 'stabs'. Stabs are where the point of the knife goes into the body followed by the length of the blade. While incised wounds tend to generate a great deal of blood, often there will be little external haemorrhaging from stabs – the danger in this case being damage to the internal organs, causing internal bleeding from which death may result.

INTRODUCTION

Using a study 3-inch lock knife, Joanne rammed the blade into throats, lungs and hearts with so much force it penetrated, in one murder, a sternum and broke nine ribs. This woman shed a lot of blood.

People have a preconceived idea of who I am, or the way a serial killer should behave.
Joanne Dennehy, letter to the author, 24th February 2014

One can partly understand the emotions that promote *crimes passionels*, so I personally feel some compassion for Edith Thompson and Ruth Ellis. However, for my part and this is only my opinion, if anyone deserved to be strung up it has to be Rose West, Myra Hindley, child nurse Beverley Allitt *and* Joanne Dennehy. At least Fred West and Dr Shipman saved us the trouble of expensive trials in committing suicide by hanging themselves beforehand. Nevertheless, we should have held street parties, inflated coloured balloons and popped them to celebrate with huzzas, hurrahs, and made merry when child killer Hindley went ashes-to-ashes, dust-to-dust, so no climbing out of a rotting coffin to haunt us again for her.

1

THE MARK OF CAIN?

*She looks like butter wouldn't melt in her mouth
until she opens her bloody mouth.*
MARK LLOYD, WITNESS AT THE TRIAL OF
DENNEHY AND STRETCH

When you pick up a book like this you might be forgiven if you expect that the person making up the subject matter possesses some evil characteristic that sets him or her apart from the rest of us. Most times, to some extent this is true, but the characteristic is not visible. It is not a physical stigma that these serial killers wear like the Mark of Cain. No, the characteristic is lodged deep within the dark souls of such individuals. These human aberrations have killed in a way by which they have demonstrated a quality of evil that transcends our comprehension through several acts of terrifyingly brutal murder. However, to several people who knew Joanne she seemed perfectly normal – at times as if butter wouldn't melt in her mouth.

Joanne is 5ft 8 in tall, and was about a size ten before she went to prison. 'Scrubbed up with a little "slap" [make-up], which she put on with a trowel,' remarked one of her few existing female friends, 'she is quite pretty, especially when she does her hair and got into her thigh-length boots with killer heels.' There are several photos of Joanne on the Internet with her hair styled. It suits her, as I think most women might agree?

In truth, Joanne came from good stock and a healthy gene pool. Her father is a handsome, no-nonsense man; her mother is attractive and could easily pass for someone ten years her junior. And, this is the dichotomy of Joanne, one that followed her everywhere. Intelligent, musically talented, sporty, well spoken when it suits her, some may say attractive; she was undoubtedly an outrageous flirt, even dangerous – the type of personality that some men, and women, are irresistibly drawn to, like pins to a magnet.

Joanne Dennehy had a full figure. However, the notorious 'on-the-run' photo of her posing on a Hereford council flat balcony, dressed in blue jeans, handcuffs dangling from a wide, black leather belt, brown suede boots, a grey cap and grey knitted sweater pulled up to expose a red bra and her self-harmed stomach do her no favours at all. She has a tongue stud, a star – or is it a green reversed pentagram, the mark of evil – tattooed on her right cheek, a pleasant face, but she is a volcano waiting to explode, for sure. Now, take a long look at her police mugshot. Here, her hair is lank, unwashed, lacking any vitality at all. Those eyes are cold as the grave and if you upset her, you might have ended up in one, too.

Those who have met Joanne Dennehy in more convivial times assure me that she attracted men simply because of her outgoing, laid-back nature. 'There was no bullshit attached to her,' one friend said, adding, 'Jo had been around the block. Okay, she went off the hook but she knew what time it was. She was "Miss Confidence", who flirted with most men. But she didn't tolerate fools lightly.'

Another person told me: 'Joanne loved animals, especially dogs, perhaps more than people. I got the impression that she couldn't hurt a fly.' But the man, who does not wish his identity to be revealed in this book, added, somewhat ominously, 'In group gatherings she often sat back and didn't participate, like she was people-watching. Jo could smell bullshit, and their lies, a mile away. It really pissed her off cos she really does hate liars with a passion. She would sit there taking it all in, then suddenly she would flip, and I mean *really* flip. Then everyone's attention would turn to her.'

The lies being told about me, about things I'm meant to have said or done are too numerous for me to care about... now you are really getting my back up.
Joanne Dennehy, letter to the author, 8 June 2014

I was also fortunate to have been contacted by a former 'girlfriend' of Joanne's. We met in a cafand the woman in question – although much older than Dennehy is now – told me about their relationship lasting but a few weeks. She summed up the affair, saying:

'We hit it off from the start. Jo was great fun. She was very protective of me. I sensed she was a butterfly but I did love her very much, Christopher. She would "glass" anyone who pissed her off, no question about it. She always had a knife, or a razor blade, on her. Yes, she did have a boyfriend. They had a couple of daughters. According to her he was a drip. Our sexual relationship? That is between Jo and me. Please respect that. I want to remember her as I knew her, *not* what is reported in the papers.'

I ended the interview by asking: 'How did you feel when you learned that Joanne had killed three men?' Her answer was diplomatically to the point:

'Me? I treat people as they treat me. Jo was good to me. I sensed she lived on the edge, I knew that she could be very dangerous. She lived life on the edge, that was part of my attraction to her. I have written to her in prison, but I've had no reply.'

John Treanor had an on-off relationship with Joanne Dennehy spanning twelve years. The father of her two daughters, he found much to love in her. At other times he witnessed the flip side of her psychopathological coin. One moment she was sweet as chocolate pudding, moments later she became the Phal from Hell.

Then there are Joanne's two daughters. As we will learn later, theirs is a tragic tale indeed. One day they may want to know their 'real mum', at once enquiring whether she is that evil after all. Blood is thicker than water, or so they say. By then, of course, Joanne Dennehy will be old and grey; hopefully a little more compassionate and mentally mature, perhaps. Somehow I doubt that day will ever come. Nevertheless, we'll meet John Treanor later. He will tell you his own story.

Joanne's parents, and her 29-year-old sister, Maria, have washed their hands of her. We cannot blame them. She has made their lives a misery; then again Joanne washed her hands of her parents when she was just fourteen years old. Just over a decade later, she falsely boasted to several people that she had spent a long time in prison for killing her father because he had sexually abused her as a little girl when that would have been the last thing on his mind.

Because she is a high-risk 'Category A' prisoner I have not met Joanne Dennehy, nor will I ever be allowed to. In the UK such visits are only granted to immediate next of kin, although I have circumvented the system in the past – notably with Michael Sams, a Category-A prisoner who, for a while, was incarcerated at HMP Full Sutton. Sams murdered Julie Dart in July 1991 and kidnapped and imprisoned estate agent Stephanie Slater for ransom in January 1992.

Approaching a red stoplight most people apply the brakes. During her ride along 'Murder Road' Joanne Dennehy chose not to. She drove on regardless of the consequences and therefore the purpose of this book, while pulling no punches, is not to condemn Dennehy but instead strives to understand her... and then crucify her.

And this will appeal to her sadomasochistic nature for her response will likely be: 'I don't give a fuckin' shit!'

So, let's start at the beginning.

2

EARLY YEARS

There was a girl we loved and then turned into a monster. I don't think you can actually describe it in any other way. I don't think I want to understand how such a human being is capable of doing so much damage. My parents doted on her. My sister was very academic and used to read books and liked to learn, and she played the flute and the recorder.
MARIA DENNEHY TO *DAILY MAIL* REPORTER
ANDY DOLAN, THURSDAY, 13 FEBRUARY 2014

Born a Virgo, Sunday, 29 August 1982, in sleepy St Albans, Hertfordshire, to security guard Kevin Dennehy and grocery store manager, Kathleen, Joanne was the first of two daughters – the second being Maria, who followed two years later. Her parents were decent and hardworking. Wanting somewhere a little larger to live, the family relocated to a semi-detached, four-bedroom house situated in Harpenden.

The present owners of 47 Longfield Road are a polite, friendly Asian couple who moved into the property four years ago and have since refurbished throughout. I spoke to them while they were seat-belting their youngsters into a silver-grey people carrier. They vaguely recall that the Dennehys had previously lived there, but a neighbour remembered, 'Yes, you mean *the* Dennehys? They were nice people. Jo went to school with my son. She seemed perfectly normal to me.'

Maria says that her sister Jo always had time for her. They shared secrets, but Maria's favourite memories are of the times when Joanne would make up lyrics to songs and sing them to her. Referring perhaps to the St Alban's address – because there has never been a tree in the back garden at 47 Longfield Road – she said: 'There was a big tree in our back garden and we would climb it and sit on the branches, singing in the evenings after school. When we were younger we did a lot of sporty things together. We even made up a secret language that we used all the time. There was a deep bond between us.'

At the time of writing, now aged twenty-nine, Maria, a former Army signaller who completed a six-month tour in Helmand Province, Afghanistan, who has also worked for NATO, hopes that Joanne, 'never sees daylight again.'

You had a perfectly decent and proper upbringing and the advantage of a good home.
Mr Justice Spencer, sentencing remark to Dennehy

Without doubt, Joanne enjoyed all the benefits of a middle-class upbringing in the Home Counties. She was a clever pupil who, initially, got on well with her teachers and her peers, although she did spend a lot of time daydreaming and looking out of windows during classes, recalled one of her tutors who does not wish to be named. 'Her English was good. She had an interest in history, although not too good at math. She was more inclined to the rough and tumble in the gym.' This is confirmed by the fact that Joanne played in the Roundwood Park School netball and hockey teams. The pretty, dark-haired girl was a GCSE student and a keen musician, with her parents paying for private music lessons. Without doubt, as Mr Justice Spencer pointed out at sentencing, her parents had invested all of their love and hard work in providing their two daughters with a good start in life.

If Joanne Dennehy had become a solicitor, I think she would have been a good one.
DCI Martin Brunning, to the author at interview 2014.

While Maria had her own ambitions so too did Joanne. Kevin and Kathleen dreamed of Jo going to university to study law and becoming a lawyer. Then something awful happened. It came completely out of blue skies when, in 1996, now aged fourteen, she met an eighteen-year-old fairground worker then ran away from home with him. Her parents were devastated.

Joanne was soon located in a Milton Keynes hostel, to be brought back kicking and shouting. Tragically, this proved to be the first rebellious act in her transformation from studious schoolgirl to drug-addled, self-harming, sadomasochistic sadistic serial murderess. She began associating with much older boys, who introduced her to alcohol, then to 'skunk' – which has been linked to mental illness and the scrambling of a user's brain – and then onto cocaine. This prompted what Maria has called a 'radical change' in Joanne's behaviour for she became increasingly rebellious, violent and argumentative.

One of the early signs that a child is reaching emotional

adolescence is that he, or she begins to exercise power. Sometimes that power takes the form of a direct confrontation or challenge to adult authority, but this challenge is normal. If the authority – in this case Dennehy's parents – responds to the challenge in a supportive fashion and does not seek to crush the adolescent, the youngster grows to accept an adult interpretation of it and the social order and can deal with it. But Joanne was unable to do so – the skunk and the booze were seeing to that.

When disappointment is constantly experienced, when a youngster's desires are thwarted and their needs go unmet, when faced with rejection, or when made to feel powerless by self-perceived, seemingly unreasonable authority figures, children, especially during adolescence, sometimes react with extreme anger and resentment towards all those who are in a position to exert control over their environment. This is sometimes referred to as 'cutting off one's own nose to spite one's face'. One way of reacting is by rebelling. Sometimes children misbehave by turning their backs on those who are most important to them. In Joanne's case she rebelled against her parents and her teachers in a case of: 'I will reject you before you reject me'. Ultimately, this kind of insubordination is self-destructive and self-negating. The child blows up over anything and even trivial incidents lead to fights, arguments and tantrums.

According to the professionals I consulted with during the research for this book, at the very heart of all of this is 'adolescent problem solving'. An adult with knowledge of life and people skills is used to solving problems while the still-maturing adolescent has very little experience of either. Joanne's parents used all their parenting skills to try and straighten out their daughter and a normal youngster would have challenged them in a healthy way.

A youngster who gets into trouble may be 'grounded' by their parents or sent to their room for an hour or so. Pocket money may be withdrawn. They may not be allowed out with their peers, and so forth. However, by the age of fourteen Joanne was hooked on alcohol and skunk. Under the influence of these toxic substances she was becoming mildly paranoid and, as the result of this, what limited problem-solving skills she did have were being eroded.

I have no doubt that Joanne's parents tried desperately hard to rein in their daughter, but they were trying to communicate with a youngster who was developing a serious behavioural disorder. Already she was evidencing the early signs of schizophrenia-like reactions. Jo was behaving aggressively and involving herself in antisocial activities which might have been red flags indicating a downhill spiral into more serious criminal activity for the months and years to follow. It became a domestic bush fire that grew and grew – a vicious circle for parents, teachers and Joanne herself alike. The more she was told: 'You must' or 'You will', the strong-willed teenager responded with more of, 'Fuck off. I'll do what I want to. No one can tell me what to do.' If a parent touched her during one of these emotional outbursts she would sometimes strike them back. She would later do this with John Treanor when he remonstrated with her during their long-term partnership.

More and more Joanne skipped school. This wild child started stealing money from her parents to buy drink and drugs. When discovered and scolded, she verbally and physically abused them. Reprimanded by her teachers she became disruptive in class. On one occasion, and drunk, she threw an empty bottle of whisky through a classroom window, shattering the glass before climbing through it herself. The former teacher explained to me: 'Her attendance record literally plummeted overnight. My other pupils were scared of her, as I was, too. But, what can one do? Joanne became uncontrollable.'

Now drinking heavily and her normal sensibilities negatively influenced by the use of skunk and alcohol, the fresh-faced teenager pursued a string of tawdry affairs with much older men and women. Joanne's teachers, and her parents, were at their combined wits' end.

So what of skunk?

'Skunk', a generic name used by the police and press, is a potent form of cannabis and its strength and speed can sometimes catch out inexperienced users. Many report that the 'stoned' effect can come on rapidly and be disabling. The results can be quite dramatic, including anxiety attacks and projectile vomiting. Other symptoms may include elation, profound relaxation, alteration of time and perception, transient hallucinations, mild paranoia and a strong desire to eat and continue eating.

Dr Ken Checinski, Senior Consultant in Addictive Behaviours, says: 'Frequent to long-term abuse of skunk can lead to acute and severe psychotic episodes (including believing strange, often fearful things and seeing, or hearing things that are not there), or trigger an underlying vulnerability to mental illness.'

Indeed skunk can, and often does, scramble the brain, most especially the developing mind during adolescence, with the associated damage to nerve cell activation being irreparable.

According to the Royal College of Psychiatrists, there is growing evidence that people with serious mental illness, including depression and psychoses, have used it over long periods of time. They add: 'There is also sufficient evidence to show that those who use cannabis particularly at a younger age, such as around the age of 15, have a higher than average risk of developing a psychotic illness,' which Joanne later developed.

So why should teenagers be particularly vulnerable to the use of cannabis? It is thought that this has something to do with brain development. The Royal College of Psychiatrists say that the brain is still developing in the teenage years – up the age of twenty, in fact. A massive process of 'neural pruning' is going on: 'This is rather like streamlining a tangled jumble of circuits so they can work more effectively. Any experience, or substance, that affects this process has the potential to produce long-term psychological effects.'

It would be totally incorrect to suggest all cannabis smokers develop mental illnesses, or turn into murderers, far from it, nevertheless, the amount of the main psychoactive ingredient, THC, in herbal cannabis varies hugely from as low as 1 per cent up to 15 per cent. The newer strains, including skunk, contain up to 20 per cent. Around the age of fourteen Joanne Dennehy was hooked on the stuff, although how she paid for the drugs is unknown. She was becoming mentally and physically toxic, and she contaminated anything, and everything, she came into contact with.

LOVE OF BLOOD

Instead of fulfilling her parents' dream of their daughter studying law, Joanne would soon take a Master's degree in Vengeance.

3

THE LOVER

I was smitten with her. At first she seemed quite normal.
A little rebellious, she had a free spirit, but nothing
out of the ordinary for a teenager. I loved her.
JOHN TREANOR ON JOANNE DENNEHY. INTERVIEW WITH
GUY ADAMS, *DAILY MAIL* 15 FEBRUARY 2014

Unemployed twenty-one-year-old John Treanor stayed with his mother in the upmarket village of Redbourn, about three miles from where Joanne Dennehy lived in Longfield Road. For those of you with an eye for historical detail, Redbourn is just off ancient Watling Street. Presently, the population is circa 6,000 and the village is recorded in the Domesday Book.

During the summer of 1997 Treanor was walking his dog through the park when a young girl ran up and patted the dog's head. 'I really love dogs,' she explained – introducing herself as Joanne, but he could call her 'Jo'. They talked for a while before parting, agreeing to meet up the following day. This was to be the start of a relationship that would endure, on and off, for twelve years. Back then John could have hardly guessed that Joanne Dennehy was to become one of the most evil serial killers the UK has ever known.

I remember Jo was having problems at school and wasn't getting on with her parents. She had got into big trouble by getting drunk on a bottle of whisky and climbing out of a school window.

John Treanor, interview with Guy Adams, *Daily Mail*, 15 February 2014

Shortly after they met, Treanor says that Joanne was eventually kicked out of the family home and wanted to move in with him at his mother's place. 'The problem was,' he recalled, 'my mum knew she was only fifteen and wouldn't hear of it, even though we weren't sleeping together. None of that happened until she was sixteen.'

Law-abiding Kevin and Kathleen were supportive and loving parents to both of their daughters and despite the serious problems they were experiencing with Joanne, I cannot for a moment imagine they would have kicked their Jo out onto the streets. She had run away from home before, therefore it is more than likely she used the lie that she had been evicted as a ruse to cajole Mrs Treanor into putting a roof over her head if, and when, she ran away again.

With the option of living with his mother no longer on the cards, John and Joanne moved to a shared house in Luton. Here, they rented a room from a drug dealer and addicts would turn up around the clock. 'It was a bad situation,' John admits. 'We had no money so we turned to shoplifting to get food.' Then Joanne fell pregnant. However, what I do not see here is any reference to John Treanor – now a 'mature' adult aged twenty-two – effectively eloping with the fifteen-year-old girl, nor can I find any reference to Mr and Mrs Dennehy reporting their daughter's disappearance to the police.

Nevertheless, shortly afterwards Treanor and Dennehy were allocated a council flat in Milton Keynes, where, in 1999, their first daughter was born. Joanne was now receiving state benefits while Treanor found work as a security guard to help make ends meet. Yet, despite these tottering steps towards normality, their relationship became strained. 'Jo was cold,' John remembers. 'It was like she didn't really want the baby, or have time for her. She was also drinking a lot more. The situation was not good.'

And it was not about to improve. According to Treanor, Joanne started having sex with an ex-convict, so John responsibly took himself and their child to live with his mother, who since had moved to Wisbech, Cambridgeshire. However, after a few months elapsed Joanne realised that she was better off with Treanor than without him, so she persuaded him to give their relationship another try.

In 2001, the couple moved to King's Lynn, where Joanne found a job picking vegetables for supermarkets. 'It was a period of stability,' recalls Treanor. 'For once, Jo seemed to be getting her act together. She was employed, things were relatively normal.'

But a leopard never changes its spots. Over time Joanne Dennehy rebooted and began drinking again, which never appealed to John because he was, and still is, teetotal. 'Back on the whisky, she was coming home paralytic, becoming ever more mentally toxic, physically violent towards me, screaming and smashing the place up. It became unbearable,' John recalled. 'It was scaring me and really upsetting my little girl.'

Then, in 2003, the straw that should have finally broken the camel's back came while in a drunken rage Dennehy accidentally shoved the toddler, who almost fell headlong down the stairs. At this point John took immediate action. 'I took my daughter and moved back to Wisbech and to my mum. I washed my hands of Jo completely,' he explains.

Joanne vanished off his radar screen for about eighteen months and then he learned that she had been sectioned under Section 2(*s* 2) the 1983 Mental Health Act. After committing a violent assault on a man she had undergone a pre-sentencing evaluation in the psychiatric ward of Peterborough City Hospital. According to Guy Adams, writing in the *Daily Mail* (Saturday, 19 February 2014), she was diagnosed with having a psychotic disorder and found to be 'emotionally unstable and prone to unpredictable behavioural explosions'. Following this she began a short prison sentence. After explaining her predicament in a letter to John Treanor, she sent him a 'Visiting Order' (VO), so that he could visit her in jail.

Upon her release from prison, in 2004, and subject to a Community Behaviour Order, twenty-two-year-old Joanne was given yet another chance to redeem herself. As part of her bail conditions her parents were contacted and they agreed to let her come home. She went back to live with them but, as might have been expected, this proved an unsuccessful rehabilitation programme. Following an argument after being caught having sex with travellers on the back lawn, Joanne flipped. She repaid her parents' kindness by causing 3,000 worth of damage to their new conservatory. Now there could be no turning back. The girl who at one time had the ability to become a high-achiever was determined to achieve quite the opposite.

Homeless, so yet again unable to stand on her own two feet, Joanne managed to persuade John Treanor to give their relationship a third go. 'I truly loved her, I truly did. I thought that if I could just get her away from the bad influences, and the drink, we could be a proper, normal family,' he explained, adding, 'She had put on weight in prison and her health wasn't great – she had changed, become harder – but for a period it was quite calm.'

It could be argued that Treanor either has the patience of a saint or that he was completely naive when it came to Joanne Dennehy. To be fair it is correct to say that sociopaths are highly manipulative. Dennehy knew that she was idolised by him. To her, this was his weakness, one that she could fully exploit. For Treanor's part, it has been suggested by several of the professionals I have interviewed that he was perhaps vulnerable – that at least his heart, if not his mind, was in the right place. Nevertheless, nothing can excuse what happened next, for in 2006 Joanne, who had been since diagnosed as 'emotionally unstable and prone to unpredictable behavioural explosions' and was now an alcoholic and drug user, a borderline sociopath with a prison sentence under her frock, fell pregnant again.

This constantly chemically imbalanced young woman then gave birth to a second child, a girl, when she could not even look after the first one. Again, there was no maternal instinct whatsoever. She didn't care; she would not kiss her daughters, cuddle them, feed them or put them to bed. These were not Treanor's only concerns either. The following year she started a lesbian relationship with a woman called Charmaine, spending days away from home with her. Constantly drunk and out of her mind on drugs, Joanne brought home men and women, had sex with them, argued and broke the place up in front of the hapless Treanor and their daughters. Not only a common law spousal abuser, she was a child abuser as well. Irresponsibly imbibing toxic substances throughout both pregnancies – the alcohol alone is very often the cause of Foetal Alcohol Syndrome – and if John Treanor's account is correct she was also psychologically damaging her daughters in every possible way after they were born by denying them any maternal love.

Joanne now took to wearing a tongue stud. She already recently had a star, which might be construed as a reversed green pentagram, tattooed on her right cheek. Some say that the 'star' was in recognition of her nickname. A reversed pentagram is a satanic symbol, which, it is claimed, attracts sinister forces to overturn the proper order of things. The two 'points' facing upwards signify the 'Goat of Lust' attacking the heavens – a variation of sticking two fingers up, if you will. And she had other tattoos on her arms, including one that stated 'Licking Legend' in reference to her sexual prowess.

'She was also sleeping with other men,' recalls Treanor. 'It was a crazy life, I didn't feel like I knew her any more. She was completely out of control. She was also cutting herself on her abdomen. One day she came round and I could see she had stuck pins in herself and she was bleeding. It was very scary.'

Self-harming is listed in the *Diagnostic and Statistical Manual of Mental Disorders* (DSM-IV-TR) as a symptom of a borderline personality disorder where self-mutilation provides temporary relief for those suffering depression, anxiety disorders, substance abuse, self-loathing and low self-esteem. Although not commonly associated with those who have sincere suicidal inclinations and follow through with it, this desperate form of behaviour is a way for the afflicted person to draw sympathy from others, much in the same way as wannabe suicides do not actually go through with the final act. It is attention seeking, nothing more, and nothing less. But it is the 'self-loathing' and 'low self-esteem' that interests me for Joanne now hated herself for what she had become and she would later project all of this onto her victims, as we shall soon see.

I would never harm a child.
Joanne Dennehy – to a pen friend.

John Treanor has been frequently described as being a loving father to his two daughters so I am not about to question his current sentiments towards his children. One might say that what went on in the past during his twelve-year, on-off relationship with Joanne Dennehy is done and dusted and best left where it was. Nevertheless, in 2009 he did what he should have done from the get-go: he woke up to the reality. He ended the relationship once and for all when a drunken Joanne suddenly pulled a six-inch serrated dagger from her knee-high leather boot and plunged it into the carpet of their home, yelling and screaming, 'I wish I could fuckin' kill someone!'

'Jo was just angry, I don't know what about,' recalls Treanor. 'But that dagger was very, very scary. It was a proper one with decoration on the handle. Obviously, it really freaked me out.' Fearing for his life and the safety of his two daughters, with his young family Treanor fled 140 miles away to Glossop, Derbyshire, where he is now raising them with his wife, Vicky. Dennehy would never see her girls again.

Maria Dennehy last saw her sister in 2005. Using the Electoral Roll she tracked Joanne down to Peterborough, Cambridgeshire. 'By then,' Maria recalls, 'Jo was doing drugs and self-harming. She had become an alcoholic and was in with the wrong crowd.'

In early April 2013 there was loud knock on Treanor's front door: it was the police. Joanne had been arrested on suspicion of committing three murders and two attempted murders. For Treanor, the nightmare was to start all over again for if anyone was truly possessed by Satan, Lucifer had a daughter named Joanne Christine Dennehy.

I do not lack control. I am not and never have been a junkie. I am not alcohol dependent!
Joanne Dennehy, letter to the author, 24th February 2014

4

THE BUNGLING BURGLAR

You have a dirty and dark mind... see you really soon,
your biggest supporter!
Love you always, love Undertaker XXXXXXX Hubby 4 Lifey
GARY STRETCH, LETTER TO DENNEHY IN PRISON

With an IQ lower than that enjoyed by a pencil, and claiming to be Joanne's personal 'Undertaker', standing 7ft 3 inches tall and weighing in at a pot-bellied 23 stone, the unedifying inmate A0939CX STRETCH Gary is now serving a nineteen-year stretch before he has any chance of parole at HMP Woodhill, Milton Keynes. Unless this forty-eight-year-old with three children of his own and previously a permanent resident on 'Benefits Street' considerably modifies his behaviour he'll never catch a bus again. However, the chances of this happening are slim because he'll probably die in jail.

Gary John Stretch was born Gary John Richards in Herefordshire on Thursday, 27 January 1966. Suffering from gigantism, which is usually caused by a tumour on the pituitary gland, he was already 7ft tall by the age of twenty and dubbed 'Stretch', or 'Lurch' after the character in the Addams Family by his schoolmates. Indeed he later changed his name by deed poll to Stretch in recognition of his stature and, commensurate with his abysmally low intelligence quotient, he was a slow learner. We know this because he spent the better part of his worthless life bouncing in and out of jail like a rubber ball on elastic string. Indeed, so frequent a guest at Her Majesty's Pleasure is Stretch, who suffers painful arthritis in his knees and back, he has his own custom-built extra-large jail bed that travels with him whenever he moves between prisons. And he needs it because standard prison beds are just 6 feet long!

As for his very early days, hard as I tried I could not find much evidence that Gaz went to school but this may be accounted for when we learn that he was always in trouble and his father, John, had kicked him out when the lad was just fifteen years old. Thereafter, he drifted into a life of petty crime. Pilfering, larceny, criminal damage, shoplifting and learning how to break into cars and how to lay tarmac on driveways then scarper with the cash before the job was done all formed part of his early criminal career. His height, however, meant that he was always getting caught, moving his long-term partner, Julie Gibbons, to say: 'We told him, "You can't disappear in a crowd, Gary, it's not the right profession for you".' Occasionally Lady Luck favoured him, though. One police identity parade collapsed because officers failed to find anyone else tall enough to take part.

It will therefore come as no surprise to learn that according to Cambridgeshire Constabulary and West Mercia Police, Gaz was a persistent criminal with extensive criminal antecedents stretching back years. Starting with a conviction for robbery and a five-year prison term while in his teens, he went on to earn himself 'an appalling criminal record,' as Mr Justice Spencer has put it. He was a housebreaker – although because of his enormous size not an entirely successful one. As one police officer quipped: 'When Stretch started to climb through a window his size 18-inch feet would follow a day later. Imagine Bigfoot trying to creep through someone's home at night, he wasn't exactly stealthy.' On another occasion he broke into an office and ate a chocolate from a box of Black Magic lying on a desk. He didn't steal anything but police found one of his fingerprints on the carton.

In 2000 'Gaz' was sentenced to a total of four years' imprisonment for handling stolen property. When he breached his licence following release from this sentence he received a consecutive sentence of two years for a house burglary. The property was the flat next door to where he was living with his then partner, Julie Gibbons, at 64 Huntley Road, Orton Goldhay, near Peterborough. It was broad daylight so neighbours recognised the awkward burglar because of his distinctive presence. They called the police and once again he was arrested.

A few of the Orton Goldhay locals recall Julie as being a quiet woman and they told me that they never saw Stretch with a cigarette. They were sure he didn't drink either but they did say he was an intimidating man who kept himself to himself. Julie confirms this, saying: 'Gary only ever drank the odd pint and was anti-drugs.' So he had nothing in common with Joanne Dennehy in this respect. 'He falls in love very easily. He's told me that he "trusted the wrong person" [Dennehy]. He has trouble judging people, he's the most loyal friend you could have,' remembers Gibbons.

Already a mother of two, Julie Gibbons, then aged thirty-eight, first met Stretch in a Peterborough nightclub in 1991. The couple spent thirteen years together and he had three children with her: Charlie (17), Garry (16) and Melanie (14) at the time of writing.

> When his son was born [Charlie] Gary cried – he's a very sentimental man, a big softy. He often cries while watching a film or something on TV.
> Julie Gibbons, *Daily Mirror* interview, 2014, and elsewhere in the media

Julie says, 'Gary was a real hands-on dad, always changing nappies and feeding the babies. If the kids were climbing trees he was probably up there with them. He was great with them but sometimes I felt like I was looking after another kid as well. He wasn't a responsible dad but he was a great dad and a caring dad.'

And Stretch himself cynically endorsed Julie's claim that he was a responsible, caring dad, just a few days before he was finally caught in 2013. Knowing that he would soon be arrested and was to spend a long time in jail, he told Joanne Dennehy: 'My kids are grown up now, so I don't care.'

Stretch and Gibbons finally split up in 2004, following his arrest for burglary, after which she moved to Yaxley, a small village several miles south of Peterborough.

In 2009, Stretch was serving time again. The previous year he had received a total sentence of fifteen months' imprisonment for harassing Julie Gibbons after threatening, via a third party, to kill her. When she was due to give evidence against him for burglary charges he had intimidated her. For this offence he was given an indefinite restraining order, all of which somewhat flies in the face of Gibbons' claim that he was 'the most loyal friend you could ever have'.

While in prison, he was accused of playing a part in the killing of another inmate at HMP Peterborough. The previous year thirty-three-year-old inmate Brian Haynes had died of a heart attack in his cell. Prosecutor John Farmer told Norwich Crown Court that Stretch had acted as a lookout while some of his fellow inmates beat up Haynes. 'He's the biggest man in the dock,' he added. 'If you have got Stretch as a sentry, he could warn you of a prison officer coming and prevent anyone from interfering.' Two prisoners were convicted of manslaughter, Stretch, however, was cleared, having convinced the jury that he was merely passing the cell door at the time. In 2010, parolee Dennehy was living in March, Cambridgeshire, and it was here that she met Stretch, also out on parole. He stayed with her, sleeping on the sofa in her bedsit, and this must have caused him sleepless nights for, as Julie Gibbons recalls: 'He couldn't sleep on a normal bed and he had to sleep diagonally, which wasn't great for me.'

It is generally agreed between Dennehy, Stretch and everyone who knew the pair, including the police, that theirs was not a sexual relationship.

But there is more to Gary Stretch than meets the eye. He would have us believe that he is simply a bungling burglar, petty thief and a fool, and all of this is correct. However, far from his later Crown Court trial mitigation, of having been manipulated by Joanne Dennehy and being terrified of her , he may have been complicit in two of the three murders, as well as the two attempted murders. Later in this book we will put Dennehy and Stretch's minds under the microscope. We will gather up tidbits of what she has said – more importantly what she refuses to say, or has hinted at on the public record – and we will do just the same with Mr Stretch to show how he may have been equally complicit.

'As big as he is, he's a coward and a bit of a wimp. Gary's just a big softie who would never hurt a fly,' says Julie. However, employing psychological offender profiling techniques used by the FBI and other agencies, I will attempt to show how Stretch may have been complicit in carrying out the actual murders of Lukasz Slaboszewski and Kevin Lee. Moreover, I suggest Dennehy could not have killed these two men without Gaz's intimate participation. I believe the pair may have combined to make an efficient killing, dead body deposition and cover-up team.

5

THE ENFORCER

*Where does discontent start? You are warm enough, but you
shiver. You are fed, yet hunger gnaws you. You have been loved,
but your yearning wanders in new fields. And to prod all
these there's time, the bastard Time.*
JOHN STEINBECK, *SWEET THURSDAY*

After serving a few short prison sentences for committing relatively minor offences to include dishonesty, shoplifting, openly carrying a razor blade in public and breaching a Community Service Order for an offence of assault occasioning actual bodily harm, Joanne Dennehy was freed again with a 46.00 'Discharge Grant' in her pocket.

While in jail she had spotted a notice offering accommodation for released offenders. It had been placed by Quicklet Limited, a firm with a portfolio of bedsit properties they rented out to those with 'limited resources'. The directors were Kevin Lee and his wife Cristina. Therefore, upon her release from jail Dennehy visited their office at 18 Crawthorne Road, Peterborough, while Stretch loitered around outside.

Here, the manipulative Dennehy told Lee and his office manager Paul Creed that she had just been released from prison, where she had served thirteen years for murdering her father because he had abused her from the age of five or six. She explained that she now needed somewhere to live. It was true, she had been recently released from jail, but the rest of her story was a complete fabrication, an attempt to gain sympathy. Her father, of course, was alive and in good health.

Paul Creed would later tell a Cambridge Crown Court jury that Joanne Dennehy had come into their office seeking accommodation. However, after taking one look at her, and noting multiple scars on her arms and stomach not to mention the green star tattoo on her cheek, he was reluctant to help. 'I did not want to house her,' he admitted. But Kevin Lee fell for Dennehy's yarn, hook, line and sinker. 'Kevin told me that as she was being honest he would give Joanne a chance,' Paul Creed went on to explain at Dennehy's trial in 2013. But this was the start of a shady business relationship that would quickly develop into a kinky, sex-for-favours affair, to be abruptly terminated by Kevin's death. However, there was much more to it than that.

Kevin Lee was a fit, good-looking man of forty-eight. He and his wife Cristina had two children, Chiara and Dino, and had lived in Fletton, Peterborough, since 1996. One of their long-time female friends told me that Kevin doted on his family: 'He would do anything for them and he idolised Cristina,' she said, adding, 'they were respected as a loving couple by everyone who knew them.'

Another family friend explained: 'Cristina is a very beautiful woman with a heart of gold. She loved Kevin to bits. She was loyal to him, never unfaithful, she stuck by him through thick and thin. He was a very lucky guy so why he would want to cheat on her with a slut like Dennehy?'

Yet Kevin Lee had a dark side – one that soon evidenced itself in cross-dressing, clandestine perverted sexual encounters with Joanne Dennehy, and he boasted about it to his buddies, too.

As one friend who knew him for years recalled: 'Kev was just one of the lads. It was like, "Hey, Have I got a great story to tell you." Then he would go on and on about how he had this young woman who could fulfill any man's sexual fantasies. He said, "I can arrange her for you too. A drink in it for her, yes?" He told me that she [Joanne] was a tart, who could not get enough sex; that she had "great tits"; that she liked to be slapped around. I just thought that Kev was bullshitting me cos his wife is drop-dead gorgeous. Now I know he wasn't lying.' 'Screw him!' added Kevin's former pal.

Like Dennehy, it is now obvious that Kevin Lee also had an alter ego. They were both Jekyll and Hyde characters, if you will. He would visit Joanne and enjoy crude and violent sex with her before returning to his family without a shred of conscience, even less any appreciation of the outcome should his family find out.

For her part, Dennehy was merely pandering to his sexual weaknesses and secretly she despised him. She knew that he was selfishly using her for his own gratification before returning to his wife so she in turn would use him. In exchange for a supply of drugs and drink Joanne had been used and abused by older men for years, so she reciprocated. However, while she did not enjoy sex as a loving act – like most psychopaths, she was emotionally dead inside – she knew that she could excite men, bending them to her will using her 'charms', and Kevin Lee was to be no exception.

Amongst Quicklet's properties was a newish townhouse converted to scruffy bedsits at 38 Bifield, Orton Goldhay. There was a similar set-up at 2 Riseholme – also in Orton Goldhay – and another property converted to maisonettes at 11 Rolleston Garth, Dogsthorpe, also in Peterborough.

John Chapman and Leslie Layton occupied rooms at 38 Bifield, however, eviction notices had been served on them by Quicklet. Dennehy 'The Enforcer' would soon have a room there, too.

11 Rolleston Garth was vacant. Sparsely furnished, it was in need of a tidy up and a coat of paint. For his part, social benefits scrounger Stretch was given lodgings at 2 Riseholme. 11 Rolleston Garth was an additional place where he could stay over when it suited him and Dennehy.

Exactly how the business/sexual relationship between Dennehy and Kevin Lee developed will always remain a mystery. The only ones who have intimate knowledge are unavailable for comment – Lee being dead and Dennehy staying quiet as a church mouse. However, it is known that she and Stretch successfully applied for Housing Benefit and Jobseeker's Allowance of 57.35 a week, but it was an earlier change in payments under the Local Housing Allowance (LHA) that undoubtedly contributed in some way to the untimely fate of two of the three murdered men.

Previously, local authorities had paid a tenant's rent directly to the landlord, thus guaranteeing payment, but in April 2008 all this changed. The UK Government decided that landlords and tenants should be made responsible for their own financial commitments rather than delegate responsibility to the local council. This decision in effect placed Housing Benefit tenants on a par with private tenants. Unfortunately, most of Quicklet's clients lacked any sense of responsibility. Many of them were ex-cons, drug addicts, alcoholics and born losers, so Quicklet often had problems collecting rent. This was now affecting the firm's business – enter 'Dennehy the Enforcer'.

> *She [Dennehy] is a monster who has taken and ruined my family's lives.*
> Cristina Lee, sentencing impact statement

According to the police – later acknowledged by a Cambridge Crown Court jury – apart from the sexual attraction, a shady business arrangement developed between Joanne and Kevin Lee, one that suited them both entirely. It was obvious that Kevin found gregarious Joanne a hot number with the morals of an alley cat, but he also realised that she had other attributes: she was callous and as hard as iron, added to which she had an enormous 'minder' in the form of Gary Stretch.

While Dennehy and Stretch kept their housing benefits for themselves, Kevin Lee also provided them with free bedsit accommodation in return for decorating several properties and tenant enforcement work in which the threatening Stretch ably assisted Joanne, and it worked something like this.

Whenever Lee had problems with a tenant, whether it was because rent wasn't being paid, or arrears, or he simply wanted the person evicted, Dennehy would move in on the pretext of doing the place up.

Regardless of their financial status all tenants have a legal right to occupy a landlord's rented premises until they are evicted by court order but this didn't suit Kevin Lee one bit. We know how Dennehy had treated John Treanor, or any other person who upset her, including her teachers and her own parents: she made their lives not worth living, but now the formidable 7ft 3in Stretch was around to back her up. There was no point in a tenant complaining to Quicklet because all Lee would say was that it was a domestic issue between tenants and therefore a matter they must resolve between themselves, so the only option left open to the tenant was to leave as quickly as they could or face the consequences. Most did, one didn't – John Chapman would be stabbed to death as he slept in his bed. That same day Kevin Lee would also die.

One of those who did leave was a man who had previously rented one of Quicklet's properties. Having been 'evicted' by Dennehy, Stretch and, to some extent by Kevin Lee, the man whom I shall call 'Mick' told me: 'I was recommended to Quicklet by Peterborough Social Services. I was on disability benefit and I had to attend meetings because I was a registered alcoholic. I once was married and have two kids. Had a great job then I lost these fingers on my right hand in an industrial accident. I went onto painkillers and I was taking drugs for years. I cannot tell you how many times I have been before magistrates. I have lost count. All drug stuff, I think. When you hit rock bottom and lose everything it is hard, mate. But as you can see from this flat, I keep everything clean. I love clean. Look, my bathroom is spotless.

'I have not had a drink for three years now. I am out of all of that, no drugs at all. When I moved into the Quicklet place it was shit, everything was a mess. So, I told Kevin Lee. I said that I could make things better, but he would have to pay me a bit to clean things up. I got no reply. So I spent some of my rent money to paint and dump rubbish what was in the garden [*sic*].

'I got into arrears with the rent and I could not pay it back so I asked for a Crisis Loan. I didn't get one. [Crisis Loans are Government or local authority short-term loans of up to 50.00 paid to help vulnerable people through a short-term crisis and are repaid through their benefits.] Then Joanne Dennehy came to see me with this big guy. They came into my room and pushed me against the wall and told me to get out. When I phoned Kevin Lee, I got no answer. Two days later the same woman came back with the same man and she put a knife to my throat. I left that place with just a bag of my stuff. I stayed at my aunt's house until I found this flat. No one deserves that.'

But the good news is this: much to the credit of Peterborough's Social Services 'Mick' was rehoused and with the support of lenient magistrates, he has been drink and drug-free ever since. And he has a bicycle – not a new one, of course – but it gets him about. He only has a small place in a council block – a kitchen, living/sleeping room and a bathroom, all of these rooms immaculate. Once skinny, pale and scrawny, 'Mick' is now tanned, fit and actively seeking work. He takes pride in himself, so the system really does work. Yet he understands, knowing today who Dennehy and Stretch are, that he could easily have been found dead in a ditch somewhere and no one would have really cared.

CHAPTER 6

COOL HAND LUKE

Vengeance is mine; I will repay, saith the Lord.
ROMANS, CHAPTER 12, VERSE 19

Joanne Dennehy came into this world destined for a life of blood and carnage and the first to die was thirty-one-year-old Lukasz Slaboszewski who, in 2005, had moved to the UK from Nowa Sl, a town on the Oder River in western Poland. Up until the time of his death he was living at 695 Lincoln Road, Peterborough. Slaboszewski was employed by DHL at a warehouse in Peterborough and he enjoyed his job. Previously he had visited his family at Christmas, and the last time he contacted them was in early March 2013. Lukasz planned to see his sisters in London, later in the month. A happy-go-lucky man who enjoyed cards and music, he was, nevertheless, trying to kick a cocaine habit and had been prescribed methadone as a substitute to cure his addiction. The police confirm that he was not a tenant of Quicklet.

Without wishing to state the obvious, to avoid a killer

you must know one is there. Like any victim falling prey to a predator, Lukasz didn't realise until it was all too late. On Monday, 18 March 2013, he bumped into Joanne Dennehy –the police are inclined to think the meeting took place in Peterborough's Queensgate shopping mall. It was a sunny day and the weather was perfect. He didn't know Dennehy, was totally unaware of her existence and never could have guessed in a million years she had bloody murder on her mind, that she had been secretly watching him or that the blood she would spill would be his own – and a lot of it too.

If anything, hazel-eyed Lukasz was a little on the shy side. Therefore, it is highly likely that the well-spoken, gregarious Dennehy made the approach. Perhaps she flirted with him because she is very good at flirting. For his part, Slaboszewski would easily have been won over by her just like Kevin Lee. Nevertheless, she obtained his mobile number and, after they parted company, sent him a number of sexually explicit text messages to which he replied. That evening he somewhat prematurely texted a friend, saying he had found an English girlfriend and that 'life is beautiful'. Lukasz was last seen alive leaving his home the following day, Tuesday, 19 March.

With Lukasz now unable to tell his side of the story, and Dennehy later giving responses of 'No comment!' to every question put to her by the Nationally Accredited interviewer DC Kim Bowen and DS Mark Jinks, DCI Martin Brunning and DS Andy Crocker are able to provide some of the known facts. There are a few obvious gaps, which I will fill in later, but it all makes for grim reading.

When Lukasz arrived at 11 Rolleston Garth, Joanne

Dennehy opened the front door. Inviting him in, she explained that she was tidying the place up for her boss (Kevin Lee). A short while later – it might have been as soon as a few minutes – Slaboszewski was stabbed once through the heart with a 3-inch lock knife. The attack appears to have taken place in the kitchen, however his blood was also found close to the inside of the front door. It had been a blitz attack, one that came without warning. And it had to be this way for Lukasz was a powerfully built man while Dennehy was small in comparison and therefore could not afford to display her homicidal intent.

The police, the CPS, the pre-trial hearing judge Mr Justice Sweeney and the sentencing judge, Mr Justice Spencer, had always assumed that Dennehy was alone at 11 Rolleston Garth when Slaboszewski was murdered. Therefore, as Stretch was presumed not to be present when the killing took place he was not charged with any offence in connection with the murder – only one of preventing the lawful and decent burial of a human body [Slaboszewski] for which he was sentenced to seven and a half years. However, on Friday, 29 March 2014, DCI Martin Brunning received – via *Daily Mirror* journalist Louie Smith – copies of correspondence dated 17 February 2013, sent by Stretch to his former partner, Julie Gibbons. The letters proved to be a bombshell, for in one of them he confessed:

> *I was in the house when the first murder was done. I was asleep upstairs at the time and came don [sic] to it in the morning. I thought if I told the police they would have done me for the murder so I stayed quiet.*

Gibbons also sent copies of Stretch's letters to Joanne Dennehy at HMP Bronzefield. Dennehy replied, adding another level to Stretch's involvement – that Stretch had actually watched her kill Slaboszewski:

> *Gaz was there in the room for the first one. I told him what I was going to do but not why. I told him to leave* [the house] *over and over before I did it. I told him to leave after. My path was set. I did not want this for Gary. My crimes, Julie, were vengeance. I knew what the outcome would be. I tried my best to make sure Gary was away from me when I set about the killings. I got him a place to stay and a job. I got him a car, which he insisted was in my name.*

Stretch's timing of his 17 February letter to Gibbons was well thought out. By that date he had already been found guilty of a number of offences and was awaiting sentencing. However, at his trial the police and the Crown Prosecution Service were in complete ignorance of the fact that he had witnessed Slaboszewski's and Lee's murders, if not actually assisting Dennehy.

In a later telephone call to Stretch, Julie Gibbons asked why Dennehy had killed Slaboszewski.

'Well, she's just that way,' he replied, 'She's off her head.'

'Well, you should have run a mile,' suggested Gibbons.

In an attempt to mitigate his involvement, again he said: 'I didn't know about it at first. I came down and there was a guy in the hallway. She said, "Oh, you need to help me get rid of him. Bin him!"'

Of course these admissions from Dennehy reveal more to us than she may have intended. The job she got for Stretch was acting for Kevin Lee as co-enforcer with her; the place for him to live was at 2 Riseholme. And the car? We'll come back to that in the next chapter.

But, what of Lukasz?

The Rolleston Garth estate is well maintained and spaciously laid out. There is ample parking and the houses, though a little unusual in design, are appealing to look at – and to live in, one supposes, come to that. The layout of the estate is in no way cramped and the gardens at Rolleston Garth are surrounded by wooden fences – certainly too high to peek over – and therefore quite excellent to hide unpleasant things from prying eyes. So, Dennehy and Stretch dumped Lukasz's body in a green wheelie bin parked in the garden to await disposal, but first transport was needed: they would have to get a car.

> Gary used to have big trouble getting into cars. It would be uncomfortable for him with his knees at near his chin [sic].
> Julie Gibbons

Shortly after the murder, Dennehy called Kevin Lee to explain that a man had been killed. According to police, whether or not she told Lee that the man had died at 11 Rolleston Garth is based on an element of conjecture. Whether or not she admitted that she was the culprit is also open to debate, but she did tell him that she needed money to buy a car to move the corpse.' Kevin handed over the cash.

According to the police, just two days after Slaboszewski's murder Dennehy and Stretch travelled by taxi to purchase a green Vauxhall Astra, registration number R660 ECT. Joanne didn't have a driving licence but Stretch did. However, while he insisted the car be registered in her name secretly he insured the vehicle under the company name 'Undertaker & Co.' but failed to tell her. He nicknamed the Astra 'The Hearse'. Later that evening the same vehicle was spotted being driven around remote areas on the outskirts of Peterborough – Dennehy and Stretch were looking for a suitable site to dispose of Lukasz's body. The place they settled on was at Thorney Dyke, a remote location close to where Stretch had lived, some years earlier.

'No one will ever find a body dumped there,' Stretch later boasted to a woman called Georgina Page, whom Dennehy had met several years earlier while living in Kings Lynn with John Treanor.

In her letter to Julie Gibbons Dennehy mentioned the Vauxhall Astra:

> *At court the judge informed me that Gary had insured it under the company name Undertaker & Co. As you can imagine that did not look good for him and I did not find it funny.*

In a dignified statement issued after his death had been confirmed, his sister, Magda Skrzypczak, said: 'Lukasz was the joker in the family, always finding something to laugh about. His mum and dad are devastated by their loss, and he also leaves two grieving sisters.'

Dennehy was rude and arrogant. She once grabbed me around the throat. When I visited 11 Rolleston Garth she lifted the bin lid to show me its contents. The body was wet and covered by a black, plastic bin liner. The sight horrified me. Jo was just standing there and smiling. I just wanted to get out of there. I wanted to forget what I saw in the bin.

14-year-old female witness at Dennehy's trial (name deleted at judge's instructions)

7

UNCLE ALBERT

She [Dennehy] *is man-woman and she'll get me out
of the house by any means. She's a madwoman.*
JOHN CHAPMAN, TO NEIGHBOUR TONI ANN ROBERTS
THE DAY BEFORE HIS MURDER

The T-shaped cul-de-sac of terraced properties in Bifield,
Orton Goldhay, can be entered only after encountering
speed bumps – countless speed bumps every fifty yards or so, and
this really does get on one's nerves. But it sets the scene, if you will,
for speed bumps do not exist in sleepy, upmarket green-wellie-
brigade Redbourn, where Joanne Dennehy first met John Treanor.

Each house in Bifield is allocated a parking space. White vans
seem to be popular. Some of the front gardens are neat and tidy,
others merely a space to dump rubbish. The residents are folk
who mind their own business, expecting others to attend to
theirs. Curtains twitch ever so gently and strangers are treated
with collective, almost tribal suspicion, when anyone wearing
a suit turns up for they are treated to the same greeting one
might afford a County Court bailiff, or collectors from a loan
company demanding an overdue debt be paid.

About a week before John Chapman's murder, Kevin Lee had allocated Joanne Dennehy a temporary bedsit at 38 Bifield. She wasn't exactly a happy person because at the time she was alleging that Lee owed her money for work that she and Stretch had carried out at 11 Rolleston Garth. Notwithstanding this, she moved in with tenants Chapman and Layton, upon whom Lee had already served eviction notices, on the pretext that she would clean the place up. Lee wanted the two men out as soon as possible so he would use Dennehy and Stretch to make his tenants' lives unbearable, ensuring they smartly packed up and left.

During the evenings of Wednesday, 27 and Thursday, 28 March 2013, Dennehy, Stretch, Leslie Layton and a man called Robert Moore were seen by neighbours sitting outside the front of the house and playing loud music. With the exception of Stretch, who was sipping water, they were rowdy, drunk, smoking dope and making nuisances of themselves. Dennehy was flirting with Layton and at one point she sat on his lap.

According to the police, widower and alcoholic fifty-six-year-old John Chapman had served for a short time in the Royal Navy and had genuinely fallen on hard times. By and large, he kept himself to himself, so much so that none of his immediate neighbours actually knew him except in passing.

By all accounts John Chapman was a good tenant of Quicklet. Occasionally, he would fall behind with the rent but he kept his room clean and tidy as best he could. However, Kevin Lee wanted to evict John and Leslie Layton by any means. Joanne Dennehy and Gary Stretch were his tools to achieve this aim but chequered as Lee's past may have been, having Chapman killed would have been the last thing on his mind.

Of all of the doors I knocked on in Bifield no one recalls No. 38 ever being festooned in yellow and black 'Crime Scene – Do Not Cross' tape, nor countless uniformed police officers wearing hi-vis jackets, men in white anti-contamination suits, or the area being jammed with vehicles sporting blue flashing lights, either.

Perhaps conveniently no one remembered the entire area being lit up with floodlights like a football stadium after dark. In fact no one recalls reading about the murder in the local Peterborough *Telegraph* newspaper, or seeing news flashes on TV. It appears that Bifield suffers collective amnesia despite the fact that the furthest front door from No. 38 is a mere sixty yards away. But there was a man who, obviously intrigued by me photographing 38 Bifield, decided to take out his rubbish, then take out more trash, retreat, only to reappear, which begged me to ask, 'Did you know John Chapman, the guy who was murdered in this house?'

'Yes, just in passing,' he replied. 'People came and went at all hours of the day and night. They smoked drugs and were always drunk. They used to sit out the front, playing loud music and shouting abuse.'

'Was John one of them?' I asked.

'He liked his drink. Perhaps sometimes he would join them for a few minutes. He was okay, but the rest of them were scum.'

Another neighbour later testified in court that Chapman was just a friendly guy who liked talking about the Royal Navy.

Toni Roberts explained, 'He was like Uncle Albert from the sit-com *Only Fools and Horses*, but without the beard.' A friend of John's revealed that he was very worried about being evicted and that Dennehy intended to get him out of the house by any means.

Externally sad-looking, yet well-stocked Virans 'Premier' Discount Supermarket is just a minute's walk away from Bifield. It is where mustachioed John bought his ready-meals, his booze, his 'Amber Leaf' rolling tobacco and his green Rizla papers.

Virans is not a Waitrose or a Tesco. There is no trolley park because there are no trolleys, but with ample parking it serves the community well. It is where the local kids congregate after dark, attracted to the security lights like moths to a flame. The owner of Virans told me that he had been there for forty years. He knew all the local people and he knew John Chapman:

'He was a harmless old guy. He came in most days, always just after 11am, when we start selling alcohol,' he recalled, while at pains to stress that it was illegal for him to sell alcohol before that time.

'He bought "Omega" lager. Most afternoons he would return and buy some more. He was always very respectful. We never saw him drunk, sort of a quiet man. He dressed okay, but who wants to dress up smart for a day's drinking?'

'Did you ever meet Joanne Dennehy?' I enquired, by way of an afterthought.

'When I saw her photograph in the newspaper I recognised her immediately because of the tattoo on her face. The murder happened over Easter, you know.' He paused to serve a customer before adding, 'She was well spoken, educated and very nice... *very* polite.'

At that point a young lad who was stocking a shelf piped up, 'Quite pretty, too!' which brought a disapproving glare from his father.

Externally, 38 Bifield is now quite unlike the police photographs in which the place seems half decent. These days it is boarded up with three-ply sheet securely screwed to the front door. The padlock is broken. There is a white utility door to the left as one looks at it. The top half smashed open. A brick-paved car stand is weed-ridden. Without wishing to seem overly dramatic, 38 Bifield smells of murder most foul. Good testimony is an estate agent's board periodically propped up, soon to be removed, because 'real murder' is not sanitised like it is on TV – all clean, neat and tidy, as in staged *Columbo* movies.

On 4 April 2013, a few days after Chapman's murder, another neighbour told Tom Kelly and John Stevens of the *MailOnline*: 'We have had so many problems with that house [38 Bifield]. The noise. The mess. We have had stuff thrown at our dog. We've just had to have our carpet and beds replaced because we had an infestation of bed bugs come from there. Kevin Lee had paid for our house to be fumigated last week.' So, this is most probably the reason why Kevin Lee had served eviction notices on Layton and Chapman.

As a resident explained to me, 'That house has got to be haunted. Who would want to live there now? It should be torn down!' – a demolition that might prove problematic because it is in the middle of a terrace.

In the early hours of Good Friday, 29 March 2013, John

Chapman was asleep in his bedsit. As usual he had been drinking. At autopsy the decedent's blood alcohol level was found to be four times the legal limit for driving. He was perhaps dreaming of catching his next big carp when Dennehy stole into his room and plunged her lock knife into the inert man. At autopsy it was determined by pathologist Dr Carey that Chapman had been stabbed five times in the chest. Two of the stabs penetrated the heart – one inflicted with sufficient force to pass through the breastbone – then she stabbed him once in the neck, severing the carotid artery. He died without a struggle.

Dennehy's first excuse for committing this murder was that previously John had caught a glimpse of her, naked, in the bath. She had asked him to leave but he didn't. Later, she changed her story, saying that Leslie Layton had killed Chapman to impress her. Nevertheless, after knifing John Chapman, at 6.34am she used the dead man's mobile to call Gary Stretch, all the while singing the Britney Spears' song, 'Oops!... I Did It Again'.

LESLIE PAUL LAYTON

*John Chapman was killed by Layton in some pathetic attempt to
impress me and Gary. I was pissed at Gary for telling Layton in the
first place things were not going to plan... in the dock at sentencing,
Layton was sitting behind Gaz. I leant over to Layton
and clearly told him, 'I may be taking your life sentence,
but you and Stretch are fuckin' idiots."*
JOANNE DENNEHY, LETTER TO JULIE GIBBONS, MARCH 2014

If I have given the impression that Gary Stretch was an idiot, try
this genetically challenged man for size, for thirty-six-year-
old Leslie 'Les' Paul Layton must have been a great source of
pride to his parents. He was a drug addict and an alcoholic, and
at this point I would ask the reader to take a peek at his mugshot,
generously supplied by the Cambridgeshire Constabulary. Layton
is a weasel-like chap with a sloping forehead indicating a poorly
developed frontal lobe. His ears are abnormally large. In the flesh
his oversized feet don't seem to match up with his spindly legs
and, like his head, none of the rest of him seems to fit together in
any meaningful way. So, now I'd like you to answer this question:
If your daughter brought our 'Les' home for tea and cakes with
Mom and Pop, would you be impressed? If not, you would be
drawing upon good science, so please bear with me here.

For centuries there have been theories that certain individuals were 'born' to be criminals, though it was not until impetus was provided by Charles Darwin's theory of evolution (published as *On the Origin of Species* in 1859) that anthropology as a science achieved popularity and was taken, with much infighting, into the service of criminologists to help understand the bewildering conduct of habitual criminals, Mr Stretch and Mr Layton being but two of them.

A pioneer in the field was Hubert Lauvergne, a stocky, short-sighted, indulgently bearded naval physician at Toulon, who, to the dismay of his long-suffering wife, made plaster casts of his patients' heads either at his laboratory, or at home while she was trying to make supper. His aim, as is almost certainly already obvious to my readers, was to demonstrate 'degenerate features of the skull', and how that novel idea popped into his own head we will never know.

Now enter the acknowledged father of anthropometric criminology, Cesare Lombroso, who would have had a field day with Gaz Stretch and Les Layton. Cutting to the chase, Lombroso's studies led him to the belief that a study of the criminal was more rewarding than a study of the crime itself and in this he laid the foundations of modern criminology. Lombroso's research is well documented on the Internet and elsewhere. Fascinating stuff, it is most invaluable for weighing up a possible suitor for your daughter in the future, perhaps.

Somewhat miraculously, though he had never been to prison Layton was a typical 'pick and mix' low-level, low-intelligence offender whose aspirations for the good life included theft from motor vehicles and general dishonesty with a smattering of shoplifting and five-fingering anything not nailed down thrown in. Therefore, we can safely assume that he did not attend church or hold neighbourly barbecues. But, perhaps I am being a little harsh because he could add up the important things in his pathetic existence, such as how much cash his benefit payments would allow him to spend on fags and booze, but that's about it apart from the fact that he was no stranger to police custody suits, the courts and a long-time resident on 'Benefit Street'.

To sum Les up, when our Creator had shuffled Layton's gene coils together he was obviously having a bad hair day, plus the fact that he was running short in the parts bin, having previously handed out large portions of commonsense, understanding, morality, wit, good looks and intellect elsewhere.

This also applied to Layton's sidekick, another halfwit called Robert 'Bob' James Moore. Aged fifty-six, Bob lived at 78 Belvoir Way, Dogsthorpe. One look at his mugshot explains everything you need to know – as in 'mentally deficient from basement to roof' springs to mind. Usually chemically imbalanced by drink, Layton and Moore could not wash a car without spending a year figuring out what a hose was, let alone how to attach it to a tap. In Layton's case he would steal your bucket and make off with as much water as it could carry. Somewhat remarkably, however, Moore had no previous criminal convictions, but like falling off a cliff, this was about to change dramatically.

It has now been established that on the morning of John Chapman's murder Layton bumped into Joanne Dennehy as she left the tenants' shared bathroom. She had been washing off

John's blood and she showed Les the dead body. In this moment Layton entered the big time for his reaction was not one of calling for help. Showing a callous indifference to the plight of his now deceased drinking buddy and housemate, at precisely 7.32am he picked up his mobile and took a picture of Chapman's blood-drenched corpse lying on the bed, after which he deleted the photo – or so he thought. In fact, although the image was no longer visible on his screen, or in his picture gallery, it had parked itself elsewhere in the device to be recovered later by forensic technicians.

That afternoon Gary Stretch turned up at 38 Bifield in the Vauxhall Astra. Leaving Gaz and Joanne to do whatever was necessary, Layton went shopping with a mate only to learn things were going badly wrong on his return.

Amongst the topics discussed while Layton was at the shops was Kevin Lee's reaction when he learned that another man had been killed inside one of his properties. While Lee had just about managed to cope with the murder and subsequent disposal of Lukasz Slaboszewski, there was no way he could have swept another homicide under the carpet, so it was decided in the spirit of 'in for a penny, in for a pound' that they would not tell him but instead they would murder him, too.

9

HANDSOME KEV

We are devastated by Kevin's death. He was a wonderful husband, loving brother and son. His naturally infectious personality touched everyone who knew him. He will be hugely missed by all his friends and family.
LEE FAMILY STATEMENT FOLLOWING THE TRIAL

Before Lukasz Slaboszewski was murdered, Kevin Lee had confided in his wife that he was having an affair. Whether or not Joanne Dennehy's name was mentioned is unknown. What brought about this confession is also unknown. Maybe it was Cristina's intuition based upon her husband's recent, suspicious behaviour had caused her to confront him. Her reaction is also unknown. According to police it seems that Kevin had told his wife that 'someone had been murdered' by Dennehy but not necessarily the recent nature of the killing, and allegedly Cristina did tell him to stay away from Dennehy for his own safety. I have written to Kevin's family to try and confirm all of this but without making a 'donation' of sorts, they refused to comment further and one must respect their wishes.

Joanne told me that she wanted to rape me while I am wearing a dress. She is like Uma Thurman from Kill Bill *and the woman from* Terminator.

Kevin Lee to best friend Dave Church, about an hour before the murder

Lee was now in deep trouble. Any right-minded man would have gone straight to the police when Dennehy first told him of a man being murdered, instead he loaned her money to buy an old car so that the body could be disposed of. Hopefully, this would be the end of the matter..

Nevertheless, like many of the men who were drawn to Joanne Dennehy, Kevin Lee could not stay away because by then he was completely infatuated with her. Then, on Good Friday, 2013, the day of his murder, he did something really foolish. Unaware that John Chapman was lying in a pool of congealing blood at 38 Bifield, he sent her an Easter card. Later the same day she phoned him and they arranged to rendezvous at 11 Rolleston Garth, but Dennehy's intentions were not focused on sex – she had a third murder in mind. Later, she admitted that the killing of Kevin Lee was premeditated and well planned. In a March 2013 letter to Julie Gibbons, she wrote:

Killing Kevin Lee was planned. I kept my mouth shut in the police station, I did not take the stand either because Gaz said it would harm him and no doubt he was right. He knew if I were to take the stand and lies were being chucked at me I'd lose my temper and tell it how it is, regardless of the outcome. Gaz knows I react badly to lies.

This letter again shows that Dennehy and Stretch may have planned to murder Kevin, who was last seen alive at 2pm that Good Friday in an HMV store in the Queensgate Shopping Mall, Peterborough. He bought four music CDs – two for his wife, the others – one featuring Bobby Womack and one by the band The xx – for Dennehy. However, what he didn't know was that Joanne was apparently furious with him. Before the killing of Lee, Stretch had confided in a teenage girl (name removed at judge's order) that Kevin hadn't paid Dennehy for work she had done at Rolleston Garth and that she was getting stressed and Lee was harassing her.

'She *will* kill him,' Stretch told the teenager, and the young girl confirmed this at Dennehy's trial.

After dropping off two of the CDs at his home, Kevin drove over to 11 Rolleston Garth in his light blue Ford Mondeo estate car, registration number Y32 0JB. There, he stripped naked and slipped into something more comfortable: a black sequined dress belonging to Joanne, to be precise.

Whatever was this man thinking of, you might ask. Kevin was serially cheating on his loving and extremely attractive wife, effectively betraying his children into the bargain. He knew that there had been a murder and he had conspired with his lover to provide her with a vehicle to dump the body. Yet, while oblivious to the fact that a second man had been slaughtered in another of his firm's properties, he bought Joanne an Easter card and a couple of CDs, then visited her, knowing she wanted to rape him while he was wearing one of her black dresses.

There has been some debate as to whether Dennehy dressed

Lee in the black dress after he had been killed, or whether he had put it on voluntarily. Based on forensic examination and the autopsy report, the police say the latter is correct. Nevertheless, some time after Kevin Lee arrived at 11 Rolleston Garth, Dennehy stabbed him five times in the chest. The wounds penetrated both his lungs and heart while the maniac alleged that she played Elvis songs and recorded everything on her mobile phone. Lee had put up the fight of his life for it later transpired that he was the only victim to suffer defensive wounds to his fingers and hands.

> *It was just me, him and a video cam, which was watched later over a meal and lots of white wine.*
> Joanne Dennehy, letter to a pen friend

With two more dead bodies at two separate addresses now to dispose of, Dennehy and Stretch had to move fast, with several witnesses seeing them engaged in the hectic clean-up operations.

When Kevin failed to return home that evening, Cristina became concerned so she spoke to her family and made a few calls. She rang Kevin's business partner, Paul Creed, also the partner of Kevin's daughter, Chiara. Paul not heard from Kevin either, however two of Kevin's friends decided to visit 11 Rolleston Garth, where they arrived at 8pm. As they entered the estate they spotted Kevin's Mondeo leaving and noticed 'something large in the rear of the vehicle'. This later transpired to be a mattress taken from 11 Rolleston Garth.

According to forensic evidence, police say that Kevin Lee's

dead body was taken away in the Vauxhall Astra – the corpse covered by a tarpaulin borrowed from Robert Moore, who, like Leslie Layton, incidentally had a crush on Joanne as well.

Kevin's body was soon dumped in a ditch at Newborough. Then, at about 8.30pm that evening, the blue Ford Mondeo estate driven by Leslie Layton, and the green Vauxhall Astra driven by a very uncomfortable Stretch, with Dennehy in the front passenger seat, arrived simultaneously at a Shell petrol station on the outskirts of Peterborough. The forecourt CCTV recorded Layton exit the Mondeo to fill a can from one of the pumps. Moments later, he was approached by Stretch, wearing a dark sweater, khaki sleeveless jacket, beige cut-off-below-the-knee shorts and trainers. Layton, who had already cast a suspicious glance at the CCTV, gave Stretch money to pay for the petrol. Inside the garage, Stretch picked up a bottle of water and was filmed swigging it and muttering away to himself. The two cars were then driven off together.

The next sighting of the blue Mondeo came at 9.15pm. A farmer found it ablaze at an isolated spot where people dumped rubbish in Great Drove, a track close to the village of Yaxley. The Cambridgeshire Fire Service attended with one appliance and the flaming car and the mattress were recorded on video before being extinguished. The incident was reported to the police and the crew left the scene, returning to their station just before 10pm.

After torching Kevin's car, the threesome returned to 38 Bifield, where Stretch and Layton carried John Chapman's corpse down the stairs and placed it in the rear of the Vauxhall, causing the suspension to drop, as a neighbour recalled.

From there they drove out to Thorney Dyke, where Lukasz Slaboszewski still lay undiscovered, and disposed of the body. Telephonic data confirms that that Good Friday night a very emotional Layton stayed with Gary Stretch at Riseholme while Dennehy slept at Robert Moore's place, 78 Belvoir Way, which he shared with his fourteen-year-old daughter.

Despite not having any previous convictions Robert Moore was now up to his neck in it. The teenager had already seen the dead body of Lukasz Slaboszewski in the wheelie bin because Stretch and Dennehy had shown it to her. She had told Moore who, being under no illusion that murder had not occurred, had supplied the tarpaulin that he knew was to be used when disposing of the bodies of the three men. Moore had also been sending sexy text messages to Dennehy because the fool was besotted with her, and now he was giving two murderous fugitives food and shelter. One couldn't make this up if one tried!

After the two friends of Kevin Lee had reported their concerns to Cristina, she contacted the police. At about 10.40pm an officer took down Kevin's details, but for the time being he could only be categorised as a potentially missing person who might turn up alive and well at any time.

There is yet another tragic tailpiece to the death of Kevin Lee to consider. I do not know the state of Quicklet's financial affairs prior to Joanne Dennehy's arrival on the scene although one suspects a cash flow problem of sorts –why else would Lee have used the services of Dennehy and Stretch to evict tenants? Intimidation and threats of violence amount to blackmail, coercion and duress, which are all indictable offences. One might add conspiracy to defraud the taxpayer by abusing Housing Benefit payments and a large dose of false accounting into the bargain, of which Kevin Lee would have been well aware.

Nevertheless, what one can say in all certainty is that without Lee at the helm of the business he incorporated on Tuesday, 2 December 2003, Quicklet went down like the *Titanic* and destroyed his family into the bargain. He was officially removed as a director on Friday, 9 May 2014, and Cristina, the former company secretary, took over her late husband's role – a paper exercise until the firm was liquidated.

During my research for this book I wrote to Quicklet, via the firm's registered office. A Mr J. R. Arnott courteously replied on behalf of certified accountants Bulley Davey – Business Recovery and Insolvency Specialists:

'In our capacity as Insolvency Practitioners we are acting on the instructions of Mrs Cristina Lee and have convened meetings of members and creditors of the company for the purposes of Creditors Voluntary Liquidation. The company is due to go into liquidation on 24th June 2104.'

This has been an incomprehensibly difficult time for all of the family as we try to come to terms with what has happened to Kevin. Nothing is the same now. This tragedy has shaken our lives to the core and we are devastated about how Kevin's life came to an end.

Cristina is devastated that Kevin has been taken away from us as a family. Initially, after discovering the circumstances of Kevin's death she felt a lot of anger but she is slowly managing to deal with it.

As a family we feel an immense pressure to fill so many voids, which no one could ever really replace. Kevin was so full of life, excitement and laughter that life now is very dull without him around.

Dino has lost not only his dad, but also his best friend – his karting mechanic and his most encouraging mentor. Dino and Chiara have, in essence, lost both parents because Cristina hasn't been able to deal with her own grief. Almost 22 months on and she is still not coming to terms with the loss of Kevin.

Cristina's brother-in-law, Darren Cray, press statement after Dennehy's conviction

10

OPERATION DARCY

Detective Chief Inspector Martin Brunning is a wonderful man.
He and his officers have been very supportive to us. They all
work very, very hard. We will never come to terms with
what our daughter has done. It is the way it is.
KATHLEEN DENNEHY, TO THE AUTHOR, WEDNESDAY, 28 MAY 2014

Making good multi-agency operational commonsense, the
Bedfordshire, Cambridge and Hertfordshire Major
Crime Unit was formed in 2012 during an amalgamation of
highly experienced detective police officers and technical
specialists drawn from three counties, together into two
operational 'hubs'. One of these centres is based at the Hex
Building, Cambridgeshire Constabulary HQ, Hinchingbrooke
Park, Huntingdon. The other is at the Hertfordshire Police
HQ, Welwyn Garden City. The Major Crime Unit's brief is
to investigate all serious crimes, to include robberies, stranger
rapes [where attackers and victim are unknown to each other]
and homicides. Martin Brunning joined the police in 1995 and
he is now the boss of Team (3).

After signing in at the front desk of the Cambridgeshire
Police HQ, and having the obligatory photograph taken and

details of my ID logged, DCI Martin Brunning, his Detective Sergeant Andy Crocker and Media Relations Officer David Old invited me into 'The Hub' at the Hex Building – an airy, expansive set-up with state-of-the-art systems and state-of-the-art investigators busy as bees. Martin ushered me into his office. Previously he had emailed me saying this was the first 'dedicated' office he'd had.

My team does all the hard work. I just take the calls.
DCI Martin Brunning, to the author at interview, 2014

Taking me briefly me through the triple murder inquiry as it had developed (and Brunning does not appreciate being interrupted when he has something to say, adding, 'It is all a bit complicated so ask your questions when I am finished'), he first explained that when Kevin Lee didn't return home he was initially treated as a possible missing person. He added that such missing person cases are not within the remit of the Major Crime Unit. However, all this soon changed when Lee's blue Ford Mondeo was found ablaze close to a railway bridge in Great Drove, Yaxley, where, coincidentally, Julie Gibbons was now living. A quick check of the registration number of the burning vehicle on the Police National Computer revealed that it belonged to a Kevin Lee, who had been reported as missing.

Early the following morning sixty-eight-year-old Terry Walker was walking his dog in the rural parish of Newborough when he spotted a body face down in a dyke by the side of Middle Road. The corpse was dressed in a black sequined dress, pulled up to expose the buttocks. An 'object' had been pushed into the anus. 'This was a degrading act of post-death humiliation. The body had been posed,' DCI Brunning explained to me during our interview. In fact, photos of the corpse were so unsettling they were later 'sanitised' before the trial jury could view them.

'At first, I thought it was a dummy,' Walker recalled. 'But then I noticed blood on the sleeves and it dawned on me that this was a crime scene, so I decided to call the police. The location is very isolated. Only dog walkers like myself come up here, it's really out of the way.'

Some time later that day, police went to 11 Rolleston Garth with a locksmith in attendance. Near to the kitchen units crime scene technicians found blood spatter – later proved to be that of Lukasz Slaboszewski. His blood was also found close to the inside of the front door – perhaps indicating this contamination was caused when his corpse was removed from the premises by Dennehy and Stretch to be placed in the wheelie bin.

On a sofa, Scenes of Crime Officers (SOCO) found more blood, which proved be that of Kevin Lee. Impressions from two sets of footwear, later proved to belong to Dennehy and Stretch, were also discovered.

Despite a half-hearted attempt by Stretch and Dennehy to clean the place up, detectives also found that blood had dripped onto the carpet, indicating the men's bodies had been moved after their deaths. The trainers Stretch was wearing when he was later arrested in Herefordshire were contaminated with Slaboszewski's blood. Another pair of trainers found at Stretch's home bore evidence of Lee's blood.

'Operation Darcy' was now launched to find Kevin's killer.

The code names for police operations are not selected by the police agency concerned, they are randomly selected from a central law enforcement database and now every UK police force was alerted to 'Wanted for Murder'. Even at the time of writing the full cost of catching Dennehy and Stretch still has to be established. With Operation Darcy one is looking at – even on the light side – a cost to the taxpayer of £300K, more likely £1 million when the meter eventually stops running. However, the cost to human life and the tragedy brought to the victims and their next of kin by these cowardly lowlifes is incalculable. The cost to the public purse in keeping Dennehy, Stretch, Layton and Moore in prison will send the final tab into orbit.

And this is where a tri-county police agency really makes sense, especially for the Police and Crime Commissioners who watch their individual budgets like hawks, for the bill for investigations such as Operation Darcy is no longer picked up by a single county. Bedfordshire, Cambridgeshire and Hertfordshire would cover the costs between them.

11

MURDER - NOT LIKE ON TV!

These days the word murder is much used with most of us unaware of its etymology. It is, however, derived from 'murdrum' (itself from Old French *murdre*) – a heavy fine imposed on the community by the Normans when one of them was killed and the perpetrator remained at large. In time, murdrum was corrupted to murder and signified the act of killing. (Old English *modhor* is an alternative derivation.)

The classic definition of murder was given by Sir Edward Coke (1552–1634), Lord Chief Justice and authority on common law:

'Murder is when a man of sound memory, and of the age of discretion, unlawfully killeth within any county of the realm any reasonable creature in rerum natura under the King's peace, with malice aforethought, either expressed by the party or implied by the law, so as the party wounded, or hurt... die of the wound or hurt... within a year and day after the same'.

Coke's definition of murder still holds good in its essential provisions, and under common law until 1957 all acts of murder were punishable by death. The Homicide Act of that year limited capital punishment to specified types of murder, such as the killing of a police officer in the execution of his duty, and the death penalty was abolished altogether by the Homicide Act of 1965, except for acts of high treason and piracy with violence.

Real murder is not sanitised as it is on TV, certainly not as in the staged *Columbo* movies with wealthy victims from silver spoon backgrounds, expensive cars and $15 million Hollywood mansions with large swimming pools. In 'Columbo Land' the scheming killers are just as well educated as their victims. Some are highly-decorated retired army generals, famous singers or fading film stars, no one so banal as a low-life drug addict park bench resident, his body pickled with cheap booze, and no rotting, stinking and bloated corpses filled with gas for Lieutenant Columbo.

Even Columbo's scruffy beige raincoat and his battered Peugeot saloon are out of kilter. Real-life UK and US detectives are immaculately groomed, wear well-tailored suits, sturdy wristwatches, spotless starched shirts and drive well-maintained cars. And, unless they are wearing wellington boots while examining crime scenes, such as the deposition site of Kevin Lee, you can see your face in their well-polished shoes. And a detective constable, with whom I spoke at Yaxley police station, reinforces all this.

I needed directions to one of the body disposal sites, but the police station is not operational as far as the public are concerned. There is a yellow telephone handset on the wall outside, which connects those with enquiries to the central Cambridgeshire Constabulary switchboard. I picked up the handset, explained to the operator who I was, what I was doing, and I mentioned Martin Brunning's name. Within two minutes the operator called back, telling me that an officer would be with me shortly – in fact he was walking towards me as we spoke. Smart as a button, courteous and thoroughly efficient he was, too. Unfortunately, I didn't catch his name or collar number, but I am sure when Martin Brunning reads this book he'll ensure my gratitude is passed on.

Nevertheless, in real life, centre stage in the dramatic theatre of murder most foul seems always set with dripping-wet alleyways and places where no sensible person would venture after dark, for none but the most foolish killer would want to advertise their intentions. Trees in the wings; black, bereft of leaves, their spindly branches pointing accusingly like a dead crone's fingers at the waning moon spotlighting the cooling body interred an a hastily-dug hole in the ground, or dumped in a ditch in the middle of nowhere, as is the case with Dennehy's victims. And here we find 'Fenland': 500 square km of extremely flat fens; naturally marshy regions within a few metres of sea level in eastern England artificially drained since Roman times, now given over to the growing of grain and vegetables. There are a lot of drainage ditches and dykes in Fenland. Many places to dispose of dead bodies with only a solitary owl to bear witness, however, what inevitably follows is an open metal draw from the filing cabinet of death – the cadaver's eyes collapsing into their sockets, lips distorted, shrunken back into a sardonica rictus grin.

Columbo's victims' teeth are all pearly white and in good condition. In real life they are not. On TV, the body is still pristine whereas in the real world the hair is matted and there are dead leaves, twigs and insect larvae entangled in the strands. There is never any excrement or urine fouling the underwear or vomit staining a T-shirt, and there is never any post-mortem lividity present in such films either. In real life a decomposing body reeks. An unmistakable smell, it can cling to anything it touches, especially when bodies are discovered in warm residences where they have lain for days.

In one particular historic case I have knowledge of a man, in the dead of night, beat to death his wife and two children before hanging himself in the stairwell. Here, their bodies remained for a week in the suffocating summer heat before they were discovered. Years later, the senior investigator explained to me:

'We went in and did what we had to do. We showered ourselves at home afterwards. We washed our shirts and socks. We dry-cleaned our suits. It was useless so we had to burn every single item of clothing we had worn in that place. I can still smell it today.'

But, hey, we all enjoy *Columbo*, and what follows would make the loveable TV cop proud. As a tribute to the remarkable actor, Peter Falk, who played Columbo, shortly before he passed away at his home on Roxbury Drive, Los Angeles, he fell asleep during an award-winning ceremony with a sign around his neck – 'DO NOT DISTURB'. How cool is that? Falk was eighty-four.

12

ON THE RUN

The prisoners seemed to me in no way morally inferior to the rest of the population though they were on the whole slightly below the usual level of intelligence, as is shown by their having been caught.
BERTRAND RUSSELL, AUTOBIOGRAPHY, 1967

The basis on which the investigation of crime stands is the assembling of a sequence of facts allowing the judicial process to be carried through to a satisfactory conclusion. It should prove that a crime was committed, and should also present evidence that a named person, or persons, was responsible for committing it. During Operation Darcy, police used every trick in the book to catch and bring to justice Dennehy, Stretch, Layton and Moore. Indeed, they employed state-of-the-art surveillance systems to great effect and forensics played a great part. So, if committing a serious crime, or any crime, is in your mind, forget it. The odds are you'll get caught.

The earliest-known treatise on forensic medicine (the word 'forensic' meaning no more than 'connected to the courtroom') is the thirteenth-century Chinese book *Hsi Yuan Lu* (The

Washing Away of Wrongs). Above all else, this work stressed the importance of examining a crime scene, stating: 'The difference of a hair is of the difference of a thousand li' – a li being a Chinese mile. This adage reflects the importance placed on trace evidence in whichever form it takes by the French criminologist Dr Edmond Locard at the University of Lyon who, early in the twentieth century, recognised the value of trace evidence and advanced his 'contact trace theory', which states simply: 'That a criminal will always carry away with him some trace from the scene of his crime, and leave some of his presence behind'.

This is the very foundation of forensic science. It is these objective traces, which the criminal unwittingly deposits as clues, along with subjective traces such as witness statements that conspire to prove the 'named person or persons' responsible for a crime. This tangible evidence will, these days, be subject to analysis and comparison in one or other of the specialised sections of the modern forensic science laboratory and the range of possible interchanges is vast.

Harry Sodeman, a distinguished Swedish scientist criminologist, wrote that 'everything imaginable may constitute a clue'. Everything that is, from earwax to ski tracks. Earwax traps dust particles from the environment and may yield information about a person's occupation, while looking at ski tracks tells the experienced observer the direction the traveller was moving – usually downhill. The list of contact traces includes blood, glass particles, dust, fibres, hair, body-fluid stains, oil, paint, fragments of vegetation and a great many more substances, restricted only by the limits of scientific detection methods – which today are very few and far between.

For instance, if archeologists can determine from the preserved body of a man buried in an icy glazier 100,000 years ago what he ate for his last supper, his diet, age and occupation, then today forensic pathologists and scientists will know more about you than you did before you died. And, believe it or not, one can get chemical fingerprints from smoke, which is especially useful when determining the crime of arson and use of an accelerant. But we'll leave these fascinating forensic issues for another day. However, what Dr Edmond Locard could never have conceived is nowadays one can pluck contact trace evidence from thin air – indeed, out of clear blue sky, even space – and it is as damning to the offender as any type of physical evidence or DNA matching. Enter stage left, your mobile provider!

From the very moment one purchases a mobile telephone, be it on contract or Pay-as-you-Go, 'Big Brother' starts watching you – yes *YOU*! The telephone providers know your full name, your address, your credit rating, if you are employed or otherwise. And you can bet your bottom dollar that buried in the small print, the very small print of the 15,000-word contract is a clause stating that your provider can share your personal data with anyone they choose – such as those firms who ring at all hours of the day informing you that you can claim thousands of pounds for the road traffic accident you never had, but it gets even better. If the CIA took an interest in a taxi trip you booked using your mobile – or 'cellphone', as our cousins across 'The Pond' insist on calling them – they can find out in minutes and plot your movements to within a yard or so.

Then there are the 'APPS'. If your suspicious partner buys one of these surveillance apps, he/she can monitor your movements via Global Positioning Satellites (GPS), 24/7. Switching your phone off while between the sheets with your lover is of no use at all. Your route to a hotel, or apartment, can be traced in a heartbeat because your phone still emits a signal. So, wherever you go, anywhere in the world Big Brother may be covertly watching you. Take this as Gospel, even more so because every phone provider has its own police liaison officer who works hand in hand with detectives investigating a crime where a mobile phone plays some part.

According to the *Mail on Sunday*, 12 October 2014, at the headquarters of every police force in Britain is a small office called the 'Telecoms Intelligence Unit' (TIU). There, police can log in directly to the mainframe computers of three of four big mobile phone companies – Vodafone, Three and EE – as well as BT and internet service providers. EE comprises the former networks Orange and T-Mobile, whose law-enforcement interface was called 'Plod' – an acronym for Police Liaison On-screen Database.

Armed with the required usernames and passwords (the method by which police do this I cannot reveal to the reader), in a few keystrokes officers can retrieve confidential data from anyone's telephone or computer use within minutes. All it takes is a couple of senior officers within the force to sign off the request and any officer can have those details on his screen.

Telecoms security expert Martin Hoskins, Privacy

Counsulting, has said: 'It's going on every hour of every day. As long as the police have the authorization for the data, the door is always open for them,' adding, 'Quick access to communication data can be a matter of life or death if, for example, you're trying to trace a child carrying a mobile phone.'

The use of electronic mobile telephone data proved crucial as forensic contact trace evidence during the early stages of Operation Darcy. It allowed DCI Martin Brunning and Team (3) of the Major Crime Unit to piece together the movements of Joanne Dennehy, Gary Stretch and Leslie Layton around the times the three murders were committed and thereafter to Robert Moore, who harboured Dennehy and Stretch for two nights while they were on the run.

This mobile phone data put Dennehy (who now had Chapman's phone in her possession), Stretch and Layton's 'Pay-as-You-Go' mobile phones near a telecommunications mast close to Yaxley at the time when Kevin Lee's Ford Mondeo was set ablaze.

Ironically, the Yaxley telephonic data only came to the notice of the police because Cristina Lee, already suspicious about her husband's activities, was concerned as to his whereabouts during the evening he went missing. She had already established that he was having an affair because Kevin had allegedly confirmed it so she checked his mobile phone statements. A well-used number was Dennehy's, although she probably did not know the name at the time. Cristina rang the number and it was that call which police would say proved that Dennehy was in the vicinity of Kevin's car when it went up in smoke.

Joanne Dennehy's name was now in the frame. Then a

second piece of electronic forensic contact evidence came about following the murder of John Chapman. She had used the dead man's mobile phone to sing a song to Gary Stretch – a mistake that all but invited her arrest. Now Stretch's name was in the frame, too.

Some time after Leslie Layton was arrested, police found the 'erased' photo of Chapman's dead body as a callous souvenir on his mobile phone. This matrix of electronic mobile phone interchanges between Dennehy, Stretch, Layton and Moore was as strong as steel wire. It provided a web from which even the spiders that spun it could not escape.

This was circumstantial evidence in its purest form because it gave the police solid links to the deaths of Kevin Lee, John Chapman, Lukasz Slaboszewski, the addresses of 38 Bifield, and 11 Rolleston Garth; later to prove that Dennehy, Stretch and Layton's mobile phones were in the near vicinity of the fire that destroyed Kevin Lee's car, and the ditches where the bodies were dumped at the relevant times in question – all proving forensic contact trace evidence can be plucked out of thin air, even space.

Edmond Locard would now be delighted – can we agree on this? But back then he would not have known about the coming advent of CCTV or the Automatic Number Plate Recognition (ANPR) system either, for the combination of telephonic data, CCTV and ANPR was to rubber stamp Denney, Stretch, Layton and Moore's downfall.

> She [Dennehy] ran her hand down my neck. It was like being touched by a rattlesnake.

Mark Lloyd, one of Gary Stretch's former criminal associates

Despite some bickering as to the exact number of cameras, current research shows that there are about 1.85 million CCTVs in use – one for every 32 people in the UK. It is thought that on average a person passes by one of these cameras at least eight times a day. While on the run Dennehy and Stretch would pass scores of them.

Unknown to police, Dennehy and Stretch, a gun tucked into the waistband of his trousers, were at the time in the green Vauxhall Astra paid for by Kevin Lee. On the night 29/30 March 2013 they stayed with Robert Moore at his council flat at 78 Belvoir Way, Peterborough

Now alone at an empty 38 Bifield, the weak-willed Leslie Layton was falling apart at the seams. As Judge Robin Godfrey Spencer later concluded: 'Over that Easter weekend Layton was undoubtedly wracked with guilt and worry at what he had done. This is why his friends, Toni Ann Roberts and Michelle Bowles, described him as distressed and upset on the Sunday evening when they spoke to him.'

Besides, where was John Chapman?

However, this guilt and worry did not extend to Layton assisting the police in getting to the truth. When first interviewed he went out of his way to try and cover not only his tracks, but those of Dennehy and Stretch too. When asked about the whereabouts of John Chapman, his take was, 'I know nuffink, honest to God. I fink I last saw him on Wednesday or Thursday.' Then, when the cops went away, the first thing he did was to text Moore, and then Dennehy, telling her the police were trying to find her.

The police visited Layton again during the afternoon of April Fool's Day – Monday, 1 April. Once again he claimed ignorance of the entire business. During this interview Dennehy phoned Layton on Chapman's mobile phone and as soon as the police left him, he called her back to update her on the progress of the investigation.

By now the murder of Kevin Lee was headline news. On the Sunday, Dennehy and Stretch drove to East Anglia. On arrival at King's Lynn they stopped off at a friend of Joanne's called Georgina Page. They talked in a matter-of-fact way about the murders, with garrulous Stretch boasting to Georgina that the bodies would never be found. Georgina would later testify that Joanne became excited and animated when she saw reports on television that she was wanted in connection with the murder of Kevin Lee (the bodies of John Chapman and Lukasz Slaboszewski were yet to be found). 'She was ecstatic,' testified Page at the trial. Dennehy then went on to explain to her that she had dressed Kevin Lee up, had 'lubricated his backside' and 'shoved something into it to make it look as though it was a sexual act'.

Before the fugitives left Georgina flat, Stretch threatened her, saying he would get his father to sort out anyone who grassed, which she took to mean that she would be killed. For her part Dennehy said that she had already accepted they would be caught and would go to prison for a long time. With this, Stretch laughed and said: 'My kids are grown up now, so I don't care.' After leaving King's Lynn he burgled a holiday home at

Diss. Amongst the property stolen was an expensive camera. Dennehy and Stretch then received another text message from Robert Moore, telling them they could stay a second night at his place. He had food waiting and wished them good luck.

By now the two of you were well and truly on the run and your behaviour was totally lawless.
Mr Justice Spencer, sentencing remarks, 28 February 2014

Early in the morning of Tuesday, 2 April, with a duvet spread across the back seat of their car, Dennehy and Stretch left Peterborough to drive west towards Herefordshire. It was a place that Stretch knew well because he had been born there and periodically lived on and off there – while not in prison, that is.

The couple were filmed by CCTV walking hand in hand at a service station in Market Harborough, south of Leicester, then later at Strensham Services where another camera tracked them to the green Vauxhall Astra bearing the registration number R660 ECT. The police immediately flagged this car as a 'vehicle of interest' and added it to the Automatic Number Plate Recognition (ANPR) system. A check through the Motor Insurers Bureau (MIB) revealed the vehicle as being insured by one Gary Stretch of Messrs Undertaker & Co. Now the pieces of the crime puzzle were fitting into place: Stretch was a known associate of Dennehy and she was wanted for murder.

From Strensham in Worcestershire they drove, via Ledbury, to Bartestree, Hereford, where they were once again seen recorded on a store CCTV before Stretch arrived back at his old haunt of Kington, on the Welsh border, and about twenty miles from Hereford. There he met up with a criminal associate called Andrew Wilmott, aka 'Moby', at his flat in Llwellin Road. This is where Dennehy and Stretch took the notorious on-the-run photos of each other on the balcony and several of Joanne sitting in an armchair, holding a lethally serrated dagger. They were soon joined by Mark Lloyd. Ironically, the first time Stretch and Dennehy saw their 'happy snaps' was after the police developed the film.

Lloyd proved to be yet another sucker who fell for Joanne's charms. Making no bones about it, he said that he became enamoured with Dennehy from the outset. He later gave evidence in court, saying: 'She ran her hand down the back of my neck. It was like being touched by a rattlesnake. If she had told me to put my head through the car windscreen, I would have done it.' But was he, just like Leslie Layton and Robert Moore before him, a little out of his depth? Mr Justice Spencer was inclined to believe so:

'I am quite sure that Mr Lloyd was not a willing passenger in the Vauxhall Astra when it set off for Hereford,' the judge said in his sentencing remarks. 'He gave evidence at the trial over a long period and, like the jury, I had good opportunity to assess him. I am also sure that before you [Dennehy and Stretch] left the flat at Kington there was an incident in the kitchen, out of sight of Dennehy, when Gary Stretch showed Mark Lloyd a handgun, which was in the waistband of Stretch's trousers. Whether it was in fact loaded, as Mark Lloyd believed on the basis of his experience of such weapons, matters not.'

Quite what experience of guns the judge is referring to is a bit of a puzzle, so I asked DS Mark Jinks for the answer. He replied, probably tongue-in-cheek: 'Lloyd worked in an abattoir but that is probably the closest he got aside from an air rifle.'

Thereafter, Dennehy and Mark Lloyd, with Stretch driving the Vauxhall Astra and their crony, Wilmott, following in a Renault, made their way towards the Oval area of the City of Hereford.

By now DCI Martin Brunning's Major Crime Unit had connected Dennehy and Stretch to the murder of Kevin Lee and suspected John Chapman might have met a similar fate, so 'Wanted for Murder' bulletins were circulated to every police force in the country, especially CID colleagues in Herefordshire, advising them that Stretch could be coming their way. For his part Stretch was easily noticeable because of his enormous height (7ft 3in), with Joanne Dennehy diminutive in comparison at 5ft 8in. They made an odd-looking and easily recognisable couple for he was a mere three inches shorter than the tallest man in the country. {At the time of writing, the tallest man in the UK is English actor and baseball player Neil Fingleton. Born 18 December 1980, Neil stands at 7ft 7.56in and he is listed amongst the tallest men in the world.]

Now we had the type of car Dennehy and Stretch were driving. Now we had a vehicle registration number. Now, using ANPR, we could track them down.
DCI Martin Brunning, to the author at interview, 2014

ANPR is a mass surveillance method that uses character recognition on images to read vehicle licence plates. Most have infrared lighting so the system also works at night. Developed in 1976 by the Police Scientific Development Branch, ANPR's first vital role in a murder case came about with the location and conviction of a criminal gang who shot dead Sharon Beshenivsky, a thirty-eight-year-old Bradford police officer, on Friday, 18 November 2005.

Now, just forty-eight hours after fleeing Peterborough, the police were in hot pursuit and there could be no hiding place: Dennehy must be arrested before she killed again.

13

ROBIN BEREZA

She just came straight at me.
ROBIN BEREZA, GIVING EVIDENCE AT TRIAL

With the precise whereabouts of Lukasz Slaboszewski and John Chapman still unknown to police, Dennehy, Stretch and the other villains in tow next surfaced in the 'Oval' area of Hereford during the afternoon of Tuesday, 2 April 2013. They stopped off in Green Lane, at a shop on a roundabout at Wordsworth Road and Westfaling Street. Here, along with Mark Lloyd, Dennehy bought rolling tobacco and some whisky. Once again her image was captured on CCTV. She was, according to the young woman behind the counter, 'in high spirits, and in a state of euphoria'.

Earlier that day the circular from colleagues in Cambridge-shire had raised eyebrows amongst the older hands in the CID office at Hereford police station. This 'focus-led intelligence' informed them that one Gary Stretch – or 'Gary Richards', as the older West Mercia detectives knew him – was linked to a murder investigation in Peterborough. To West Mercia Police, 'Richards' from Kington was a known criminal who had often been arrested before he left the area. The intelligence also suggested that Stretch might be 'making for home' in the company of Joanne Dennehy, prime suspect in the murder of Kevin Lee.

At about 3.35pm, former fire service employee sixty-three-year-old Robin Bereza was walking – rather than opting for his usual jogging – his Labrador called Samson along Westfaling Street. The previous evening he had celebrated his thirty-sixth wedding anniversary with his wife, Pam. He was in high spirits but then, just as he approached the junction at Holmes Street, a car pulled up behind him. Bereza described what followed to the jury at the joint trial of Dennehy, Stretch and Layton:

I felt a blow to my right shoulder. I did not immediately realise that I was being attacked. I turned around and saw this lady. She just stared straight through me. I kicked her and made contact. It had no impact on her. She just came straight towards me and I thought she was just going to mug me.

I ran into the road. I put my hand to my jacket and saw all this blood and then it triggered and I thought, 'You just want blood'. She tried to come for me again. I kicked her again, but still she didn't react. I asked her, 'What are you doing?' She said, 'I'm hurting you. I'm going to fuckin' kill you.'

Dennehy pursued Bereza down the road, continuing the attack, but she eventually desisted because of the arrival of another car on the scene, waiting to turn into a side road. Gary Stretch had driven the Astra slowly behind Dennehy and he beckoned for her to get back into the Vauxhall. Leaving Robin with a stab to his right shoulder and another to his chest area, a smiling Dennehy casually strolled back to the Vauxhall, and Mark Lloyd saw her kiss Stretch on the cheek, then heard her say, 'Thanks.'

Although Dennehy had only managed to inflict two stabs to Robin Bereza she caused him potentially fatal injuries. The deep wound to his back penetrated the chest wall, causing a haemopneumothorax as well as bruising to the lung and fracturing a rib. Had the blood and air not been promptly drained from his chest through expert medical treatment, Bereza's life would have been endangered. The other stab shattered his shoulder blade and fractured the bone in an upper arm. It was only by pure chance that the nerves in the arm were not irreparably damaged with a drastic loss of function.

'The attack has had a profound effect on Robin Bereza, emotionally and psychologically,' remarked Mr Justice Spencer at sentencing, 24 February 2014

Mark Lloyd went even further with this graphic account:

Dennehy struck Robin Bereza like in the film Pyscho, *thrusting and putting her whole weight behind it. The blade of the knife was as black as the handle with blood. She stank of blood. Afterwards, Gary drove off very, very calmly. It was as if they had just stopped for a McDonald's.*

Mark Lloyd, giving evidence against Dennehy and Stretch at trial

Despite his wounds Robin Bereza staggered home and managed to dial 999. At 3.42pm police took a call from West Midlands ambulance control saying that a man had been repeatedly stabbed in Westfaling Street. Robin was initially taken to Hereford Country Hospital before being airlifted to the Queen Elizabeth Hospital, in Birmingham. Bereza gave a description of his attacker as a woman with a star-like tattoo on her cheek.

14

JOHN ROGERS

*You've had your fun, now I want mine. I don't want to kill a woman,
especially not one with a child. Find me another man with a dog.*
DENNEHY TO STRETCH IMMEDIATELY AFTER THE
ATTEMPTED MURDER OF ROBIN BEREZA

About nine minutes after the attack on Robin Bereza, with a
crime scene perimeter being set up in Westfaling Street,
Stretch zeroed in like a heat-seeking missile on another potential
victim. It was fifty-six-year-old John Rogers out walking his
grey lurcher dog called Archie along a footpath close to the
River Wye, and between Golden Post and the Belmont Estate,
Hunderton, Hereford. This was a cul-de-sac location Stretch
knew well as a place for dog walkers. It was very close to where
his grandmother used to live.

Giving his evidence at the joint trial of Dennehy and Stretch
in 2013, a gaunt-looking Rogers told the jury:

*I felt a punch in my back. I assumed it was a friend, or
a neighbour just messing around. I turned around. I saw
the woman who had struck me just standing there. She*

started stabbing me in the chest. I asked her, 'What's this all about?' She replied, 'You're bleeding. I better do some more.'

I said, 'Just leave me alone, please. Please leave me alone,' but she didn't. She didn't seem to be showing any emotion. She didn't seem to be enjoying herself. She just seemed like she was going about business.

I fell to the ground but the attack continued. I was just waiting for it to stop. There was loads and loads of blood. As I lay there, I thought, 'This is where I am going to die.'

Rogers had been stabbed more than thirty times. He had deep wounds to the chest, abdomen and back; both lungs had collapsed. His bowel was perforated and exposed. Had he not received the most expert and prompt medical treatment he would have died from those injuries. So severe was the force of the wounds that nine ribs were fractured. He also received defensive wounds to his hands and arms that could have resulted in irreparable nerve damage. Like Robin Bereza, he too has suffered grievous emotional and psychological harm.

As John lay there, and before members of the public began gathering around him in a desperate attempt to save his life, Dennehy left the scene, taking Archie with her. Like Bereza, Rogers was rushed to the Hereford County Hospital and then airlifted to Birmingham. He spent six hours in surgery and five days in the Intensive Care Unit. Rogers has been left with significant nerve damage and suffers mental trauma, always remembering that he came within an inch of losing his life, at once ever grateful that his dog was returned safe and sound to him. Today, he is a shadow of his former self. He no longer has the dexterity to play the guitar, and he was a keen musician. The psychological trauma has been just as devastating, and perhaps even greater. As Mr Justice Spencer commented: 'Only through the love and devotion of his wife has he been able to get through the ordeal at all.'

Joanne Dennehy's sadistic excuse for attempting to murder Robin Bereza and John Rogers was: 'It was a kind of fetish. I am ashamed of the brutality and the fear that I heaped upon those two victims. It was drunken cruelty, plain and simple, compelled by my lack of respect for human life. I tried to kill more times than Bonnie and Clyde. My only regret is that those two guys lived, this is no fault of mine.'

15

THE ARRESTS

I suppose I am Britain's most wanted man?
GARY STRETCH, TO POLICE ON HIS ARREST

After the attack on John Rogers, the Vauxhall Astra travelled over the Old Bridge spanning the River Wye and into South Hereford, where Stretch joined up again with Andrew Wilmott, then parked up in Newman Close to meet a buyer interested in the stolen property. When that deal was done he and Dennehy hoped they could stay on the run, at least a little longer.

With West Mercia Police now fanning across Hereford, every patrol in the area was given details of the green Vauxhall Astra – that it had a 'Used in Crime' marker on it and the descriptions of its occupants. Almost immediately two officers spotted the vehicle as they drove into Newman Close. The Astra was parked up, with Joanne Dennehy, out of her mind on drugs and drink, sitting in the front passenger seat, Archie in the back. She was waiting for Stretch, who was at a house close by.

According to DS Mark Jinks: 'At that time the Force was in the process of changing their call sign structure, as such the officers were identified individually by their collar numbers only. Joanne Dennehy was arrested by PC 1268 Andy Mowen, who was crewed with and assisted by PC 1268 Paul Hunter.'

Even for Gaz, with a police car, its blue lights flashing, now parked up alongside the Vauxhall Astra, Dennehy in 'La-La Land' and a dog yapping in the back seat, the penny would have dropped. Peering out of the window he was desperately trying to process the scene unfolding in front of his very eyes. There were matters of distinctness, organisation and differentiation to deal with; matters under such dire circumstances that only a shifty criminal such as Stretch can resolve in nanoseconds, so he took to his toes. Realising the game was almost up, he jumped into the Renault with Andrew Wilmott and they sped off along the A480, back towards Kington although they were soon to be spotted by other officers recognising the now-known villains. A chase ensued before the car was stopped, some sixteen miles away near the village of Almeley in Hereford. Stretch's two associates were arrested, but he himself was already out and running. However, unlike Robin Bereza's dog Archie, he was never genetically bred for speed – or climbing through windows, come to that – and so he soon found himself out of breath and wheezing in a field surrounded by police. Exhausted, he brazenly walked up to armed West Mercia officers, who were being briefed to track him down, and said: 'I suppose I am Britain's most wanted man?' He was taken into custody just twenty minutes after the stabbing of John Rogers.

THE ARRESTS

I have maintained my guilt throughout even though I had a case for diminished responsibility.
Joanne Dennehy, letter to the author, 24 February 2014

All of the arrested individuals were taken to Hereford police station, where they were processed; their belongings were itemized, DNA swabs and photos taken, as were fingerprints. Dennehy thought the whole thing was hilarious and joked with officers that it could be worse but the CCTV footage of her being booked in reveals more about her psychology than just her words and body language.

Impatiently, she drums her fingers on the sergeant's desk then flicks back her hair as she coquettishly flirts with the officer. Laughing out loud, she flashes broad smiles to those around her. She is more concerned about her clothes than the two men she left for dead a short while ago. When an officer tells her that her clothes and personal possessions will be seized, before she is taken away to be strip-searched, Dennehy asks: 'So, what are you going to give me afterwards, tracksuit and plimsolls – fucking glamorous, that is!'

She then complains that she does not wish to wear a suicide suit – prison issue clothes specifically designed so that prisoners cannot self-harm themselves. 'Don't put me in a suicide suit,' she grumbles. 'I'm good with my own clothes. Those shorts are massive, the paper suit will wrap around me twice. I'm not having it!'

She asks the duty sergeant, 'Am I suicidal? No. Am I cheery now? Yes. Would you be cheery if you were up for attempted murder and murder? No, but I'm still smiling. What am I up for, attempted murder and murder? Attempted murder and murder is nothing. It's like going down for a Sunday roast, easy. It could be worse.'

After being strip-searched she returned to the sergeant's desk wearing a dark suicide suit. The killer moans: 'Why can't I have a T-shirt? I'm in a suicide suit, it's huge. Can I not get a T-shirt, seriously? I do need a T-shirt because this is massive, like a tent.'

When a PC tells her the outfit looks good on her, she replies, 'Thanks for that, that makes me feel so good. Real sexy.' She then flashes the officer a dazzling smile and stands in front of the CCTV camera for a further sixteen minutes as her booking is completed. During this time she does not ask if Robin Bereza and John Rogers survived. She does, however, express concern about the welfare of Archie.

'What's going to happen to the dog?' she asks. 'He's lovely, he's lovely.'

Dennehy then turns on the charm again. She tells the desk sergeant, 'You've got very distinctive eyebrows. You can't say they are not strict eyebrows. Up and down, I love your eyebrows.'

The officer replies, 'Good, we like cheery Joanne even though I am strict.'

With a hint of a lesbian flirt, Dennehy also tells a pretty WPC standing behind her left shoulder: 'You are so tiny,' to which the officer replies, 'Oh, thank you. I have never been called "Tiny". Thanks.'

Dennehy responds with: 'You are welcome. Not bad for a murderer.'

She is then asked several more questions to include details of her address.

'At the moment I have been on the run,' she replies, while admitting she is drunk: 'Half a bottle of whisky this morning, expensive stuff. 80 a bottle,' she boasts.

When Dennehy refuses to take out her tongue stud it has to be removed by a male officer wearing protective blue gloves.

She tells him, 'You are a decent copper, I'm a crap criminal. You'll read about it in the newspapers shortly. You will think, "That's the girl I arrested. I know her".'

Then, as she is led away to the cells she performs a 'chicken walk', saying, 'I'm The Incredible Hulk. I could be big, fat and ugly.'

One of the officers present explained to me: 'She was out of her box. She was considered a security risk and a danger to herself.'

Therefore, Dennehy was detained under Section 2 (s 2) of the Mental Health Act 1983 and sent to a secure unit outside Hereford to be assessed. Psychiatrists soon learned that she had been sectioned once before. Between 18 and 21 February 2012, she had been admitted to a Peterborough psychiatric unit, where she was diagnosed as having a psychotic disorder and found to be, 'emotionally unstable and prone to unpredictable behavioural explosions'. But after this arrest she would stay in the Herefordshire unit for a week before being released into the custody of the Cambridgeshire Constabulary.

'Wilmott pleaded guilty to handling the stolen property,' recalls DS Mark Jinks.

Between 8.13pm and 11.21pm – allowing for breaks and tape

changes – DS Jinks interviewed Gary Stretch at Thorpewood Police Station, Peterborough, on Wednesday, 3 April 2013. The following day he was interviewed again between 4.10pm and 7.21pm, allowing for breaks and tape changes. As DS Mark Jinks explained to me: 'Stretch was fairly frugal with the truth. Whilst he placed himself at both scenes and as the driver of the car, he did not accept that he knew what she [Dennehy] was about to do. He denied seeing or knowing that she had stabbed either man in Hereford, only becoming aware after she returned to the car after the second victim had been stabbed. He maintained that position throughout the trial but declined to give evidence from the witness box. His account was never going to stand scrutiny, especially given the account of Mark Lloyd, who was a key witness at the trial. He was in the rear seat of Dennehy and Stretch's car at the time of both attacks.'

DS Mark Jinks interviewed Joanne Dennehy on Friday, 12 April, between 8.30pm and 10.15pm. Commenting on the interview, DS Jinks says: 'Despite being generally cooperative and attentive throughout my time with her, she simply answered "No comment" to all questions.' Dennehy was duly charged with the attempted murders of Robin Bereza and John Rogers on Saturday, 13 April 2013.

Master criminal Gary Stretch was initially charged with carrying out the burglary, but as time passed, stealing a camera and a few bits and bobs would be the least of his worries. When the green Vauxhall Astra was searched police found Dennehy's knife with John Rogers' blood on it. There was also blood from Kevin Lee, and the Easter card he had given to Dennehy a few days earlier.

They [the dead men] *shouldn't have pissed me off. They shouldn't have flirted with me.*
Joanne Dennehy, in a letter to a friend

At 11am, 3 April, the day following Dennehy and Stretch's arrest in Hereford, a Cambridgeshire farmer found two corpses lying together in a drainage ditch at Thorney Dyke. The ditch runs parallel with a footpath alongside the River Nene, and just a few miles from where Kevin Lee's body had been found. This was an area Stretch also knew intimately – for a time he had lived close by, on the B1040 Thorney to Whittlesey road.

One of the bodies (Slaboszewski) exhibited signs of advanced decomposition, the other body (Chapman) much less so. But now everything added up to a short-lived, nevertheless chilling thought: a psychopath was in the area and he, or she, could be a serial killer. If that person was not caught there might be another killing for such offenders rarely stop until they are caught. However, Dennehy had tried to kill again, not once but twice. Much to the relief of DCI Martin Brunning and his team he was delighted to learn that she and Stretch were now under lock and key.

16

THE CHARGES

*Kevin Lee was an established landlord. He was always
friendly and polite with our staff. We never had a problem
with him. We're surprised someone would want to hurt him.*
ESTATE AGENTS BAIRSTOW EVES, WHICH MARKETED
LEE'S PROPERTIES

Leslie Layton had already been arrested and charged with
conspiring to pervert the course of justice with respect to
John Chapman, so he appeared before Peterborough Magistrates
at 10am on Wednesday, 3 April 2013. He pleaded 'Not Guilty'.

Chris McCann, CPS head of the Complex Case Unit East
of England, then issued a press release, saying: 'I have advised
Cambridgeshire police to charge Gary Stretch, aged 47, in
connection with the deaths of three men in Cambridgeshire,
March 2013.'

On Friday, 5 April 2013, Gary Stretch was brought before
Hereford Magistrates. In addition to the burglary offences
and handling stolen property he was further charged with:
'Encouraging or assisting in the commission of indictable
offences, believing that one or more will be committed (under
the Serious Crime Act 2007)'.

On Friday, 31 April, he was also charged with: 'That between 17 March and 4 April 2013 and between 27 March and 4 April 2013, it is alleged that within the jurisdiction of the Central Criminal Court, without lawful excuse Gary Stretch conspired together with Leslie Layton and others to prevent the lawful and decent burial of Kevin Lee, John Chapman and Lukasz Slaboszewski'. Another charge followed; that of the attempted murder of Robin Bereza on 2 April, at Hereford. He pleaded 'Not Guilty' to all of the charges.

Perhaps one of the most recent cases of prevention of the lawful and decent burial of a dead body was when Hans Kristian Rausing, heir to Hans Rausing, who owns the multinational food and packaging company, Tetra Pak, was charged with the offence following the 17 July 2012 discovery of the corpse of his wife, Eva Rausing, at their London home. He was given a suspended prison sentence, but this common law offence has no maximum penalty. It is an offence that can vary enormously in its severity, the most important factor being the intention of the offender.

In Layton's case the intention was to obstruct the course of justice by concealing a body so as to make it difficult to bring home a charge against a person responsible for the death. In such a case a sentence at the top of the scale was required. Layton would soon get just that.

On Monday, 15 April 2013, Robert Moore was charged with assisting an offender and lying to police for which he would later earn three years imprisonment. He appeared before Peterborough Magistrates on Monday, 22 April, and pleaded 'Not Guilty'. Later, after Dennehy flip-flopped her original not guilty plea, in December 2013 Moore pled guilty.

On Wednesday, 8 May 2013, Joanne Dennehy was charged with three counts of murder, two counts of attempted murder, and three counts of prevention of the lawful and decent burial of a dead body. She was remanded in custody to appear before Peterborough Magistrates on 30 May, when Crown Prosecutor Cheryl Williams told the Bench that the matter was too serious to be dealt with by them, that the case had to be referred to the Crown Court. Representing Dennehy, Martin Newman said there was no application for bail and no plea by his client at the present time.

On Tuesday, 4 June 2013, prosecutor Chris McCann announced: 'That between 27 March 2013 and 4 April 2013, it is alleged that within the jurisdiction of the Central Criminal Court, without lawful excuse Leslie Layton conspired together with Gary Stretch and other persons to prevent the lawful and decent burial of the dead bodies of Kevin Lee, John Chapman and Lukasz Slaboszewski.' Layton would appear before Peterborough Magistrates on Wednesday, 5 June. McCann then issued a warning to the media: '...and this decision to charge was taken in accordance with the Code for Crown Prosecutors. Leslie Layton now faces very serious criminal offences and has the right to a fair trial.'

Joanne Dennehy would next appear before Mr Justice Sweeney at Cambridge Crown Court on Thursday, 6 June. Here, Chief Crown Prosecutor for the East of England, Grace Ononiwu, said that Dennehy was charged with three counts of murder: that of Lukasz Slaboszewski, on or about March 21, and Kevin Lee and John Chapman, on or about March 29, 2013. The Prosecutor added: 'Joanne Dennehy now stands charged with very serious offences and the right to a fair trial.'

All four defendants (the men via video links from prison) next appeared at Cambridge Crown Court on Friday, 6 September. For legal reasons Dennehy did not enter any plea at all. However, Stretch, Layton and Moore pleaded 'Not Guilty' to all charges.

17

DAVID HEMING – THE CORONER

On Tuesday, 16 April 2013, David Heming, the Senior Coroner for Peterborough, opened the inquests on Slaboszewski, Chapman and Lee, then immediately adjourned until Monday, 19 May.

As Heming explained to this author: 'Dear Christopher, I literally opened the inquest for ID evidence and provisional cause of death, and suspended it (the power now contained in Schedule 1, para 2 Coroners' and Justice Act 2009). I then issued *"Form 121"*, which is a document indicating that the inquest would not be resumed.'

For a little medico-legal background there is some dispute over the exact date of origin of the English office of coroner, and, although the first mention of the modern equivalent dates from an ordinance of 1194, requiring every shire to elect an officer to 'keep the pleas of the Crown', it is reliably thought that as a Crown office it was first instituted following the Norman conquest, and when murdrum/murder was introduced.

The *De Officia Coronatoris*, a stature of 1276, enumerated the Coroner's duties and obligations. The Coroner – then called 'The Crowner', his full title being *custos placitorum coronae*, or keeper of the King's pleas, suits, or causes, was so-called because his special duty was to keep pleas, suits or causes which more particularly affected the King's Crown and dignity, and were determined either by the King in person or by his immediate officers.

As one of the King's officers – and a poorly paid job it was, too – his function was not so much to hear and determine causes as to keep a record of all that went on in the county in any way connected with the administration of criminal justice and, above all, to guard what may be called chance revenues falling to the King. The collection of such revenues depended to a great extent on the diligence of the Coroner in seeking for such things as the forfeited chattels of felons, deodands (a thing that had caused a person's death and was forfeited to the Crown for a charitable purpose, meaning 'something to be given to God': abolished 1862), wrecks, royal fish and treasure-trove.

So, if you are caught pillaging a wreck, stealing fish from the Crown's estate, shooting a swan or looting a field of Roman god coins expect to be hauled before the Coroner.

In his early days the chief functions of the 'Crowner' while guarding the King's revenues were the holding of inquests on view of the body in cases of death due to violence or accident and those dying in prison. Following the 1926 Coroners (Amendment) Act a person is only eligible for appointment if he/

she is a solicitor, barrister or a medical practitioner of five years or more experience. In practice most posts are held by solicitors, and apart from in cities and large towns, the appointments are part-time. Full-time coroners are usually qualified in medicine *and* the law, and their appointment is for life.

According to Mr F. G. Hails, former Coroner for the City of Stoke-on-Trent: 'The office of coroner in England has been adapted to keep pace with the legal machinery and needs of the times, and it is probably now the most effective machine of medico-legal investigation to be found in the world.'

18

ON REMAND – 'MY DEVIL IN THE FLESH'

I love & respect Gaz. I never forced him to do anything he didn't want to.
JOANNE DENNEHY, LETTER TO JULIE GIBBONS,
MARCH 2014

Inmates held on remand before trial in the UK are permitted to correspond with co-defendants, or anyone else for that matter. After conviction, the Ministry of Justice puts restrictions in place and correspondence may be curtailed and is always vetted by a prison's censors.

For his part Stretch had been busy writing letters to Julie Gibbons. He had told her that he had only gone along with Dennehy because he feared not only for his life, but she had threatened the lives of Julie and their children as well. 'I did this to protect you,' he wrote.

At the same time, however, Stretch had also written love letters to Dennehy, now held on remand at HMP & YOI Bronzefield. In turn, Joanne generously forwarded his letters to Julie, who bravely replied. This left Stretch – who obviously

111

wanted to have his cake and eat it – with some explaining to do, putting himself out on a limb.

Starting on Friday, 19 September 2013, less than a month before Joanne Dennehy stunned the Crown Court and her own barrister by admitting guilt, Stretch sent a series of fawning messages to the woman he nicknamed 'My devil in the flesh', adding, 'I can't wait to see your sexy smile and evil eyes'. Chillingly, he signed one note: 'Always yours, I love you Joanne – your personal undertaker'.

The letters, exclusively obtained by Louie Smith of the *Daily Mirror*, revealed another badly spelt note:

'Yo Wifey, thanks for your letter babe, I'm writing this letter sat in the court cells today, waitin for the verdict. The case has all been about the Serial Killer called J.d. We are the new bonnie and clyde [*sic*], so they say. Your not a killer you're a woman with major issues (lol) issues being bloodthirsty. Hey hold on your not a vampire are you? How's the book coming on, I want the copywrites [*sic*] ok'.

He continued by asking Dennehy if she had been keeping up with the case on TV, and in the newspapers, so he penned, 'there will be lots of interest when it comes to the sentencing,' which, when it eventually came, left him bitterly disappointed.

Excitement completely overwhelming his already limited literary skills, Stretch continued: 'They will be here just to see you, so stand strong it'll soon be here babe then you'll get to say your thing the speach [*sic*] of a lifetime to be heard all over the country, so make it a bloody good one. So looking forward to seeing you babe, well your sexy smile and thoughs evil eyes of yours oops evil meant to angeleyes (*lmfao*) [laugh my f***** a***off]. You have a dirty and dark mind. See you really soon, your biggest supporter! Love you always, love Undertaker xxxxxxxx Hubby 4 Lifey'.

In another letter, Stretch writes: 'Love you always you nutter and greatest woman I know or will ever know babe. Forever as one with you and I, love Undertaker xxxxxxxx'.

In another letter Stretch tells Joanne: 'Rite [*sic*] stop blaming yourself for me being in this with you, it was my own choices (sic) babe, cause I'm my own person I can make up my own mind, so get off that trip'.

He then writes: 'Mad choices have been my undoing, it's not your fault you did tell to leave [*sic*] but I never. I'll do anything 4 you, which I have already proven to you'.

Wrestling clumsily with his vocabulary and losing the battle, in his letters Gaz repeatedly flirts with Dennehy, referring to her as 'sweetbitch', 'bad girl', 'Angel in sheep's clothing' and 'you are the one woman I ever trulely [*sic*] loved'. In a moment of tender weakness Stretch reveals that perhaps unsurprisingly the pair did not get the chance to consummate their love while on the run.

Stretch also joked about the killings, beginning one letter with: 'hiya S.K. [Serial Killer]' and describing Joanne as 'the dreaded knife wheeling [*sic*] madwoman [*sic*]'. He quipped: 'Yeah you be in good hands marring [*sic*] a undertaker, it's a dieing [*sic*] trade'.

In an exchange of inane correspondence Stretch and Dennehy described their routine while on remand. He revealed that he passed the time watching TV and playing video games, listing his favourite film as the horror movie, *Jigsaw*. Not to be outdone, Dennehy replied that her favourite was the ultra-violent torture movie, *Hostel*, and he replied; 'hostel you sure: that's tame'.

Stretch also discussed music and mentioned pop groups, including the Spice Girls, S Club 7, Pussycat Dolls and Take That. Then he added: 'Hiya babe, hope your doing okay, was good to see on videolink the other week, will see you in court on the 18th Nov for sure. Never forget babe, whatever happens babe (loyal 4 life)'.

Undaunted by the lack of an affectionate response from Dennehy, on the day before his trial Stretch wrote:

'Just had a lovely shower babe, wished you could joined [*sic*] me, you could have washed my back for me and visa versa [*sic*], well I'm sure other things would have happened as well, any guesses babe. Never ever forget my loyalties will always be with you, I told you in the very beginning you can always count on me no matter wat (sic) my devil in the flesh. My legal team think I will get a straight sentence of around 12-18 years. OK angel I off now hope to hear from you really soon. Always yours – hugs and Kisses from me to you. Love you. Love. BABYBOY'.

Then, quite omitting the fact that he had known Dennehy for several years, Stretch added: 'I just wish I'd got the chance to really show u how much I loved you, I am sad I never got the chance to make love to you babe. I one of those men that didn't just want to fuck you [*sic*]. Since day one, making love to you was my dream and now it will always be a dream never to come true.'

Stretch's carefully crafted prose continued unabated with:

'You will never know how much I really loved you babe, and that's a proper shame. You will never meet another like me babe, that I know for sure. Always yours, I love you Joanne, your personal Undertaker, love The Drive'.

Who could resist such a charm offensive, dare I ask. But it certainly propelled Joanne to repay Gaz's undying love by forwarding his letters to Julie Gibbons, after which she replied to Joanne, asking if it were true that she and her children might have been killed by her.

'I have a right to some answers,' she stated. 'Can you tell me, why Gary? Did you plan to involve him or was he there at the right time for you? Did you ever consider what would happen to Gary when you involved him in this mess?'

In response Dennehy enclosed the letters from Gary Stretch in her blunt reply:

Dear Julie, I have received your letter. I would like to set a matter to rest. Gary did not go along with me out of fear for you. Mine and Gary's relationship was based on past background. I had no idea you even existed until in court my legal team informed me of a recorded phone call to you. Not long after meeting Gary I made it clear I was not the sort of person one should pursue. He chose otherwise.

The Gary I know, love and respect seems to differ from yours. I told him a million times to get away from me and the situation but he flat out refused and got annoyed with me when I did.

I had reasons for my actions and your view of me is understandable, but wrong. I tried my hardest to prove that I had not manipulated him, but if you know him as well as you say you do you will know he has his own mind.

I know Gary tells you what he needs to for his own needs but I resent the fact he used 'threat to you' as an excuse as I told him as we chatted from our cells at court as I said I knew nothing of your existence.

I love Gaz and contrary to what he now tells you he has strong feelings for me. There was no sexual relations between us as he admits in his letters. My love for Gaz is platonic. I would never force him to do anything and I'll be informing him of our correspondence.

An apology would be pointless and meaningless, the effects on your life, having not known you or about you are the responsibility of Gary.
Signed: J. Dennehy.

Totally betrayed, Gibbons never replied to Dennehy but she has been quoted in the Daily Mail, 2014, and elsewhere in the media as saying:

Gary was saying all long that she [Dennehy] was evil and he didn't want anything to do with her. He always said he only went along with her because he was scared for me and the kids. It was a real shock to find out that she has strong feelings for him. She's a good-looking girl, he's nearly fifty. He falls in love very easily but I can't understand why anybody would want to be in a relationship with Dennehy. He's just attracted to her looks and can't believe his luck that someone so much younger than him has shown an interest. He has fallen in love with a serial killer. Can't he see how dangerous she is? I used to feel responsible for Gary but not anymore – I am going to cut off all contact. Now, all he has to look forward to is visiting her in prison through a sheet of glass when he is seventy years old. I really hope it was worth it.

But Stretch's letters to crafty Joanne proved another mistake. At his trial this correspondence would show that far from living in fear of Dennehy, as his barrister, Karim Khalil QC, claimed in mitigation for his client's behaviour (that Stretch merely conspired with Dennehy out of fear for his own life and that of the safety of Julie Gibbons and their children), the opposite was patently obvious to judge and jury.

Sometimes a man can meet his destiny on the road he took to avoid it, but this was not so with Gary Stretch and it is often said that to really get inside the head of a sociopath you have to think like one.

Despite his size Gary Stretch was a weak, pathetic individual, who was often seen talking, grumbling and muttering to none other than himself. He was a loser from day one. Streetwise Joanne knew it. Stretch was also malleable, like the far more intelligent Kevin Lee and just about every other man who came into contact with her. However, where he really slipped up was in writing to Julie Gibbons with a pack of lies, claiming Joanne was threatening him, that she would kill Julie and her kids if he did not go along with her. This was patently untrue for, as we now know, Dennehy does not appreciate people who tell lies – although, because of her sociopathic disorder, she does not accept, nor ever will accept, that she has ever told a lie in her life and she appears to have convinced herself of this even today.

I replied to Gary once since your first letter, telling him how sick it made me feel to hear he claimed I was a threat to you or your family. I informed him that out of respect for you. I no longer wish for contact. There is something you must understand, I am incapable of harming females or children. I think that's why Gaz's lies cut so deep.
Dennehy, letter to Julie Gibbons, March 2014

When Julie Gibbons sent Joanne Dennehy the five letters from Stretch, it was like a red rag to a bull. Stretch was now blaming her for his predicament. To Dennehy this was the ultimate act of two-timing betrayal. Now she would dump him in a heartbeat without conscience, just as she did Slaboszewski, Lee and Chapman. In this instance, as will soon become apparent, she would turn on Gary, who had now passed his sell-by-date', then post him in a hand basket to serve nineteen years in jail, for his letters to her, and Julie, provided a one-way ticket for Stretch, who didn't even see it coming.

Dear Mr Berry-Dee
Re: Our Client – Gary Stretch.

Mr Stretch has asked we contact you regarding your letter to him of 24th March 2014.
Mr Stretch thanks you for your interest but declines your offer to take part in your project.

He asked you [*sic*] respect his wishes and not contact him any further regarding the matter.

Yours faithfully

Richard Brown & Co. – Solicitors, Broadway, Peterborough

19

THE TRIALS

I've pleaded guilty and that's that, you bastard!
JOANNE DENNEHY, TO MR JUSTICE SWEENEY

Murder trials have frequently been linked to theatre and there is much in the comparison. The courtroom itself is like a stage set and many of the chief participants, bewigged and gowned, may fairly be said to appear in costume. The chief component of any drama is conflict and this is certainly at the heart of any murder trial, where arguments about truth and falsehood, good and evil, swing this way and that. The accused is corralled and guarded in the dock, the judge perched on the commanding heights of his bench, and a procession of bit part players gives evidence from the witness box. Above all, during the last century there lurked over the murder trial the shadow of the gallows – murder was a capital crime and those accused of it stood in peril of their lives.

Life and death are the very essence of all drama and tragedy, but the sight of the judge putting on his black cap and uttering

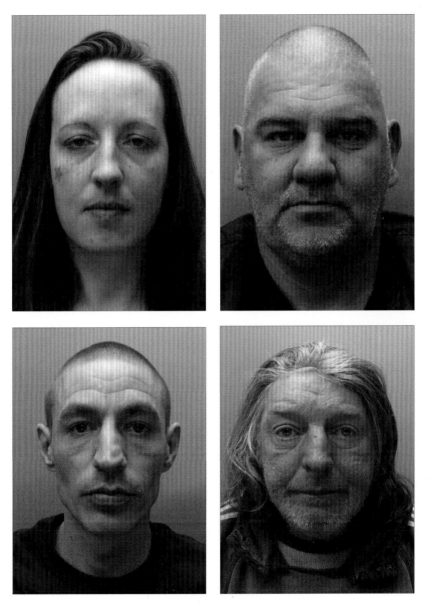

Above left: Joanne Christine Dennehy. ©*Cambridgeshire Constabulary*

Above right: Gary John Stretch – Dennehy's main partner in crime.
©*Cambridgeshire Constabulary*

Below left: Leslie Paul Layton – accomplice. ©*Cambridgeshire Constabulary*

Below right: Robert James Moore – accomplice. ©*Cambridgeshire Constabulary*

Main: Middle Road – body deposition site of Kevin Lee.

©Cambridgeshire Constabulary

Above left: Kevin Lee – third victim murdered 29 March 2013.

©Cambridgeshire Constabulary

Above right: Lukasz Slaboszewski – first victim murdered 19 March 2013.

©Cambridgeshire Constabulary

Below right: 78 Belvoir Way – home of Robert Moore.

©Cambridgeshire Constabulary

Main: Thorney Dyke – body deposition site of Lukasz Slaboszewski and John Chapman. ©*Cambridgeshire Constabulary*

Above left: No. 2 Riseholme – where Stretch lived.

©*Cambridgeshire Constabulary*

Above right: John Chapman – second victim murdered 29 March 2013.

©*Cambridgeshire Constabulary*

Below right: 38 Bifield – where John Chapman was killed.

©*Cambridgeshire Constabulary*

Above: An artist's impression of Gary Stretch (*second left*), Leslie Layton (*fifth left*), Robert Moore (*centre*) and Joanne Dennehy (*right*) in court.

© *Elizabeth Cook/PA Wire*

Inset, middle: DCI Martin Brunning – led Operation Darcy.

© *Cambridgeshire Constabulary*

Below: John Rogers (*left*) and Robin Bereza – attacked by Dennehy and Stretch in Hereford on 2 April 2014. © *Ben Kendall/PA Wire*

the dreaded death sentence is long gone. Indeed, the case of Dennehy, Stretch and Layton must rank as the most uninspiring judicial murder hearing in British criminal history and it came in two parts.

The trial of Dennehy, Stretch, Layton and Moore was held at Cambridge Crown Court, September 2013. The sentencing for all four defendants would come later and was to be held before Mr Justice Spencer, a Presiding Judge of the South Eastern Circuit, in Court Two at the Central Criminal Court, Old Bailey. They were both pretty much open and shut affairs because all four defendants were as guilty as sin.

Dennehy's case started on Monday, 17 November 2013, at Cambridge Crown Court. The next day, wearing a set of handcuffs, and another pair attaching her to a female officer, she passed a note to her barrister and turned the tables in a shock statement by pleading 'Guilty'. This drew gasps of amazement from the court and shook her barrister, Nigel Lickley QC, who was moved to say: 'The course of this arraignment is not one we had anticipated.'

Following a short adjournment, during which Mr Lickley went down to the cells to take further instructions from his client, the case was called back to court.

'It is incumbent on us to tell the court whether the pleas will be maintained or changed,' Mr Lickley said. 'To that end, arrangements have been made to see Miss Dennehy hopefully on Friday this week. If that is possible we will inform the court on Monday.'

Dennehy then interrupted. Laughing and smirking, she told the judge: 'I'm not coming back down here again just to say the same stuff. It's a long way to come to say the same thing I have just said. I've pleaded guilty and that's that, you bastard.'

Clearly unimpressed, the judge stepped in: 'She has pleaded guilty to a large number of counts, clearly, intentionally, and in the circumstances if there is to be any application for a change [of plea] then I will consider it but otherwise she has pleaded guilty.'

> *I think Joanne did that to control the situation. She likes people to know she's the boss.*
> Maria Dennehy, following her sister's unexpected guilty plea

Despite the overwhelming evidence against him Gary Stretch was not going down without a fight. His defence was one of mitigation: he had been terrified of Dennehy and he had only gone along with her because he was fearful for his life and the lives of Julie Gibbons and their children, an excuse that the jury of eight men and four women would find hard to believe.

Karim Khalil QC, representing Stretch, said: 'My client had been taken in by the evil of a woman who described herself as a monster.' He added, 'While playwrights or authors would have dared pen such a ghastly tale of criminality, Joanne Dennehy's killings were reminiscent of a Jacobean tragedy.'

The judge was impressed and allowed himself a courteous smile. The labels 'evil', 'monster', 'playwrights', 'authors', 'ghastly tale of criminality' and 'Jacobean tragedy' struck accord and now sensing this, Mr Khalil rose to his theme with a flourish: 'Shakespeare and Jacobean writers understood how one foul deed could beget a sequence of tragic circumstances.' Then he took up a book, sniffed and then paused to allow the court to take in his performance, before putting it down again.

'People like Dennehy surrounded themselves with people they knew to be weak or who they could bend to their will,' he said. 'In such circumstances, ordinary people behave in ways that they would have thought inconceivable. The question is this, may there have been a reasonable fear of death which caused Mr Stretch to act as he did for there is no doubt that he was Dennehy's nodding dog.'

This was courtroom theatrics at its best and worthy of any advocate. The term 'nodding dog' had not passed through the judge or the jurors' minds without interruption, for John Treanor had told police that Joanne first met him while he was walking his Alsatian. The corpses of Lukasz Slaboszewski, John Chapman and Kevin Lee were eagerly sniffed out by dogs owned by Terry Walker and the Peterborough farmer. In trying to kidnap Labrador Samson, Robin Bereza was almost killed, while Dennehy and Stretch did manage to steal John Rogers' dog, Archie. Dennehy's alleged love of canines had backfired on her, for the creatures had indeed bitten back and played their part in her undoing.

Representing Layton, Mr Christopher Morgan QC argued the same 'terrified of Denney' defence, as did the QC representing Moore. However, none of this washed. The judge summed up the case against each defendant to the jury: 'Stretch, Layton and Moore had been willing participants in the disposal of Joanne Dennehy's bodies and attempts to cover up her crimes.' But he added that the defence had claimed in mitigation that the accused were acting under duress. 'They say,' added the judge, 'that you should not underestimate the evil and malign influence of Dennehy. And if you, the jury, believe the men were in fear of death or serious harm, they could claim they were acting under duress, they should be found not guilty.'

Then came the knockout punch. 'The key test,' the judge suggested, 'is would a *reasonable* person placed in the defendants' situation have been driven to act in the way the defendants did?', before concluding, 'Neither man has given evidence in his own defence.'

The jury retired to consider their verdicts on Tuesday, 4 February 2014.

On Monday, 10 February, Gary Stretch was found guilty of one count of conspiracy to attempted murder and three counts of preventing the lawful and decent burial of three human bodies.

On Wednesday, 12 February, Leslie Layton was found guilty of two counts of preventing the lawful and decent burial of three human bodies.

All four defendants would be sentenced by Mr Justice Spencer at the Central Criminal Court, Old Bailey on Friday, 28 February 2014.

20

SENTENCING

'I have taken your murder sentence for you.
You and Stretch are fuckin' idiots."
AN INFURIATED JOANNE DENNEHY TO STRETCH AT TRIAL,
UPON LEARNING THAT STRETCH HAD INSURED THE ASTRA UNDER
THE NAME 'UNDERTAKER & CO.'

Dressed in a pink athletic vest, her hair tied back in a ponytail with a purple scrunchie, nose stud and a sleeveless top, Joanne Dennehy, although seeming agitated, laughed and smirked from behind the glass-fronted dock. Next to her, wearing a blue T-shirt, was Stretch. Nine guards in all surrounded the four defendants but the smile was soon to be wiped off her face.

At one point Dennehy turned to Stretch and Layton and she was clearly heard to say: 'I have taken your murder sentence for you. You and Stretch are fuckin' idiots.' Stretch seemed uninterested in the proceedings and was yawning while repeatedly glancing over his shoulder at Dennehy.

Judge Spencer described Dennehy as a sadistic serial killer and sentenced her to a natural life term. 'Bollocks!' shouted Dennehy before being taken down.

She would also earn the distinction of becoming the first woman in British criminal history to be sentenced to full life in prison by a sitting judge, and this has proved to be the first occasion that the term 'serial killer' has been used by a judge in any British criminal proceedings.

Sarah Murnane, High Court Judges Clerk to Mr Justice Spencer, has provided the material that follows for inclusion in this book.

The Queen
-v-
Joanne Christine Dennehy
Gary John Stretch
Leslie Paul Layton
Robert James Moore
In Cambridge Crown Court sitting at the Central Criminal Court
28 February 2014
Sentencing remarks of Mr Justice Spencer

Joanne Dennehy, Gary Stretch, Leslie Layton and Robert Moore, you may remain seated for the time being.

Joanne Dennehy, within the space of 10 days at the end of March last year you murdered three men in cold blood. Although you pleaded guilty you have made it quite clear that you have no remorse for those murders. With the help of one or more of your co-defendants you dumped the bodies of your three victims in remote rural areas around Peterborough hoping they would not be found. Only a matter of days later

126

you attempted to murder two more men, this time openly on the streets of Hereford, victims chosen entirely at random. Miraculously they survived. You claim to feel remorse for stabbing those two men nearly to death. I have no hesitation in rejecting that suggestion. You are a cruel, calculating, selfish, and manipulative serial killer.

You Gary Stretch actively assisted Joanne Dennehy in dumping the bodies of all three men she had murdered, making use of your local knowledge. You were her driver in Hereford and stopped the car to enable her to get out and attempt to murder two more men. You knew exactly what she was likely to do. The jury convicted you of attempted murder as well.

You Leslie Layton actively assisted Joanne Dennehy and Gary Stretch in dumping the bodies of two of the three men she had murdered. One of them was your housemate. The other was your landlord. You had every opportunity to distance yourself from these crimes. Instead you chose to go along with them. When the police were trying to find your missing housemate and needed your help as a member of the public, you repeatedly lied to them to cover your own tracks and to protect Joanne Dennehy and Gary Stretch. Had you told the truth, it is possible they would have been arrested before the attacks in Hereford.

You Robert Moore gave shelter and assistance to Joanne Dennehy and Gary Stretch for two nights when you knew or believed she had committed those murders and that he had helped her dump the bodies.

I have to sentence each of you for your part in these appalling offences. Before I do so, however, I need to set out the factual basis on which I sentence you all.

Your first victim, Joanne Dennehy, was a 31 year old Polish man, Lukasz Slaboszewski. He had come to this country in 2005. Somehow you met and befriended him. Within a matter of days of meeting him you murdered him. He texted his friend to the effect that life was beautiful now that he had you as his girlfriend. You lured him soon afterwards to 11 Rolleston Garth in Peterborough, where you had been living. There can be no doubt that you lured him there specifically to kill him. You stabbed him once through the heart. Whilst you decided how to dispose of his body permanently, you put the body for the time being into a wheelie bin. You made a point of bringing a 14 year old girl whom you had befriended to 11 Rolleston Garth where you opened the bin and showed her the dead body. You deny doing this, but the detail of her account is so clear and compelling that I find it impossible to accept your denial. That conduct is an aggravating feature of the murder and of the charge of preventing the lawful and decent burial of the body. You set about acquiring a vehicle specifically to dispose of the body. With money you borrowed for the purpose from your landlord and third victim, Kevin Lee, you bought a Vauxhall Astra, travelling with Gary Stretch by taxi to collect it. This was within two days of the murder. Later the same evening, you and Gary Stretch were driving around remote areas on the outskirts of Peterborough looking for a suitable site to dump the body. The site chosen was Thorney Dyke, close to where you, Gary Stretch, had lived some years earlier. You boasted to Georgina Page that no one would ever find the bodies dumped there.

The second man you murdered, Joanne Dennehy, was John Chapman. He was 56 years old. He was murdered a week or so later, probably in the early hours of Friday 29th March, Good Friday. You stabbed him to death in his own bedsitting room at 38 Bifield where by now you were also living. John Chapman was a kindly, harmless and inoffensive man who had served his country in the Royal Navy but had fallen on hard times through his weakness for alcohol. You, Joanne Dennehy, were well aware of that vulnerability and exploited it. You, Gary Stretch, and you, Leslie Layton, met and drank with John Chapman at 38 Bifield only a matter of days before he was murdered. You, Leslie Layton, lived in another bedsit room on the same floor of the building. You, Joanne Dennehy, said or hinted to Georgina Page when you visited her a few days later that you had killed this man because he came into the bathroom when you were having a bath and would not leave. I bear in mind that it is a feature of your psychopathic personality that you are a pathological liar. There is clear evidence that you had threatened John Chapman that you would get him out of the house by any means. Eviction notices had been served on the tenants at 38 Bifield by your landlord and third victim Kevin Lee, someone you wanted to lead to believe you were helping. You had only just moved into 38 Bifield. John Chapman described you to another tenant, Toni Ann Roberts as "the mad woman". It was she whom he told that he was having problems with you, and that you had said you would get him out of the house by any means. I am quite sure that this, once again, was a planned and premeditated killing.

You stabbed John Chapman to death in his own bed sitting

room. You stabbed him once in the neck, severing the carotid artery, and five times in the chest. Two of the stab wounds penetrated the heart, one of them inflicted with sufficient force to pass first through the breast bone. There was no injury to suggest that John Chapman had attempted to defend himself. His blood alcohol level was four times the limit for driving. It may even be that you stabbed him as he lay asleep on his bed.

You, Leslie Layton, had a photograph of John Chapman's dead body on your mobile phone, a photograph taken at 7.32am that day, not long after the murder. You were never asked about that photograph by the police in interview, because it had been deleted from your phone and had not then been retrieved by forensic analysis. You had the opportunity at your trial to give evidence and tell the jury, if it was truly the case, that you did not take that photograph, did not delete it, and knew nothing of it. You did not give evidence. Instead the theory was put forward by your counsel in his closing speech that the photograph might have been taken by Joanne Dennehy using your phone and that she might have deleted the image without your ever knowing it was there. That was only a theory. There is no evidence to support it. Bearing in mind how critical the evidence of this photograph was to the prosecution case against you in rebutting your defence of duress, and how important it would have been for you to challenge it, I am quite sure that the reason why you chose not to give evidence about this photograph was that you knew it was you who took it and you who deleted it.

Soon after you had murdered John Chapman you, Joanne Dennehy, were using the dead man's mobile phone. I strongly suspect that it was you who was using it as early as 6.34am to call Gary Stretch, an hour before the photograph was taken, but I cannot be sure of that as the telephone schedule shows that from time to time over the previous few days John Chapman had himself called Gary Stretch, albeit never so early in the morning.

When you, Leslie Layton, were confronted with the body of John Chapman early that Friday morning your reaction was not to call for help but to photograph the body for your own purposes as a morbid souvenir. That showed a callous indifference to the plight of your housemate. When Gary Stretch came round to 38 Bifield soon afterwards that morning you were able to leave the house, free of threat or fear, and you went out shopping with a friend. You could and should have raised the alarm then, but instead you chose to meet up again with Gary Stretch later that afternoon knowing that the body of John Chapman still lay upstairs in the room where he had been murdered. You played your part in helping to dump the body of John Chapman later that night, in the same ditch at Thorney Dyke where the body of Lukasz Slaboszewski lay undiscovered. I shall return to that.

The third man you murdered, Joanne Dennehy, was your landlord Kevin Lee. He was 48 years old, a much loved husband and father. By a combination of bad judgement on his part born of genuine compassion and desire to help you, and the strange fascination that you held for him, as you did for other men, Kevin Lee became infatuated with you. Over a period of several months you led him to believe that you had been grossly abused as a child and even that you had killed

131

your own father and served many years in prison as a result. That was pure fantasy. You had a perfectly decent and proper upbringing and the advantage of a good home. Kevin Lee befriended you, gave you employment in his property letting business and provided you with accommodation in a series of bedsits in the houses his company owned and rented out. Your relationship with Kevin Lee became so close that you felt able to confide in him that you had committed the first murder. You were to tell Georgina Page later that it was because he had seen the body that you had to kill Kevin Lee. That may be part of the reason, but it was only part. I am quite sure that the reason you murdered Kevin Lee in the way that you did, and dumped his body in the way that you did, was to gratify your own sadistic lust for blood.

Like your first victim, you lured your third victim Kevin Lee to 11 Rolleston Garth specifically in order to murder him. You had whetted his appetite sexually by telling him that when he came to see you that Friday afternoon you were going to dress him up and rape him. That is what he told his best friend Dave Church when he met him that afternoon on business less than an hour before his fatal rendezvous with you at Rolleston Garth. It was not the first time Kevin Lee had described to Dave Church the sort of extreme sexual activity you and he were taking part in together. You stabbed Kevin Lee five times in the chest. The wounds penetrated both lungs and the heart. This time there were injuries to suggest that your victim tried to defend himself.

With two dead bodies now to dispose of, at two separate addresses, you, Joanne Dennehy, and you, Gary Stretch, were seen by various witnesses engaged in the cleaning up operations. Then in the evening, with you as well now, Leslie Layton, the three of you set about dumping these two bodies and covering your tracks. You, Leslie Layton, I am quite satisfied on all the evidence, were a wholly willing participant in getting rid of the bodies and setting fire to Kevin Lee's Mondeo car. The three of you travelled to another remote rural area on the outskirts of Peterborough at Newborough to dump the body of Kevin Lee. You, Joanne Dennehy, had indeed dressed Kevin Lee in a black sequined dress of your own. As a final humiliation, his body was dumped in the ditch still wearing that dress, with his naked buttocks exposed. I have studied the photographs of his body as it was found in the ditch, rather than rely on the sanitised photograph which, quite properly, was all the jury were allowed to see. I am quite satisfied that Kevin Lee's body must have been deliberately positioned or deliberately left that way, with his bare buttocks prominently exposed upwards, still wearing the sequined dress.

I am prepared to accept, however, that you, Leslie Layton, played no part in that and, as you told the police, did not get out of the car on that occasion. But you, Leslie Layton, were active in driving the Mondeo, probably with Kevin Lee's body in the boot, and as the CCTV clearly showed you were prominent in obtaining petrol with which to set fire to and destroy the Mondeo. This was done on an area of waste ground at Yaxley quite deliberately chosen, I am sure, to be as far away as possible from where Kevin Lee's body had been dumped, out beyond the other side of Peterborough.

The three of you then returned in the Astra to 38 Bifield

where the body of John Chapman was loaded into the car. You, Leslie Layton, admitted in interview that you played an active part with Joanne Dennehy in carrying his body downstairs from the top floor. It was probably his body that you, Gary Stretch, were seen carrying to the car and putting in the boot, causing the suspension to drop. The three of you drove out to Thorney Dyke where John Chapman's body was dumped in the same ditch where the body of Lukasz Slaboszewski still lay. This time you got out of the car, Leslie Layton, and must have seen there was another body already there. The jury rejected your defence of duress. You had ample opportunity in the course of that day to distance yourself from Joanne Dennehy and Gary Stretch. It was fascination not fear which led you to stay with them and help them to dispose of the bodies. That is why you had no qualms about accepting Gary Stretch's offer to stay at his flat overnight.

You Gary Stretch, also relied on the defence of duress before the jury. Whatever the true nature of your relationship with Joanne Dennehy there is not a shred of evidence that you were ever in fear of her. Had you been, you would not have dispensed with the gun which I am sure you had in your possession when you went on the run to Hereford two days later.

You, Leslie Layton, and you, Robert Moore, were more than willing to give Joanne Dennehy and Gary Stretch whatever assistance they wanted in evading the police, even though you knew full well that murders had been committed and bodies dumped. Leslie Layton told the police that it was from your house, Robert Moore, that the tarpaulin was borrowed in which to wrap or carry the bodies that Friday. I do not sentence you on the basis that you lent them the tarpaulin knowing why it was needed. That allegation has never been made. But you knew that the body of the first victim had been stored for a while in a wheelie bin at 11 Rolleston Garth, close to where you lived. That much is apparent from what you told the probation officer, although you made no comment in interview when the police questioned you on the topic. It is quite clear, not least from the text messages you sent her, that you were besotted with Joanne Dennehy and prepared to do almost anything to indulge her. Knowing what she and Gary Stretch had done you were willing to put them up in your house and willing even to expose your young daughter to their influence. When they could not return to their own accommodation because the police were looking for them, you provided them with food and shelter for two nights running, Saturday 30th and Sunday 31st March.

Over that Easter weekend you, Leslie Layton, were undoubtedly wracked with guilt and worry over what you had done. That is why your friends Toni Ann Roberts and Michelle Bowles described you as distressed and upset on the Sunday evening when they spoke to you. That did not stop you trying to cover your tracks, however, nor did it induce you to go to the police and tell them what you knew about the disappearance of John Chapman, which was, by now, headline news in the media. Instead, when the police came to see you on Sunday 31st March and again on the afternoon of 1st April you lied time and again in denying all knowledge of what had become of John Chapman. You said you had not seen him since the previous Wednesday or Thursday. In fact on the Friday night you had helped to dump his dead body in a ditch. You said you had not seen Joanne Dennehy since the previous Wednesday. You lied to the police in a determined attempt to pervert the course of justice. The jury rejected your defence of duress. By now Joanne Dennehy and Gary Stretch were far away in East Anglia. All you had to do was tell the police the truth if you had the remotest concern for your own physical safety. I am sure you did not. You were thinking only of yourself and your friends in crime. Whilst the police were speaking to you that Monday afternoon you had several calls from Joanne Dennehy, calling you on the phone of the dead man the police were asking you about. As soon as the police had left, you rang Joanne Dennehy back, no doubt to report the progress of the police investigation as you knew it, as she had requested you should in a revealing earlier text message you neglected to delete from your phone.

On the Monday evening, you, Joanne Dennehy and Gary Stretch, paid a visit to Georgina Page in King's Lynn. There you both talked in a matter of fact way about the murders. It was there that you, Gary Stretch, boasted that the bodies would never be found. You, Joanne Dennehy, became excited and animated when you saw reports on television that you were wanted. Ecstatic was the way Georgina Page described you to the jury. You told her that when you dressed Kevin Lee up you had lubricated his backside and shoved something up it to make it look as though it was a sexual act. I am quite sure that you, Gary Stretch, did threaten Georgina Page before you left her house, saying that you would get your father to sort it out if anyone grassed on the two of you. Georgina Page told the jury that she understood by this that if she went to the police she might be killed. You, Joanne Dennehy, said that you knew the two of you would get caught and go to prison for a long time. You, Gary Stretch, laughed and said "My kids are grown up, so I don't care". The two of you returned to Peterborough and spent a second night at Robert Moore's home.

Early on Tuesday morning, 2nd April, you set off together from his home for Hereford. You chose Hereford because it was somewhere Gary Stretch knew well. You had burgled a house at Diss in Norfolk the previous day. This time you burgled another house in Herefordshire looking for valuable electrical items you could sell easily. By now the two of you were well and truly on the run and your behaviour was totally lawless.

You met up with other criminals at a flat in Kington, about 20 miles from Hereford on the Welsh border. The two of you, and the rest of the group you met, agreed to sell the stolen property to someone in Hereford with whom there would be a rendezvous. One of the men in the group you met was Mark Lloyd. He gave evidence at the trial over a long period and, like the jury, I had a good opportunity to assess him. I bear in mind the need for caution in relation to his evidence. However, I am quite sure he was not a willing passenger in the Vauxhall Astra when it set off for Hereford. I am also sure that before you left the flat in Hereford there was an incident in the kitchen, out of sight of Joanne Dennehy, when you, Gary Stretch, showed Mark Lloyd a hand gun which was in the waistband of your trousers.

Whether the gun was in fact loaded, as Mark Lloyd believed on the basis of his experience of such weapons, matters not.

His evidence that you were in possession of such a gun was not challenged in cross-examination, although I accept that it was your counsels judgment not to challenge it. I accept too that you had denied in interview having such a gun, but you told many important lies in your interviews, so that denial counts for very little. Nor did you give evidence to contradict Mark Lloyd's evidence about the gun, where any denial would have been tested.

I am sure that you did have such a gun in your possession, and sure that you led Mark Lloyd to believe you had it with you to rob a drug dealer if you could find one. You left the flat and disposed of the gun somewhere before the journey to Hereford began. That is significant in itself because it shows you were not truly in fear of Joanne Dennehy and did not consider that you needed a gun for your own protection against her. It is more likely, in my judgment, that you realised you were bound to be apprehended by the police sooner or later and did not want to compound your criminality by being caught in possession of a firearm. The fact that you had access to such a gun is, however, relevant to the danger you may pose to the public. I shall return to that.

Either before the journey to Hereford began, or during the course of the journey, I am quite sure that you, Joanne Dennehy, said words to the effect that Gary Stretch had already had his fun, in the sense of carrying out the burglary, and now you wanted your fun. I am also sure that you said earlier, at the flat, that you had killed three people, that Gary Stretch had helped to dispose of the bodies, and you had to do some more. By the time you arrived in Hereford I have no doubt that you had already formed the intention of killing at least one more man, at random, by stabbing him to death, and that you Gary Stretch knew perfectly well that this was bound to happen. In the event two men were nearly killed, not one.

On the jury's verdicts you, Gary Stretch, either shared Joanne Dennehy's intention to kill the two men she stabbed in Hereford or at the very least realised that she would stab them with the intention of killing them. On the facts of this case there is no real difference. One way or the other you foresaw the inevitability of what was going to happen and you played your part in bringing it about.

I am quite sure on the evidence that it was you, Gary Stretch, who spotted the first victim, Robin Bereza, as you drove down the road. He was walking his dog ahead of you on the nearside pavement. You lied to the police in interview in suggesting that you had pulled up only after passing him and you lied in suggesting that you did not see what happened because it was taking place behind the car. The truth, I am sure, is that you decided to stop the car when and where you did, pulling up before you reached him, in order to give Joanne Dennehy the advantage of surprising her victim by attacking him from behind. Whether you actually uttered the words 'Will he do?' as Mark Lloyd told the jury is less important. The fact is that you initiated the opportunity for the attack.

You, Joanne Dennehy, claim that you were under the influence of alcohol when you carried out this attack and that you feel remorse for what you did. You had undoubtedly been drinking whiskey from a bottle during the journey that day but despite the expert's back-calculation of your possible alcohol level, I reject entirely any suggestion that you were so inebriated that you were unaware of what you were doing or that you were disinhibited by the alcohol you had consumed. Only a minute or so before the first attack you and Mark Lloyd went into the Green Lane store, as shown on the CCTV. You appear to have been in high spirits and, from the way you were behaving towards the young woman behind the counter, you were possibly in a state of euphoria at what was in prospect, but there was no indication at all that you were grossly affected by drink.

Robin Bereza was 63 years old at the time, a retired fireman who had kept himself fit. That afternoon he had chosen to walk his dog rather than go jogging. You attacked him from behind, taking him completely unawares. You stabbed him first in the back then a second time in the right upper arm. When he turned to face you and asked what on earth you were doing you told him "I want to hurt you, I am going to fucking kill you". He tried to fight you off, kicking out at you. You pursued him into the road, continuing the attack, but eventually you did desist, probably because of the arrival of another car at the scene waiting to turn into a side road. You, Gary Stretch, had driven the car slowly behind Joanne Dennehy and beckoned to her to get back into the car. You did and said nothing to show any disapproval or surprise at any stage at what she was doing. I accept the evidence of Mark Lloyd that you exercised some degree of physical restraint over him, for otherwise I am sure he would have got out of the car and distanced himself from what was going on. You Joanne Dennehy calmly got into the car, looking across and smiling at the driver of the other car waiting to turn right at the junction where this was taking place.

Although you managed to inflict only two stab wounds to Robin Bereza you caused him potentially fatal injuries. The deep wound to his back penetrated the chest wall causing a haemo-pneumothorax as well as bruising the lung and fracturing a rib. Had the blood and air not been promptly drained from his chest cavity by expert medical treatment, his life would have been in danger. The other stab wound shattered the shoulder blade and fractured the bone in the upper arm. It was only by pure chance that the nerves in the arm were not damaged irreparably with a drastic loss of function. The attack has had a profound effect on him emotionally and psychologically, and I shall return to this.

You, Joanne Dennehy, were not satisfied with the outcome of this first attack. You had not succeeded in your objective of killing another man. You required Gary Stretch to find you another victim and you, Gary Stretch, were happy to oblige her. It was no coincidence that the second victim was another man walking his dog. Using your local knowledge you, Gary Stretch, drove to a cul-de-sac adjacent to a path well used by dog walkers. As you told the police in interview, it was close to where your grandmother used to live. This time your victim was a 56-year-old man, John Rogers who lived nearby and who was taking his dog for a walk. He had only gone a few yards down the path when you attacked him from behind, stabbing him in the back. When he turned round you stabbed him repeatedly. You pushed him backwards for several yards, stabbing him all the time. When he fell over you continued to stab him to the front and to the back. It was a relentless and frenzied attack with only one purpose, to kill him. You left him for dead, picked up his dog, and left the scene. As he lay there helpless he thought he was dying. You accept that you thought you had killed him. That is what you told the police officer who arrested you a few minutes later.

You stabbed John Rogers more than 30 times. He had deep wounds to his chest, abdomen and back. Both lungs had collapsed. His bowel was perforated and exposed. Had he not received the most expert and prompt medical treatment he would have died from these injuries. So severe was the force of the stab wounds that nine ribs were fractured. He also received wounds to his hands and arms which could have resulted in irreparable nerve damage. He too has suffered grievous emotional and psychological harm, to which I shall return.

The death and destruction for which you are responsible, Joanne Dennehy, has caused untold distress to the families and friends of the men you murdered and to the victims who survived and their families. Many of those affected are in court today. I have read and taken into account the victim personal statements from John Chapman's brother-in-law, from Kevin Lees widow, and from Robin Bereza and John Rogers. The cruel and aggravated circumstances of Kevin Lees death in particular have been very hard indeed for his loved ones to bear. They are here in court as a tribute to his memory and to see justice done. You, Joanne Dennehy, described yourself to Kevin Lee as a monster for what you had done in the past. Kevin Lee's widow describes you as a monster who has taken and ruined her family's lives. Robin Bereza speaks of his inability to grasp the reality that anyone could be so evil as to attack someone in this way for no reason, someone you had never met. The experience has totally shaken his confidence and turned a robust former fireman into a nervous shadow of his former self. The lives of his wife and family have likewise been turned upside down and it is only with their love and support that he has been able to come to terms at all with the enormity of this experience.

John Rogers acknowledges that he owes his life to those who came to his assistance so promptly and the doctors who treated him so expertly. He continues to experience the physical consequences of the attack. For example he no longer has the dexterity to play the guitar, and he is a keen musician. The psychological trauma has been just as devastating, and perhaps even greater. Only through the love and devotion of his wife has he been able to get through the ordeal at all.

Having set out the factual basis on which I pass sentence, I now deal with each of you in turn.

JOANNE DENNEHY

First you, Joanne Dennehy. For murder there is only one sentence, life imprisonment. But I am required to determine the minimum term you must serve. Parliament has laid down different starting points for the minimum term, depending upon the seriousness and circumstances of the case. In your case only two starting points could conceivably be appropriate, either a whole life order or a term of 30 years. If the latter, the gravity of your offending is such that the minimum term would have to be very substantially in excess of 30 years.

The issue in your case, therefore, is whether or not there should be a whole life order. Any question as to the lawfulness of such a sentence has been dispelled by the recent judgment of the Court of Appeal in the case of *McLoughlin* [2014] EWCA Crim 188. My duty is to apply the provisions of paragraph 4 of schedule 21 to the Criminal Justice Act 2003, and to consider whether the seriousness of the offence (or the combination of the offence and one or more offences associated with it) is exceptionally high. If the seriousness is exceptionally high, the appropriate starting point is a whole life order. Paragraph 4(2) provides that cases that would normally fall within this category include the murder of two or more persons where each murder involves a substantial degree of premeditation or planning, or the abduction of the victim, or sexual or sadistic conduct.

For the reasons I have already explained, I am quite sure that each of these three murders did involve a substantial degree of premeditation or planning. I am sure on the evidence that you lured your first victim Lukasz Slaboszewski to 11 Rolleston Garth specifically in order to kill him. I am quite sure on all the evidence that you murdered John Chapman not on the spur of the moment because he had been watching you in the bath but because by then you had got a taste for murder and, as you had told him, you were prepared to do whatever it would take to get him out of the house. I am quite sure that you lured Kevin Lee to 11 Rolleston Garth that Friday specifically in order to kill him. I am also quite sure that his was a murder which involved sexual and sadistic conduct on your part. It is true that there is no medical evidence at post mortem of sexual interference, but the whole circumstances of the killing bear out what he told his friend he was expecting, namely that you were going to dress him up and rape him. You admitted as much to Georgina Page. The way in which his body was dumped was part of the playing out of your sexual and sadistic motivation.

Quite apart from meeting the threshold of seriousness in the examples given in paragraph 4, there were other aggravating features to these three murders. First, each of them involved stabbing with a knife or knives that you took to the scene for that very purpose, even if only within the same building. Second, having murdered Lukasz Slaboszewski and having put his body in a wheelie bin, you made a point of inviting a 14 year old girl to come to 11 Rolleston Garth specifically to show her the body in the bin. Third, John Chapman, although not physically disabled, was to your knowledge a particularly vulnerable victim on account of his alcoholism and you exploited that vulnerability. Fourth, you went to great lengths to dump each of the three bodies in a remote area where you hoped it would not be found. Fifth, having committed these murders and dumped the bodies, and knowing that you were wanted by the police, you attempted to murder and very nearly succeeded in murdering two more men, selected at random, by stabbing them repeatedly. Although there are separate counts which cover the dumping of the bodies and these two attempted murders, the overall criminality of your conduct in this case must be reflected in the minimum term you are required to serve. The starting point for your minimum term must therefore be a whole life order rather than 30 years. Your counsel submits that a whole life order is not necessary in your case because the minimum term would in any event be so long.

In addition to the most recent decision of the Court of Appeal to which I have referred, I have also considered carefully the guidance in this area given by the Court of Appeal in the case of *Oakes* [2013] 2 Cr App R 22. In particular I bear in mind that a whole life order should be imposed only where the seriousness of the offending is so exceptionally high that just punishment requires the offender to be kept in prison for the rest of his or her life. I am required to consider all the material facts before concluding that a very lengthy finite term will be not be sufficiently severe. I bear in mind that a whole life order is reserved for the few exceptionally serious offences in which, after reflecting on all the features of aggravation and mitigation, the court is satisfied that the element of just punishment and retribution requires the imposition of a whole life order. I also remind myself that I am setting the penal element of the sentence only. I am not concerned with risk to the public on release. That is a matter solely for the parole board or, very exceptionally, for the Secretary of State.

I have considered your criminal record. You are now 31 years of age. You have been in and out of prison in recent years serving short sentences, mainly for offences of dishonesty, although I note that in 2012 you were convicted of possessing a bladed article in a public place, razor blades, and later in the year you received a community order for an offence of assault occasioning actual bodily harm. I have read the psychiatric report on you from Dr Farnham, dated 26th October 2013. I note that his assessment is that you suffer from a severe emotionally unstable personality disorder, and from an antisocial personality disorder. In his opinion you also suffer from paraphilia sadomasochism, a disorder of preference for sexual activity involving the infliction of pain or humiliation or bondage. It is Dr Farnham's assessment that you suffer from a psychopathic disorder, that is a personality disorder characterised by superficial charm, callous disregard for others, pathological lying and a diminished capacity for remorse.

You have not sought to put forward any partial defence to murder based upon your psychiatric condition. You very strongly declined the opportunity to do so by the firmness of your guilty pleas to all counts on the indictment when you were first arraigned on 18th November last year. Your counsel accepted in mitigation that you do not have the normal range of emotions and you do not form personal attachments. Others end up suffering because of your personality and that risk is removed by your being in custody. I do not consider that your personality disorders or psychiatric condition afford any mitigation in this case.

You have shown no genuine remorse. Quite the reverse. In the letter you have written to me you say in terms that you do not feel any remorse for the murders, and to claim otherwise would be a lie. You claim in that letter, and this formed part of your counsel's mitigation, that you do feel remorse for the attempted murders. You say that you are ashamed of the brutality and fear you heaped upon those two victims and that the attacks will always be a great source of regret. The only reason you can offer for the attempted murders is 'drunken cruelty plain and simple, compelled by my lack of respect for human life'. As I have already made clear, I reject your protestations of remorse for these attempted murders. I note that you told the psychiatrist that you killed to see how you would feel, 'to see if I was as cold as I thought I was. Then it got moreish and I got a taste for it'. It is very significant, in my judgement, that from a single stab wound to the heart to kill your first victim you progressed by the end to the frenzied attack on John Rogers when you so nearly killed him, stabbing him more than 30 times. You told the psychiatrist you saw the killings as a kind of fetish and that you were sadistic.

I have considered very carefully all the circumstances of this case, and all the features of aggravation and mitigation, including your guilty pleas. I am quite satisfied that the seriousness of these murders is exceptionally high and that the element of just punishment and retribution requires the imposition of a whole life order. Even if, contrary to my conclusion, any of the three murders did not involve a substantial degree of premeditation or planning, the overall circumstances of the three murders, taken in combination with the attempted murders and the dumping of the bodies, plainly makes this a case of exceptionally high seriousness and one of the rare cases which requires a whole life order.

Having regard to the Sentencing Council guideline for attempted murder, I am satisfied that each of these attempted murders, if they stood alone, falls into the highest category in level 1, where the sentencing range after a trial is 27-35 years custody and the starting point 30 years. There must be life sentences for the attempted murders. Had the offences of preventing the lawful and decent burial of a body stood alone, the appropriate total sentence for those three offences, after a trial, would in your case have been at least 16 years imprisonment, but you did at least plead guilty, for which you are entitled to credit although it makes no difference overall.

Joanne Dennehy for these three cruel and brutal murders I sentence you to life imprisonment and the term you will serve is a whole life order. That reflects the seriousness not only of the three murders but also the two attempted murders and the three offences of preventing the lawful burial of the bodies of your three victims. For the two attempted murders, there will be concurrent sentences of life imprisonment. For each of the offences of preventing burial, there will be concurrent sentences of 12 years imprisonment.

GARY STRETCH

I deal with you next, Gary Stretch. I have to sentence you for three offences of preventing the lawful and decent burial of the bodies of the three men who had been murdered, and for two offences of attempted murder. They are all very serious offences indeed, for which a very lengthy sentence of imprisonment is inevitable.

I consider first the three counts of preventing lawful and decent burial. It is a common law offence for which there is no maximum penalty. These were offences at the very top of the scale of seriousness. I have been referred to a number of authorities. In particular I have been assisted by the guidance of the Court of Appeal in the case of *Godward* [1998] 1 Cr App R (S) 385. This is an offence which can vary enormously in its seriousness. The most important factor is the intention of the offender. If the intention was to obstruct the course of justice by concealing a body, so as to make it difficult or impossible to bring home a charge against the person responsible for the death, then a sentence at the top of the appropriate scale is required. That is plainly the position here. The case of *Skinner*, referred to in *Godward*, tends to suggest that any of these three offences on its own would have merited a sentence of at least 7years imprisonment after a trial.

Although Joanne Dennehy initiated these offences, you played a leading role in selecting the sites where these three bodies were dumped. In particular you had lived near Thorney Dyke and boasted to Georgina Page that no one would find the bodies. Just how close you came to achieving that objective is demonstrated by the fact that the farmer who found the two bodies in the ditch at Thorney Dyke on 3rd April had for several days been working in that area of his land without spotting them. I am quite sure that you carried out reconnaissance of the outlying rural areas around Peterborough to find suitable places to dump the bodies. You helped to clean up the scenes of the murders. You helped to load the bodies into the car. You drove the car to the scene. As I have already made clear, I reject entirely any suggestion that you were in fear of Joanne Dennehy. On the contrary, you were revelling in helping her and in the publicity of being described as 'Britain's most wanted'. You were luxuriating in the notoriety which you enjoyed through your association with Joanne Dennehy and her crimes. Taking account of totality, and passing concurrent sentences to reflect the overall criminality of the three offences, the overall sentence for these three counts of preventing the burial of the bodies, if the offences stood alone, would be 15 years imprisonment.

I turn to the two attempted murders. For the reasons I have already explained, on the facts of this case there is little difference between the alternative mental states which the jury were required to consider. Joanne Dennehy had to your knowledge already murdered three men. She was talking that day about wanting her fun and doing more. It was therefore obvious to you that if and when she found another victim she was bound to try to kill him. For that reason there is precious little difference between a shared intention to kill on the one hand and a realisation that there was a real risk she would kill, with the intent to kill, on the other. I am quite satisfied that you knew perfectly well that when the opportunity arose she would attempt to kill again.

You did not wield the knife, but you played a crucial part in facilitating these two dreadful attempted murders. As I have already set out, you stopped the car where and when you did specifically so that she could get out and attack Robin Bereza from behind, catching him unawares. In that sense you both assisted and encouraged Joanne Dennehy to commit the offence, fully believing and expecting that she would stab her victim to death. You knew there were no half measures with Joanne Dennehy. You said or did nothing to stop her. Quite the opposite. You sat and watched what she was doing, and beckoned her back to the car when the time was right. For the reasons I have already explained, I am quite sure as well that you exercised some physical restraint on Mark Lloyd for a short time at least in order to stop him leaving the car and raising the alarm.

When Joanne Dennehy made it clear that she wanted a second victim you drove her to a spot where you knew, from your local knowledge of Hereford, that dog walkers were to be found. It was no coincidence that John Rogers, walking his dog, was the next victim. Again, you assisted and encouraged Joanne Dennehy to commit that second and very nearly fatal attack, knowing perfectly well that murder was what she intended. Had either of these two victims died, you would have been facing a life sentence for murder. The starting point for your minimum term for one such offence of murder would have been 25 years, and if both men had died, the starting point would have been at least 30 years.

Both victims survived, but these two attempted murders are still offences of the utmost seriousness, and at the very top of the scale under the Sentencing Council guideline. Your counsel submits that your culpability was markedly less than Joanne Dennehy's and that this means that these were, in your case, at most level 2 offences. I disagree. In my judgment they are plainly level 1 offences, that is to say offences of a kind which would attract a starting point of 30 years for the minimum term had the charge been murder. That is equivalent to a determinate sentence of 60 years. In both cases, for the reasons I have explained, the victim has suffered serious and long term physical and psychological harm. That means that under the guideline the starting for these two attempted murders would be a determinate sentence of 30 years imprisonment, with a sentencing range of 27 to 35 years. That would be the appropriate level of sentence for someone with no previous convictions whatsoever.

You have an appalling criminal record, albeit mainly for offences of dishonesty. That record, however, includes many convictions for dwelling house burglary where the potential for confrontation with a householder is always a risk. You also have a conviction for robbery as a young man, for which you received a custodial sentence of 5 years. That, I am told, arose in the course of a house burglary. More recently in 2000 you were sentenced to a total of 4 years imprisonment for handling stolen goods. When you breached your licence following release from that sentence you received a consecutive sentence of 2 years for a dwelling house burglary. In 2008 you received a total sentence of 15 months imprisonment for harassment of your former partner, threatening via a third party to kill her. When she was due to give evidence you intimidated her to try to prevent her giving evidence. As a result there is an indefinite restraining order in force against you. These offences show a violent, aggressive and impulsive side to your character, which you try to hide by portraying yourself as a harmless failed burglar who is always caught because of his enormous size.

Your counsel has submitted that your sentence for these two attempted murders should be significantly shorter because you were only a secondary party and not a principal offender. It is well established on the authorities that for murder the starting points in schedule 21 apply equally to secondary parties as to principals, although the starting point may well have to be adjusted to reflect a secondary party's lesser culpability on the facts of the particular case: see *Attorney General's Reference (No.24 of 2008)* [2009] 2 Cr App R (S) 41. The same reasoning applies to the situation here. I accept that your culpability was substantially less than that of Joanne Dennehy in these offences, but it was still very great. If the two attempted murders stood alone the appropriate total sentence for you for those offences would be 27 years.

The offences you committed in Hereford amounted to entirely distinct criminality from the offences you committed in Peterborough. Consecutive sentences are therefore required as between the two sets of offences. On what I have indicated so far, that would make a total of 42 years. Because the offences are so distinct and so serious, and because I have not treated either set of offences as aggravating the seriousness of the other, only a modest further reduction for totality is appropriate. I therefore conclude that if a determinate sentence were the appropriate course to follow in your case, these offences together would merit a total determinate sentence of 38 years, made up of 13 years concurrent for each of the prevention of burial offences and 25 years concurrent for each of the attempted murders. If 38 years were your sentence, you would serve 19 years before release on licence.

However, I have to consider whether a determinate sentence is appropriate at all or whether it is necessary to pass a sentence of life imprisonment or, alternatively, an extended sentence of imprisonment.

Because you have been convicted of offences of attempted murder I am required by law to consider whether you are a 'dangerous' offender, in other words whether there is a significant risk to members of the public of serious harm occasioned by the commission by you of further specified offences, which for practical purposes means serious harm from any significant offence of violence. In making that assessment I must take into account all information available to me about you and about the nature and circumstances of these offences of attempted murder and the other offences of which you have been convicted, including information about any pattern of behaviour of which any of those offences forms part.

I bear in mind that these attempted murders are offences at the very top of the range of seriousness. You were convicted as a secondary party, not as a principal, but these offences demonstrate your willingness to involve yourself in the most serious violence. Second, I bear in mind that likewise the offences of preventing burial were of the most serious kind, committed in order to interfere with the course of justice. They did not involve any violence but they demonstrate a willingness to assist a triple murderer to evade justice. Third, you have a previous conviction for a serious offence of robbery, albeit a very long time ago, and a more recent conviction for harassing your ex-partner by indirectly threatening to kill her, compounded by intimidating her, or attempting to intimidate her, into not giving evidence against you. Fourth, you are an inveterate house burglar, where the risk of conflict with a householder is always present. Fifth you threatened Georgina Page with violence, albeit indirectly, if she went to the police. That was not just for bravado because Joanne Dennehy was present. Sixth you were prepared to arm yourself with a handgun whilst you were on the run from the police, although you disposed of the gun without using it, and I accept there is no other evidence you have ever possessed or used a firearm.

Your counsel rightly urges upon me the most powerful point

in mitigation against the imposition of a sentence based on dangerousness, namely the fact you committed these offences in the thrall of Joanne Dennehy. That opportunity will never arise again. I have considered carefully the guidance of the Court of Appeal in the recent decision in *Saunders* [2013] EWCA Crim 1027, and the circumstances in which a life sentence may be appropriate and necessary for its 'denunciatory' value reflecting public abhorrence of the offence, and where the notional determinate sentence would be very long indeed, as here, measured in very many years. However, I would first have to be satisfied that there is a significant risk that you would commit further offences of violence if at large and a significant risk of serious harm to members of the public as a result.

I have considered very carefully all the submissions, both written and oral, made so powerfully by your counsel, but despite those submissions, I have no hesitation in reaching the conclusion that there is a significant risk of serious harm to members of the public from the commission by you of further specified offences. I accept that these offences of attempted murder in which you played a full part arose from the special circumstances of your association with Joanne Dennehy. However, having seen the way she attacked the first victim, you encouraged her to attack again, knowing that she was likely to kill. That persistence on your part, as well as hers, demonstrates all too clearly your potential for causing serious harm to the public in the future, particularly in the light of the other factors I have just identified. I therefore conclude that the threshold of dangerousness is clearly met.

That being so, the next question, under s225(2) of the

2003 Act is whether the offences are together so serious as to justify a sentence of life imprisonment. In my view they are. A very long determinate sentence would not in my judgment be sufficient to protect the public. Nor would an extended sentence be appropriate bearing in mind the very long custodial term which would dwarf even the maximum extension period of 5 years. I bear firmly in mind that a sentence of life imprisonment must always be a last resort. But in my judgment, this is a case where a life sentence is required in order to reflect public abhorrence of these offences of attempted murder committed jointly whilst you were seeking to evade arrest for helping to dispose of the bodies of three men already murdered by Joanne Dennehy.

As the Court of Appeal made clear in *Saunders*, it remains open to the court to pass a discretionary life sentence even where the pre-conditions for a sentence under section 225 of the Act are not met. Had that been the position in your case (which I stress it is not), I would in any event have passed a discretionary life sentence on that alternative basis, having regard to the overriding need to protect the public from you indefinitely.

Gary Stretch for each of the offences of attempted murder the sentence is life imprisonment. You will serve a minimum term of 19 years, that being one half of the determinate sentence which would otherwise have been appropriate. That term of 19 years reflects the criminality not only of the attempted murders but also the three offences of preventing burial. For those offences there will be concurrent terms of 15 years imprisonment. You will receive credit against the term of 19 years for the time you have already spent on remand which, by my calculation, is 332 days.

The effect of this sentence is that you will serve 19 years in prison before you are even eligible to be considered for parole. It will then be a matter for the parole board to decide if and when it is safe to release you, and if you are released you will remain on licence for the rest of your life.

LESLIE LAYTON

I deal with you next Leslie Layton. I have to sentence you for preventing the lawful and decent burial of the bodies of two of the men Joanne Dennehy had murdered. I also have to sentence you for perverting the course of justice by lying to the police when they were trying to find what had become of John Chapman, one of the men who was murdered. For the reasons I have already explained, these offences of preventing burial are at the very top of the range of seriousness. Had they stood alone, each individually would have merited a sentence of 7years or more. You were actively involved in dumping these two bodies, but your involvement spanned a single day, Friday 29th March. I am satisfied that you played a subordinate role to Gary Stretch and Joanne Dennehy, although you were a perfectly willing participant.

It is an aggravating feature of the offences that you had already taken that photograph of John Chapman's dead body on your mobile phone. That casts a flood of light on your attitude towards the fate of your housemate and on your lack of concern or respect for human life and for the decency and dignity of a body after death. You had every opportunity to distance yourself from what you were being asked to do but chose to go along with it. You assisted physically with the removal of John Chapman's body from the house. You travelled with each of the bodies to the separate sites where they were dumped. You were prominent in setting fire to and destroying Kevin Lee's vehicle, as a further way of preventing the circumstances of his death being discovered and hence preventing his lawful and decent burial.

Yours was also a serious offence of perverting the course of justice. You lied to the police repeatedly in what you knew to be a murder investigation. You did so to cover your own tracks and to protect Gary Stretch and Joanne Dennehy. You had no reason to be in fear of them because they were far away in East Anglia when the police came to see you, as you well knew. Whether they would have been apprehended sooner had you told the police the truth, we shall never know. It is certainly possible they could have been arrested before committing the offences in Hereford. That is an illustration of the potential seriousness of your offence.

You are now 37 years of age. You have previous convictions for offences involving vehicles and for dishonesty but you had never been to prison before. These offences are wholly outside your normal league. You were caught up in the excitement and fascination of these appalling murders committed in one case quite literally on your doorstep by a woman who undoubtedly exercised some psychological influence over you and other men with whom she came into contact, including her victims. But that does not excuse what you did. Nor do you have the mitigation of guilty pleas.

I have had regard to the guidance in the authorities to which I have been referred and in particular *Tunney* [2007] 1 Cr App (S) 91 and *Gonsalves* [2008] 1 Cr App (S) 40, both of which involved perverting the course of justice in homicide cases. They emphasise the need to consider three factors in particular. First, the seriousness of the substantive offence. Here it was murder. It could not be more serious. Second, the persistence of the offender's conduct. Here you persisted in these false statements over a period of two days, although the most extensive lies were told on the afternoon of Monday 1st April. Third, the effect of what you did on the course of justice itself. Here your attempt was unsuccessful in the sense that the police soon discovered the truth of what had happened, and John Chapman's body was in any event discovered, fortuitously, two days later. There must plainly be a consecutive sentence for the offence of perverting the course of justice because it involved quite separate and distinct criminality from the two offences of preventing burial.

Leslie Layton. Were it not for the fact that I must bear in mind the totality of the sentence I am passing upon you, the individual sentences would have been longer. For the two offences of preventing the lawful and decent burial of bodies you will serve concurrent sentences of 10 years imprisonment. For the offence of perverting the course of justice you will serve a consecutive sentence of 4 years imprisonment. So your total sentence is 14 years imprisonment. You will serve one half of that sentence in prison and upon release you will be on licence for the remainder of the sentence and liable to recall if you commit any further offence or breach your licence.

ROBERT MOORE

I deal finally with you, Robert Moore. You had the good sense to plead guilty to the two counts you faced, although your guilty pleas did not come at the first reasonable opportunity so you cannot expect full credit. It is clear to me from the pre sentence report that you do not fully understand even now just how serious your conduct was in giving shelter to Joanne Dennehy and Gary Stretch for two nights when you knew they were wanted by the police for the most serious of offences.

You are 56 years of age and a man with no previous convictions whatsoever. I am prepared to accept that you came under the spell of Joanne Dennehy and were flattered by her attention. You must have known the sort of woman you were getting involved with when you were made aware that the body of one of her victims was in a wheelie bin at her address close to your home. You admitted to the probation officer that you knew that. You kept in close touch with Joanne Dennehy and Gary Stretch by phone in what might be described as a fawning manner, texting that you had food waiting for them. When Joanne Dennehy and Gary Stretch went on the run in East Anglia you texted them that the police were after them and you wished them luck. They returned to your home again that night.

When you were interviewed by the police you repeatedly lied about your involvement in helping Joanne Dennehy and Gary Stretch. Had you not provided them with shelter for those two nights and had you instead done your duty as a citizen by telling the police straightaway what you knew, it is possible that they would have been arrested earlier, and before the offences in Hereford were committed. Again, we shall never know but it illustrates the seriousness and the potential consequences of what you did.

The maximum sentence for the offences to which you have pleaded guilty is 10 years imprisonment. I have had regard to the guidance in the authorities in this area, notably *R v Elfes* [2006] EWCA Crim 2799 and *Attorney General's Ref (No: 16 of 2009)* [2009] EWCA Crim 2439. In both those cases, however, the duration and value of the assistance was greater than in your case. I also take into account your good character and the health issues which are revealed in the pre-sentence report. I have had the opportunity to observe you in the dock during the sentencing hearing at Cambridge two weeks ago as well as in the dock here today. I accept that you are genuinely remorseful.

Had you been convicted of these two offences after a trial, the sentence would have been four years imprisonment. As it is you pleaded guilty at a late stage, but that took courage. You will receive credit of one-quarter for those pleas.

Robert Moore for each of these offences you will serve a sentence of 3 years imprisonment concurrent. That means you will released when you have served one half of the sentence and you will remain on licence for the rest of the sentence.

Following the verdicts, Chris McCann from The Crown Prosecution Service and DCI Martin Brunning gave press interviews:

The men were not under duress as they claimed. Stretch and Layton willingly assisted Joanne Dennehy in disposing of her three victims and in covering up the crimes she committed. The fact that Leslie Layton photographed one of the deceased victims is testament to the warped nature of these crimes and those that committed them.

I would like to thank Mr Bereza and Mr Rogers for giving evidence in this trial and reliving what must have been a terrible experience for them.

I hope the two victims and the families of Mr Slaboszewski, Mr Chapman and Kevin Lee can take comfort from the fact that the perpetrators of these crimes have been brought to justice and will be punished for what they have done.

Chris McCann, Crown Prosecution Service

This has to be one of the largest and most complex investigations in my 20 years experience.

Three men were brutally murdered in Peterborough and two men stabbed in West Mercia. Today their killer and her willing accomplices have now been brought to justice.

Joanne Dennehy is a sadistic serial killer with a fearsome personality. She manipulated men into doing what she wanted.

I am relieved she is facing a substantial period of time behind bars.

Her accomplices not only fuelled her violence but also assisted her in those cruel crimes, by helping her to dump the bodies. Stretch drove her around and he helped her pick her next victims without a thought of the impact on them or their loved ones.

Moore sheltered Joanne Dennehy and Gary Stretch while they were on the run and lied to police about their whereabouts, while Layton was prepared to help Dennehy and Stretch with their criminal activities, helped them dump the bodies and did everything to assist them to avoid being caught.

The actions of Dennehy and those who helped her have had a devastating impact on the families of those killed and the surviving victims.

DCI Martin Brunning

But there is some good news, and we must thank Martin Brunning's Bedfordshire, Cambridgeshire and Hertfordshire Major Crime Unit and West Mercia Police for bringing it to us. From the 19 March 2013 murder of Lukasz Slaboszewski through to the killings of Kevin Lee and John Chapman, to the murderous attacks on Robin Bereza and John Rogers, just 16 days elapsed before Dennehy and Stretch were arrested, which, as far as I can determine, is a world record in solving a serial homicide case. This is remarkable testimony to the efficiency of UK law enforcement when such crimes are reported then solved. There is no hiding place, nor will there ever be a hiding place for killers such as Joanne Dennehy and those who conspire to conceal such heinous crimes.

Of course the victims of Joanne Dennehy cannot speak

for themselves. Kevin Lee, Lukasz Slaboszewski and John Chapman, but they still provide cherished memories for the bereaved left behind in the wake of Joanne Dennehy and Stretch's homicidal legacy. They were assisted by Leslie Layton and Robert Moore, who will almost certainly be sponging off the taxpayer as soon as they are released from prison.

Kevin's fifteen-year-old son, Dino, so named because of the lad's love of fast cars and the Ferrari name, is becoming a Go-Kart champion, determined to honour his father, who was his mentor in racing. Dino's twenty-five-year-old sister, Chiara, is also heartbroken, for no one deserves to lose his, or her parent, in such terrible circumstances, whatever the issues may be. In an email, dated 4 July 2014, to this author, Chiara makes it clear that she is the spokesperson for the family and all media enquiries should go through her. She intimates that there has been much interest from the press, other writers and TV, and has whittled these enquiries down to just two, based on some form of donation towards Dino's budding career as a racing driver. This is not something that either myself as author or my publisher deems to be appropriate.

Robin Bereza and John Rogers are two of Dennehy's victims who lived to tell the tale. Through their accounts, we can start to appreciate how Lukasz Slaboszewski, Kevin Lee and John Chapman met their fate.

Bereza and Rogers described how the blitz attacks came from nowhere for both described an initial 'punch' while feeling no invasive pain. In shock, Robin Bereza calmly asked Dennehy why she was doing this to him. Callously, she replied: 'I'm hurting you. I'm going to fuckin' kill you.'

Similarly in shock, John Rogers asked Dennehy: 'What's this all about?' She replied, 'You're bleeding. I better do some more.'

Therefore, we might easily overlay Dennehy's murderous and highly successful method of killing onto the deaths of the three men. Simply put, their murders came from nowhere and were totally unexpected and at a time and a place where they felt safe and secure.

How could Slaboszewski have suspected his new English girlfriend would stab him to death on their first date when, as he had previously texted a friend, 'Life is beautiful'?

How could Lee have envisaged that, having sent Dennehy an Easter card and bought her a couple of CDs, soon afterwards he would end up dead in a ditch in an unseemly manner?

How could John Chapman, aka 'Uncle Albert', have known that when he fell asleep, his worst nightmare would come true – that Dennehy would evict him from 38 Bifield whatever it took, and he would never wake up again?

And, when Robin Bereza and John Rogers took their dogs for a walk, they could never have imagined that they were walking to within a heartbeat of their own graves.

Now we are beginning to understand the true nature of the beast that is Joanne Dennehy and that of her cohort, Gary Stretch. Both Robin Bereza and John Rogers described the coldness of Dennehy when she attacked them. Naturally, they could not understand her motive, nor would any of us.

Bereza described how 'she looked right through me' while Rogers recalls that she 'didn't seem to be showing any emotion. She didn't seem to be enjoying herself, she just seemed like she was going about business'.

SENTENCING

Such chilling observations but let's stop and rewind for a few moments to enquire how Joanne Dennehy is being punished in prison. This, I guarantee, will give sleepless nights for my 19 May 2014 Freedom of Information Request (FOI) to the Ministry of Justice, copied to HMP & YOI Bronzefield, came back with no explanation at all as to why female inmates were allowed to put on a show, costing *circa*170,000 of taxpayers' money, entertaining hundreds of guests who paid up to 40 a ticket to see the likes of Dennehy prance about in their undies for a *Sister Act*.

21

WHOOPI, IT'S A SISTER ACT!

This place is a dump. The food is crap.
JOANNE DENNEHY, TO ANOTHER INMATE AT
HMP BRONZEFIELD, APRIL 2014

They say a picture paints a thousand words, but it would be irresponsible of me, and my publisher, to include in this book the graphic photos taken of the decomposing dead bodies of Lukasz Slaboszewski, Kevin Lee and John Chapman, in situ in the ditches, or at autopsy. Indeed, even if one were permitted to publish these pictures, I would not do so for this would serve no purpose other than to bring additional heartbreak to their next of kin and indeed also to the parents of Joanne Dennehy, who are innocent victims of their daughter's heinous crimes, too. Besides, we all wish to remember a lost loved one as he/she was in life, not in death. Added to which so disgusting are the photos of the deceased Kevin Lee, the trial judge and the sentencing judge ordered the pictures be photographically sanitised in a certain area.

My Canadian friend, the award-winning actor and novelist,

WHOOP, IT'S A SISTER ACT!

Alan Scarfe, aka Clanash Farjeon, writes in his book, *The Autobiography of Jack the Ripper*: 'The murders [of Jack the Ripper] were variously described as "ferocious butchery, virulent savagery and beyond comprehension"'. He adds: 'People always say "beyond comprehension" when they cannot bear to admit that they comprehend all too well.' And to me this perfectly sums up Dennehy's murders.

Since being incarcerated Joanne Dennehy has risen through the inmate ranks and has now attained the lofty position of cleaner in the segregation unit (The Block) at HMP Bronzefield, Surrey. As might be expected, she claims that she is top dog there, bragging in badly spelt notes to a pen friend:

> *Girls on the spurs being scared of me? Lol no around me they become pro-asse lickers. Down here I get to see the naughty girls, plastic gangster-ett's and the one's who think their the bollox* [sic].

So why am I including this letter here and what significance is it to us in trying to understand Dennehy's mind? In fact it deserves to be included for the note signifies a great deal since her correspondence to me is well laid out. Written with a good hand and an eye for detail and punctuation, she uses perfect grammar and there is not a misspelling anywhere. Then, when we compare this to her letters to Gary Stretch and her lesbian pen friend, we see the flip side for Joanne Dennehy is a literary chameleon. This manipulative woman puts on a different persona to impress whosoever she is dealing with at any given time.

Jean Elliott is a graphologist and she analysed Dennehy's writing in the *Daily Mirror* (Friday, 21 March 2014):

The script is of a very immature writer, rounded with letters so close together that they touch, with no spaces between them. Her fields of interest are narrow and the ego over-inflated to the extent she may consider herself important, by demanding attention and taking it as her right that others will bend to her ways. The bumping letters suggest that, with regards to her feelings, she expects those around her to be telepathic. On the other hand, she prefers to follow orders as she does not like making decisions.

I agree with some of this, however, in Dennehy's mail to me I see no 'bumping letters' and there is space between the words, although the script is admittedly somewhat juvenile. I cannot say any of the halfwits involved with Dennehy had any telepathic receiving device in their heads – far from it, I would suggest. That Dennehy prefers to follow orders does not resonate with me either: sociopaths do not follow anyone's orders, they issue them.

Jean Elliott is also at pains to report that in her experience: 'her [Dennehy] inner nature is introverted with her spontaneity curbed but there are times when such writers find comfort by behaving in an unconventional way.'

Lady (in Britain) a title of honour borne by various classes of women of the peerage.
Collins English Dictionary

However, Elliott says: 'This *lady*, [author's italics] however, is reluctant to allow her emotions free expression and can use control to the point of cold-heartedness', none of which I can truly understand. A 'lady' she most certainly isn't! Nevertheless, Elliott suggests the left slant of Dennehy's handwriting shows 'a protective attitude towards herself and she has taken the ideals and values from her mother figure.'

Elliott concludes her analysis with: 'the writer is very self-involved, which can border on conceit, an individual who is self-centred and makes great issues out of trivial things. The personality is self-absorbed, dwelling on past experiences rather than looking forward to the future – which often frightens her. The danger to this person is boredom and confinement in her own self-centred world.'

But I digress. Having seen the note to her pen friend, I wrote to Joanne asking for an explanation to which I received this curt reply: 'The lies being told about me, about the things I'm meant to have said or done are too numerous for me to care about. Prime example: My views on Bronzefield.'

Before her sentencing, and while on remand, Dennehy had plotted to escape after being rejected by Anna Chambers, a lesbian inmate, with whom she became infatuated. Twenty-nine-year-old Anna is serving a prison term after attempting to hold up a petrol station with a knife in 2013.

She [Dennehy] didn't like it when people said she killed three people. She liked to boast she had killed five and did not like it when people said she had failed.
Anna Chambers, inmate at HMP Bronzefield, 2014.

A former inmate who does not wish to be named said: 'Anna was just nice to her [Dennehy]. But Joanne wanted Anna to be her girlfriend, but she told her "no" as she has a girlfriend on the outside. As soon as she said she did not want to be with her, that was it. Jo said that she would kill her [the girlfriend on the outside].'

But was this threat to escape and kill another person for real? Certainly the Prison Service thought so because they were obliged to issue the following press statement:

In September 2013, searches by staff uncovered intelligence which could have been interpreted as an escape plan. The matter was dealt swiftly with no security breaches and a prisoner [Dennehy] was relocated to the segregation unit (The Block).

Did Ms Dennehy kill more than three times? Five, seven, even ten have been bandied about. My officers have done all they can to find out. No one can rule out the possibility of more victims but we are sticking with three murders.
DCI Martin Brunning, to the author at interview, 10 June 2014

This may sound archaic but most right-minded folk would say that the punishment should suit the crime – an eye for an eye, that sort of stuff. Most certainly women in the US who have committed similar offences would now be on Death Row. However, this is not the case in the UK, far from it.

WHOOP!, IT'S A SISTER ACT!

*So yep Im sentenced Woop! Woop! Got what I expected
and as you can imagine Im cool with it [sic].*
Joanne Dennehy, letter to a pen friend, 2014.

*Working with organisations such as the Pimlico Opera can
have a positive impact on rehabilitation and help offenders
lead law-abiding lives on release.*
Ian Blakeman, Director of Commissioning National
Offender Management Service

As West End London stage productions go, a later version
of *Sister Act* performed at HMP Bronzefield was carried out
on the cheap – if one can call 175,000 or thereabouts cheap!
And, I would hazard a guess that if the internationally famous
Hollywood actress Whoopi Goldberg (who starred in the
original 1992 movie of the same name) learned of this, she
would be none too pleased, for the Bronzefield star was none
other than one Gholda James.

A former Dominican Republic Next Top Model contestant,
18-year-old Gholda James from Pointe Michel had previously
been in contact with law enforcement and had become of
interest to HM Customs & Excise Special Investigations and
other agencies. In 2013, she was jailed for trying to smuggle
90,000 of cocaine into the UK but was now cast in the lead
for Bronzefield's version of *Sister Act* as Sister Roberts. I have
Ms James's criminal CV in front of me as I write and to put
her into perspective, it is such characters who bring drugs into
the UK, simultaneously wrecking the likes of school kids like
Joanne Dennehy.

Supporting Miss James in this production, and also scantily clad in fishnet stockings, suspender belt and black stilettos, was Sarah Anderson, who is serving a life sentence for the blitz, multiple stabbing of a woman following an argument in a South London public house.

Nigerian air hostess Temitayo Daramola, incarcerated after attempting to smuggle 600,000 of cocaine on a flight to London from Lagos in the summer of 2013, unashamedly paraded herself alongside a female child abuser alongside twenty or more of the most dangerous women offenders, plus an extended cast of professional actors and opera singers, all accompanied by a thirteen-piece orchestra.

According to the media, leading Pimlico Opera designer Halla Groves-Raines had secretly created the stage without public or government financial scrutiny and professional choreographers trained the prisoners for two weeks. According to press reports, although not publicly advertised, with prison officials ordering a ban on publicity amid fears of public outrage, on the order of prison director Charlotte Pattison-Rideout the show went ahead, with tickets oversubscribed. During seven nights, between the end of February and the start of March 2014, at least 300 people attended each show, paying up to 40 a ticket to watch killers, sex offenders, drug smugglers, thieves, con-women and those due for deportation prance about in very little, all in the name of 'rehabilitation'.

Rehabilitation for what, you are entitled to ask. A job in a pole dancing club or a strip joint, perhaps even a drugs rehabilitation clinic in Nigeria... Pull the other one! They might perhaps have been more constructively rehabilitated breaking rocks in a granite quarry, or breaking sweat through some other form of manual labour.

Absent from the on-stage cast of criminal performers was the subject of this book, namely Joanne Dennehy. She was serving teas, coffees and light refreshments to 'distinguished guests' – all part of her rehabilitation into a free society to which she will never return. As for Rose West... Previously, she had been secretly removed from HMP Bronzefield, having been granted 'Rule 43' Protective Custody at her own request after Dennehy threatened to kill her, too. To confirm or deny both of these matters I wrote to HMP Bronzefield but received no reply.

> *Most victims' families will be horrified by this. Yes, rehabilitation is part of the programme in prison but there must be more appropriate ways. They are in there enjoying themselves when the bereaved families are totally devastated. I think it is very insensitive.*
> Rose Dixon, CEO of the national charity Support after Murder and Manslaughter (SAMM)

Thank you, Rose Dixon, so quite why Joanne Dennehy is complaining about the conditions at Bronzefield is unclear. Opened in 2004, housing some 527 women, the facility has three main residential units, each holding 135 female inmates in almost idyllic surroundings. Therefore, Bronzefield is perhaps the most modern of such facilities within the British Criminal Justice System, which the Ministry of Justice (MoJ) refers to as its estate.

HMP & YOI Bronzefield is run by Sodexo, a French food

services and facilities management multinational corporation with headquarters in the Paris suburb of Issy-les-Moulineaux. According to Sodexos internet web site, at the time of writing, the companys assets are circa 111.40 billion and it employs around 415,000 people worldwide, making it one of the wealthiest organisations in the world. However, during the research for this book I discovered that in August 2013, Sodexo Justice Services had previously been criticised in an official report by the Chief Inspector of Prisons for subjecting a female prisoner to 'cruel, inhumane and degrading treatment', something that the chief executive of the Howard League for |Penal Reform said 'appears to amount to torture', at HMP Bronzefield. In brief, the woman was kept segregated from other prisoners in an 'unkempt and squalid' prison cell for more than five years. Indeed, there have been two such inspections; the first being published by the Independent Monitoring Board's Annual Report for the period August 2011–July 2012, and then a visit by the Chief Inspector of Prisons, Nick Hardwick, which is mentioned by Hannah Minnock writing in *The Solicitor Online*, 11 August, 2013. The full reports are easily available on the Internet.

Subjected to both official enquiries, it is fair to say that HMP Bronzefield was thoroughly examined and mostly exonerated by HM Inspector of Prisons, who went on to say perhaps a few improvements could be made, but it was Dennehy's allegations about the food, aligned with the vast expense of the *Sister Act* production, that demanded I dig deeper. Well, it is 170,000 of taxpayers' money we are talking about here, and since another official report also confirmed that Sodexo were not feeding their prisoners properly it was right for me to enquire how the company could afford to put up such a large amount of cash for a stage production. So I submitted a Freedom of Information Request (FOI) to the Ministry of Justice on 19 May 2014.

The reply, dated 28 May 2014, follows, and despite the apparent 'transparency', it leaves much more to be answered:

No UK taxpayers' money was used to fund this stage production.

That no UK taxpayers' money was used to provide overtime for prison staff during the duration of this show.

That HM Ministry of Justice, HM Government, or any of its agents and servants were, in any way complicit in this stage production.

So, the British taxpayer – who funds Sodexo Justice Services, a company contracted by HM Ministry of Justice – is being fobbed off here, for of course the British taxpayer was ultimately left to foot the bill for the *Sister Act* show. As a nation we have all contributed to prison staff overtime and the bottom line that 'HM Ministry of Justice, HM Government, or any of its agents and servants, were not in any way complicit in this stage production' is a complete falsehood. If the Ministry of Justice is unaware of what is going on inside their prisons, this department needs a wake-up call. But it gets worse, and I owe this much to the next of kin of Joanne Dennehy's deceased victims.

My FOI request also made mention of the security clearance procedures carried out by Sodexo Justice Services on the fee-paying guests who attended the *Sister Act* show. I am talking about hundreds of guests here, each one having to comply with the National Policy covering Visitors to Prisoners *(PSI 16/2011)* Providing Visits and Services to prisoners, and *(PSI 15/2011)* Management of Security at Visits, with regard to those individuals producing the stage production.

The reply from Ministry of Justice official Roger Davis simply stated:

This applicant [Christopher Berry-Dee] for a Freedom of Information request under the 200 [*sic*] Act has knowledge, by way of fact, that many ticket paying guest [*sic*] attended this show 'Mingled' with offenders, having never associated with, or been known to each other. The Ministry of Justice will provide confirmation, by way of a hardcopy reply:

That Sodexho [*sic*], inter alia, the Sodexho [*sic*] Corporation, fully complied with the national policy covering Visits to Prisoners (PSI 16/2011) providing Visits and Services to Prisoners, and PSI 15/2011 Management of Security at Visits, with regard to guests attending this stage production?

Sadly, this official response to my FOI request merely confirms that apart from the fact that Mr Davis has not a clue what he is talking about, he might be advised to study the English language. Worse still, he cannot even spell the name of the company to whom the MoJ contracts out to run HMP Bronzefield. He has also completely overlooked the fact that for a person to be accepted for a prison visit takes careful vetting, not only by the Ministry of Justice but the Home Office too. Even magistrates are vetted before visits, but in this case we are talking about hundreds of fee-paying guests and the MoJ refuses to say how these guests were selected, how the show was advertised to them, how much cash was lost, or to identify the guests.

Added to which there is the matter of Joanne Dennehy serving light refreshments to distinguished guests. Two correctional officers and several inmates have told me that this is true. The MoJ neither confirms nor denies this, nor can HMP Bronzefield, who, while enjoying the British taxpayer's generosity, has no comment whatsoever to make.

The Sister Act *show you have described to me is news to me, and my officers. It is the first I have heard of this.*
A diplomatic DCI Martin Brunning, at interview with the author, 2014

22

MAD, BAD OR SAD?

I had a case for diminished responsibility.
JOANNE DENNEHY, LETTER TO THE AUTHOR,
24 FEBRUARY 2014

Combined with all of the overwhelming physical and circumstantial evidence stacked against her, with Joanne Dennehy having maintained her guilt from the outset, her legal team had just one defence and it would have been a flimsy one at that. They would use her previous psychiatric evaluations in an attempt to prove some form of mitigation: that she had committed her crimes while labouring under a mental illness, therefore there was the defence of diminished responsibility.

Dennehy had been twice diagnosed by psychiatrists as having a 'series of acute personality disorders', however readers will have guessed from the outset that she is not a socially inclined individual – far from it.

David Wilson, Professor of Criminology at Birmingham City University, followed her prosecution and says: 'It is impossible to say with certainty whether a person is born a killer or becomes a killer, but most criminologists believe that it is a messy combination of the two.'

This statement, of course, boils down the Nature versus Nurture argument, so popular a decade or so ago. Today, we are inclined to quantify it as Nature *and* Nurture – a mix of both, if you will.

Professor Wilson also says: 'A person can be born with a genetic makeup that means they have the potential to kill – but it is not a given that they will go on to fulfill that potential. For that to happen, certain sociological and psychological circumstances need to be in place. In Dennehy's case, they clearly were. She had disengaged from all the institutional structures that usually provide a stabilising influence – family, education, work, and so on. In addition, she was giving full rein to her paraphilia – her obsessive interest in atypical sexual practices – with her use of hardcore pornography and her pursuit of sadomasochistic sex. And the dividing line between reality and fantasy was further blurred by her persistent use of drugs. She also had a strong narcissistic streak – she craved notoriety and she enjoyed the power that killing gave her, and which she lacked in every other area of her life.'

However, for criminologists seeking to untangle Joanne's twisted mind and the nature of her crimes, her descent into barbarism is all the more shocking given the respectable nature of her childhood, a brief history of which has already been outlined in this book. Therefore, we can only speculate on how her mind worked, starting with the psychiatric evaluations of Dennehy when she was twice sectioned under the Mental Health Act. Summing this up, if a wax effigy of her were to be displayed in the Chamber of Horrors at Madame Tussauds, it would wear a label saying:

> *Joanne Dennehy*
> *Serial Killer*
> *Prone to unpredictable, sadomasochistic, emotionally unstable behaviour well seasoned with sundry psychotic disorders.*
> *PLEASE DO NOT TOUCH THIS EXHIBIT!*

With all this in mind, one might reasonably ask whether Joanne Dennehy is mad, sad or bad, beginning with questions as to her sanity and whether she was mentally competent to stand her trial. There are, in fact, two 'insanity' defences:

That, because of a disease of the mind, an offender does not know the nature and quality of the act; and

That even if one did know the nature and quality of the act, because of a disease of the mind one did not know it was wrong.

In pleas of diminished responsibility – as Dennehy herself has alluded to – it is for the defence to establish a defendant's insanity 'on balance of probabilities'. It is for the jury to decide, and the guidelines for their use are embodied in the M'Naghten Rules, which in part state: 'Every man is presumed to be sane, and to possess a sufficient degree of reason to be responsible for his crimes, until the contrary be proved to their [the jury's] satisfaction'.

On 20 January 1843, in Downing Street, a Glasgow wood-worker named Daniel M'Naghten drew a pistol, then shot and killed Edward Drummond, secretary to the Prime Minister, Sir Robert Peel, who was, ironically, the founder of the Metropolitan Police. The lead ball had been intended for Sir Robert himself but M'Naghten seems to have been unfamiliar with the Prime Minister's appearance and to have shot the first likely candidate.

At his subsequent trial before judge and jury at the Old Bailey, it transpired that he had had, with no apparent justification, an unreasoning suspicion that 'Tories' were persecuting him. Not only had murder had been committed on the open street, but Her Majesty's PM could so easily have been the victim. There was then a certain tinge of self-interest in the disquiet voiced by Parliament when the jury returned a verdict that M'Naghten was insane and should therefore be merely confined to a mental hospital. Great, too, was the public discomfort at this verdict, and it was subsequently contested in the House of Lords.

Their Lordships decided to require Her Majesty's judges to advise them on the matter – an ancient right of the House, though seldom exercised. The joint answer given by fourteen judges formed what became the M'Naghten Rules and reads in essence as follows:

> *Jurors ought to be told in all cases that a man is presumed to be sane, and to possess a sufficient degree of reason to be responsible for his crimes, until the contrary be proved to their satisfaction.*

Joanne Dennehy therefore knew the nature and quality of her acts. She understood that what she was doing was wrong so she was mentally competent to plead her case and stand trial, but what of her claim that she had a case for diminished responsibility?

> *Prosecutors prosecute. They do not ask juries to return a verdict of acquittal.*
> Lawton J in *Price* [1963] 2 QB I at 7

Borrowed from the law of Scotland dating back to 1867, the Homicide Act 1957, s. 2, introduced into UK law a new defence for murder known as 'diminished responsibility', which entitles the accused not to be acquitted altogether, but to be found guilty of manslaughter. In the US it is called 'Second Degree Homicide'. By s. 2 (2) the Act expressly puts the burden of proof on the prisoner and it has been held that, as in the case of insanity, the required standard of proof is not beyond reasonable doubt but on balance of probabilities. Therefore consideration of this defence is, strictly speaking, out of place here for it is not a general defence but applies only to murder. In practice, however, the scope of the new defence is almost the same as insanity, for the Rules themselves are rarely relied on outside murder cases. Except in murder, the prospect of indefinite and possibly life-long confinement in a facility such as Broadmoor is far worse than the ordinary punishment for the crime. Similarly, it is reasonable to suppose that defendants generally prefer a conviction for manslaughter to an 'acquittal' on the grounds of insanity.

For her part Dennehy did not plead diminished responsibility although she had told me in her 24 February 2014 letter that she may have had this defence available to her. It was not for the prosecution to interfere, and it is highly doubtful whether Mr Justice Sweeney had the discretion to call evidence of diminished responsibility. Even if he had, he could not call such evidence against the wishes of Dennehy, who had just made her intentions perfectly clear in telling him to 'Fuck off!' Therefore, her only option now is to appeal and a U-turn on confession is unusual.

According to Shula de Jersey, a solicitor from Slater & Gordon lawyers, anyone who has been convicted of a crime has the right to make an application to the Court of Appeal. In this situation – where the person has already pleaded guilty – there would have to be grounds for appeal. For example, the person could claim they made a confession or confessed under duress. In Dennehy's case she admitted her guilt the moment she was booked in at Hereford and against the advice of her legal team, she maintained her guilt throughout.

'This is a very unusual situation,' says Shula de Jersey, 'and I have never heard of someone admitting a murder then retracting it. The court would look at the evidence and decide whether to overturn the conviction. Even if it was overturned, the person who is suspected could still be charged as police may investigate further and pass a file to the Crown Prosecution Service, which would then consider if charges could be brought.'

This would only happen if it was in the public interest and there was a reasonable chance of a conviction. Prosecutors would have to take into consideration that the individual making the allegation is serving life in prison and may not be considered a reliable witness.

23

FREEDOM: AN
IMPOSSIBLE DREAM

Responding to a Freedom of Information request (FOI), according to the Ministry of Justice it costs the British taxpayer 37,163 a year to keep an inmate in prison. At the time of writing, Joanne Dennehy is housed in the high security unit, at HMP Bronzefield, and she has also served time in 'The Block', more commonly known as 'The Hole', for planning an escape. For prisoners worldwide, 'The Block' is the end of the road. Prove that you can walk on one level and onto the next, it is a form of 'carrot and stick' behavioural modification unit where, if you toe the line you get out, if not, you stay in.

Block time is hard time. You lose all privileges – no TV, no radio, no newspapers. It is all about control. Behave, and you walk on grass otherwise you spend yard time on concrete, for days, weeks, even years. From time to time Dennehy may fight the system, but the system will break her because it always wins. The regime can take even the most heinous psychopathic killer apart at the seams.

Dennehy is neither mad nor sad. She is undeniably evil, but how is she dealing with the prospect of spending the remainder of her life behind bars? After just fifteen months in custody already she is a shadow of her former self. If she lives to the ripe old age of seventy-five she still has forty-four more years of incarceration to go, and will have cost the taxpayer in excess of 1.5 million to keep under lock and key. With acres of time in front of her and freedom an impossible dream, mentally she is disintegrating and without doubt psychologically she will implode for a full life tariff imposed brings no hope at all.

I have met many offenders serving natural life, or who are on Death Row, some now executed throughout the United States, so I have witnessed first hand the devastating effects that a 'no hope existence' brings. It is like a slowly developing disease; almost cancerous from its onset when the reality of the punishment sinks in and usually, after the first six months, getting worse through a pitiless chain of hours, days, months and years until death supervenes.

I've got respect for myself. Always did have. Weird, right?
Serial killer Aileen Wuornos, at interview with the author shortly before her execution

Like Joanne Dennehy, US serial killer Aileen 'Lee' Carol Wuornos had always been slightly off the wall. Bisexual, incorrigibly fearless, a heavy drinker and drug-user, she was easily moved to violent outbursts and handed out vicious attacks that left truckers and leather-clad bikers three times her size cowering under the onslaught. As just one example out of dozens of recorded incidents, on 13 July 1976, Lee, aged twenty, went to Bernie's Club in Mancelona, where she flaunted her body and started to hustle at the pool table. Some time after midnight, barman and manager Danny Moore decided he had seen enough of her. She was drunk, rowdy, shouting obscenities, uttering threats to other patrons and being generally objectionable. Danny casually walked over to the pool table and announced that he was closing it down. As he was gathering up the balls, he heard someone shout, 'Duck!' He turned just in time to see Lee aim a ball at his head. It missed him by inches, but it had been hurled with such force that the missile became lodged in the wall.

When Deputy Jimmie Patrick of the Antrim County Sheriff's Department arrived, Lee was charged for assault and battery and hauled off to jail. She was also charged on fugitive warrants from the Troy Police Department, who had requested that she be picked up on charges for drinking alcohol in a car, unlawful use of a driver's licence and for not having a Michigan driver's licence.

Now executed, Aileen Wuornos was, and still is undoubtedly the US female version of the late Theodore 'Ted' Bundy, if only in the notoriety ratings. Unlike Joanne Dennehy, serial killer Lee was born on the wrong side of the track in a Leap Year on 29 February 1956, in Clinton Hospital, Detroit, Michigan. Her parents were dirt-poor; her nineteen-year-old handyman father, Leo Dale Pittman, was a kidnapper, rapist and child abuser who, fifteen years later, committed suicide by fashioning a noose from a bed sheet and hanging himself in prison. Lee's mother was sixteen-year-old Diane Wuornos, but little else is known about her. Lee was farmed out to live with her grandparents.

The grandfather, factory worker Laurie Wuornos, systematically beat Lee with a wide, brown leather belt that she kept clean with saddle soap and conditioner at his bidding. Stripped naked and forced to bend over the kitchen table, the petrified child was frequently thrashed with the doubled-over belt. Sometimes she lay face down, spread-eagled naked on her bed, to receive her whippings and all the while her grandfather screamed at her that she was worthless and should never have been born. 'You ain't even worthy of the air you breathe!' he would shout as the belt tore into her flesh time and again.

Around the age of eleven, Lee learnt that her 'parents' were indeed her grandparents. But by now the worm had turned and she had an unacceptable temper. Lee's volcanic explosions, which were unpredictable and seemingly unprovoked, inevitably drove a further wedge between herself and her grandparents, just as in the case of Joanne Dennehy and her real parents.

Although from totally different backgrounds – Joanne comes from a solid, middle-class family, while Lee was raised in a brutally incestuous environment we can immediately draw comparisons between Dennehy and Wuornos, for both were going completely off the rails aged around fourteen. Lee became pregnant and was sent to an unmarried mothers' home to await the birth of her child. The staff found her hostile, uncooperative and unable to get along with her peers. She gave birth to a baby boy, who was put up for adoption in January

1971. However, in July of the same year, Lee's grandmother, Britta, died. Lee dropped out of school, left home and took up hitchhiking and prostitution.

While there is no suggestion here that Joanne Dennehy was a prostitute in the true sense, we do know that while just ten years old Aileen swapped sex for cigarettes and alcohol supplied by older men. We also know that Joanne was already sleeping with men much older than her and she had been introduced to alcohol and skunk in return for sexual favours at fourteen.

Aileen's case is a tragic one, more so for after she left home she completely spiralled out of control and fell in with a lesbian lover called Tyria 'Ty' Jolene Moore, after meeting her in a Daytona gay bar in 1986. Lonely and angry, Lee was ready for something new and when it came to the push, this included murder.

There is a comprehensive chapter on Aileen Wuornos in *Talking with Serial Killers*, and her complete story in my book *Monster*, both published by John Blake – the latter accompanied the movie of the same name starring Charlize Theron.

When I met Wuornos in February 1998 she was sharing Death Row with several faces familiar to students of murder most foul in the US, including Judias 'Judy' Buenoano. Popularly known as 'The Black Widow', she had been on 'The Green Mile' since 1985. Buenoano was convicted of poisoning her husband, drowning her quadriplegic son by pushing him out of a canoe, and planting a bomb in her boyfriend's car. Gone were the painted manicured nails and the fashionable dark suits for the woman who used to swan around Pensacola, Florida, in a Corvette. Now, aged fifty-four, she looked like a frightened eighty-year-old. Her head shaved, she was strapped into 'Old Sparky' on 30 March 1998 at Florida State Prison, Starke.

But back to the end game for Joanne Dennehy. Interstate hooker Wuornos shot and killed six men out of the hundreds with whom she slept, but only those who had sexually insulted and abused her were murdered. Dennehy killed simply because she could, and it pleased her. Unlike Wuornos, she had a love of blood.

As Lee explained to me:

I've got respect for myself. Always did have. Weird, right? They were so-called pillars of the community. Pushing religion and Jesus Christ down my fuckin' throat. One was a probation officer. One was engaged to be married. One was simply a drunken asshole. One was an ex-cop. They all wanted to slap me around some, treat me like my grandfather did. So, I got really fuckin' wild and shot them away. Period.

Sadistic Joanne Dennehy killed because she wanted to see what it was like to kill and, as she told a psychiatrist prior to her trial, 'It got kind of more-ish.'

When I met Lee Wuornos, who was forty-six years old but looking a good two decades older, the condemned woman, wearing an orange T-shirt and blue trousers, was a mere 5ft 4in in height and according to her medical records weighed 133lb. The characteristic strawberry-blonde hair still framed her face but her eyes were bloodshot. From the moment she was born a helpless bundle of humanity, the seedy side of life always chewed on Lee. Her once attractive looks, the slim figure previously offset by skimpy, cut-off denim shorts and a tight gingham shirt were now replaced by a bloated body and a face that life had not treated lightly. She had a scar between her eyes and burn scars on her forehead. Her body was marked by a long cut along her left arm indicating self-harm and a cruel appendectomy wheal crossed her abdomen.

The cell in which Lee was confined measured 8 by 10ft. It was painted a dull-looking pink, the ceiling quite high, maybe 10ft, which made the room seem larger and more airy than it really was. Lee had a black and white television set, placed above a stainless steel toilet bowl, on a varnished brown shelf. Her furniture consisted of a grey metal footlocker that doubled as a desk, but no table and only a single chair, which she allowed me to sit on for a short while.

I also noted a dirty, lime-green cupboard at the foot of her metal bed. It contained her clothes and personal possessions. Everything had to be locked away at bed inspection time, between 9 and 11am. The only view of the outside world was a parking lot and a high fence, festooned with glittering razor wire. There were no bars at her cell window but a steel door with a small hatch separated her from the rest of the cellblock. It was costing the State of Florida $72.39 a day to keep Wuornos fit and well – well enough to be strapped to a gurney and injected with the 'Goodnight Juice' that would send her to perdition.

Unlike Joanne Dennehy, who frequently complains about the conditions at HMP Bronzefield, describing her conditions on Death Row, Lee Wuornos told me: 'The food ain't all that bad. We're served several meals a day. At 5am, 10.30 to 11am, an' 4pm to 4.30. They cook it in here. We get plates and spoons, nothing else. I can take a shower every other day, and we're counted at least once an hour. Everywhere we go, we wear cuffs except in the shower and exercise yard, where I can talk to my cellies. Lately, I like to be by myself. Apart from that, I am always locked up in my cell. I can't even be with another inmate in the common room.'

Wuornos spent her last, solitary days reading books on spiritual growth and writing lengthy letters. Her lifestyle, unlike that of Dennehy, was to be spartan and monotonous; and the days and years would roll indistinguishably past her locked cell door.

Death does not scare me, Chris. God will be beside me, taking me up for him when I leave this shell. I know that the end will be painful, I am sure of it. I have been forgiven and am certainly sound in Jesus's name.
Aileen Wuornos, to the author

Having refused a last meal, Lee drank a single cup of coffee before she was taken to the death chamber. By now she had completely lost her mind. Asked by the warden if she had any last words, she said: 'Yes, I would like to say I'm sailing with the rock, and I'll be back, like Independence Day, with Jesus. June 6, like the movie. Big mother ship, and I'll be back.'

Asian (be it Japanese, Chinese), French (No, you just can't get decent foie gras in prison). Seafood (hey, I'm from the

shore). I fail to cite Italian, as that is my 'ordinary food'.
Melanie McGuire, describing her favourite food to the author in correspondence

Another female lifer who mentally and physically disintegrated when she entered 'No Hope Land' is Melanie Lyn McGuire, aka 'The Ice Queen'. Like Joanne Dennehy, McGuire enjoyed a solid, stable upbringing. She was highly educated and became the mother of two adorable children but then in 2004 she spiked her husband's drink, then shot Bill in the head, chopped him into large pieces and stuffed the remains into suitcases before dumping them in the Chesapeake Bay which is surrounded by the states of Maryland and Virginia. The jury had her measure and the media dubbed her 'The Ice Queen' because she was so cold and emotionless throughout her trial.

As a 5ft 3in, 121lb brown-eyed, brown-haired nurse, she was known for her kind and generous nature. And as a wife and a mother she seemed to have a perfect life. In fact, she and Bill had just realised their perfect dream – buying their own $500,000 upscale house in Ashbury, Warren County, New Jersey. But behind that seemingly idyllic picture were secrets that would soon surface, revealing a murder, chilling in its calculation and its cruelty:

1 count of murder – life
1 count of disturbing/desecrating human remains – ten years
1 count of perjury: false statement – five years
1 count possession of a firearm for unlawful purposes – life
   She would never be a free woman again.

The depravity of this murder simply shocks the conscience of this court. One who callously destroys a family to accomplish their own selfish ends must face the most severe consequences that the law can provide.

Superior Court Judge Frederick De Vesa, sentencing Melanie McGuire, Thursday, 19 July 2007

Unlike Joanne Dennehy, Melanie McGuire had genuine blue-chip class, however beauty is only skin deep. McGuire was undeniably pretty when the camera's gaze caught her in the right moment. With her lustrous dark hair, pixie-like profile and almost vulnerable features, she was certainly not unattractive. Nevertheless, in her police photo she already appeared emotionally drained. When her sentence was confirmed she collapsed into the arms of her attorney, Joseph Tacopina, sobbing and saying: 'I didn't do it. I didn't do it... My babies, my babies,' meaning her two sons.

Melanie will be eligible for parole after serving 85 per cent of her sentence, or when she is one hundred years old. At the time of writing she is only forty-two. She has been in prison just seven years but with everything forever lost and virtually no chance of walking the streets again, already she resembles a withered crone.

I enjoyed taking care of those old people.

Cathy May Wood, to the author at interview

Married mother of two Catherine 'Cathy' May Wood and unmarried Gwendoline Gail Graham were bisexual serial killers who, in 1986, smothered to death patients in their own beds at the Alpine Manor Nursing Home, Grand Rapids, Michigan. Alpine Manor was the finest nursing home in the area. Clean, quiet, comfortable and humane, it serves as 'a model of efficient and considerate long-term care for the elderly' according to the home's promotional literature and yet five of these vulnerable individuals were killed by the very people they depended on most: their nurses.

The arrests only came about after weeks of investigation by a persistent detective, a probe that produced no physical proof but revolved around a high-stakes psychological shell game with an evasive Cathy Wood. Ultimately she spun a hypnotic tale of her relationship with Gwendoline Graham, one riddled with violence and bizarre sex. Wood claimed to have been manipulated by Graham and said they had killed the patients as part of an eternal love pact in an attempt to spell 'MURDER' with their victims' names. The authorities believed Wood's self-described role as a tragic accomplice dominated by a diabolical Graham. After a year in the courts both women were imprisoned for life – in Gwendoline's case with no possibility of parole.

As part of a twelve-part television documentary series called *The Serial Killers*, I met both women. First, I interviewed Cathy Wood. It was obvious from the outset that this woman was a psychopath – one moment a control freak shedding crocodile tears before bursting into laughter moments later. Playing the 'little girl lost, butter wouldn't melt in my mouth' role, at once avoiding eye contact with me and indeed the camera most of the time, she was grossly overweight but otherwise a picture of good health. Wood protested her innocence and blamed everything on Graham. Then, as she left the room, she was overheard telling another inmate: 'That fooled the dumb fuckers!'

I interviewed Gwendoline Graham at the Huron Valley Women's Facility. We met in a large, empty communal room. Unlike Wood, who will eventually be released from prison, Graham was stooped and frail, a pathetic physical and mental wreck. Emotionally unstable, she had resorted to self-harming and her body was covered with burns from lit matches. Every time I posed a question, she asked me to repeat it. She spoke very quietly and when I asked her to speak up, she whispered, 'Christopher, I cannot even stand the sound of my own voice.' It was as if she was sobbing her heart out inside for Gwen is living in 'No Hope Land'. At the time of writing she is only fifty-two.

It is my opinion that Joanne Dennehy, like Lee Wuornos, Judy Buenoano, Melanie Lyn McGuire 'The Ice Queen' and Gwen Graham, will go the same way, too. With all of these women – and of course this also applies to male killers – their self-esteem and grandiosity, their entire psychopathological infrastructure simply crumbles away like weathered cement once they enter prison. Physically and mentally they disintegrate until The Grim Reaper, in whatever form He takes, gives them their just deserts.

As with most murderers there are greater and lesser degrees of evil attached to these offenders. Just as it would be wrong to address a petty shoplifter with the same degree of condemnation as a violent mugger because both steal property, it might be said that the crimes of some murderers are considerably more evil than others. It is this indifference to the value of human life, and the high level of certainty that they would kill again with no qualms should they be set free, that separates the truly heinous monsters from those who have killed only once and whose crime was committed in the heat of the moment.

Joanne Dennehy is a sado-sexual serial killer and such a person may be defined as a serial murderer if he/she has killed three times or more, with a cooling-off period between the events, as distinct from a mass murderer who commits all of the killings at one place during a single event, or a spree killer who embarks on a continuum of slaughter lasting hours or even a day. Of course there are exceptions but the mass murderer and the spree killer are usually caught, or shot dead by police, soon after their crimes have been committed. It is if they have a death wish. However, it is the serial killer who is more terrifying simply because no one can predict when, or where, the offender will strike next. We know such a person is loose in society, a wolf in sheep's clothing, and he/she could be just about anyone – and in the case of Dr Harold Shipman a local GP.

The universal definitive definition of a serial killer is based upon research carried out by the FBI's Behavioral Science Unit, Quantico, Virginia, and it is unambiguous: 'The offender will have killed at least three times with a "cooling-off period" between all of the events'.

With regard to Joanne Dennehy – and much as she will rail against this – the facts are that she murdered Lukasz Slaboszewski with a cooling-off period of eleven days before she killed Kevin Lee and John Chapman – the latter two victims within the same day and with no cooling-off period in between these murders. That Dennehy attempted to kill another two men in Hereford – and I need to be coldly specific – matters little in her scheme of things because, by the Grace of God, this wannabe serial killer failed. Therefore, as much as we are all fascinated by serial murderers, Joanne ascribes to be a serial killer when she was an emerging one and she came within a single stab of achieving her aim. When I presented her with this she went berserk and it prompted an observation from DCI Martin Brunning, who drily remarked that I was 'pushing her buttons'.

Moreover, Dennehy professing to police that she and Stretch were the next 'Bonnie and Clyde' defies belief.

Amongst other things Bonnie Parker and Clyde Barrow were cop killers and somewhat successful bank robbers who evaded police dragnets and survived shootouts for over a year until they were shot dead in an ambush at Arcadia, Louisiana, on 23 May 1934. As a killing team, if we can call them such, Dennehy and Stretch struggled all of a few days to resist the clutches of the law. Bonnie and Clyde held up banks to stay on the run. Stretch stole a few electrical items, including a camera from a holiday home, to achieve the same purpose, only to be caught red-handed when he attempted to sell the swag.

24

MOTIVE

*Christopher, it is no secret that I do not regret my actions
but I have refused to give motive or make excuses [for the crimes].
I have maintained my guilt throughout.*
JOANNE DENNEHY, LETTER TO THE AUTHOR, 24 FEBRUARY 2014

Who really cares whether or not Joanne Dennehy refuses to give us her motive for killing? But she has generously spared us the earache of hearing any mitigation; none of this bad potty training, or, 'I fell off a swing and bumped my head, it damaged my frontal lobe', malarkey from Jo. Even more graciously, she has left God out of it altogether. No orders from Him to kill some chappies, thank Heavens.

Proof of motive is never necessary in the proof of the crime. Absence of any discoverable motive is of little consequence in deciding whether or not the prisoner committed the crime, for even the most brilliant jury is helpless in deciding the mental processes which actuate the criminal.
His Honour Mr Justice Christmas Humphreys, MA,

LLB (Cantab), author of *Seven Murderers*, published by William Heinemann Limited, London, 1931

Most serial murderers revel in keeping secret their motives and Joanne Dennehy is no exception, for her fields of interest are narrow, her ego over-inflated to the extent she may consider herself important. She takes it as her right that others will adapt to her ways, which several men did in becoming accomplices in murder. However, now that she is under lock and key, and when most of this controlling element is stripped away, she can only fall back on denying us her motive for murder – her last power trip. So, we should not concern ourselves that a fragment of her needing to control us mere mortals, whom she regards as simpletons, still exists within Dennehy's warped mind and her anger and incandescent rage will always radiate from her like hot coals in a kitchen stove. And, I am sure that she will commit murder again for she has nothing to lose. Someone in that prison will upset her, and she will watch and wait until the time is right, then kill once more.

As Professor of Applied Psychology David Canter, the UK's most celebrated offender profiler, wrote in the foreword of my book co-authored with Robin Odell, *Ladykiller* was devoted to the emerging serial killer John David Guise Cannan, responsible for multiple rapes, also most probably of the murder of Sandra Court (May, 1986, Christchurch, Dorset), and the sex killings of estate agent Suzy Lamplugh (July 1986, London), and Shirley Banks (October 1987, Bristol):

The authors [Berry-Dee and Odell] have used skills which any psychotherapist would be proud. They have demonstrated that no simple formula will ever capture the complexity of any one individual, even less surmise the range of variations that distinguish one killer from another. The inner recesses of the psyche of people who commit the ultimate crime will continue to remain enigmatic. Cannan, always at the centre of his own personal drama, driven by forces of which he is only dimly aware. Here we can see the mind of a murderer probably more starkly than he can ever see himself.

So, Joanne Dennehy will always remain enigmatic, at least to herself, for now she has the remainder of her time behind bars to reflect on her life and crimes. Yet she still cannot see the wood for the trees, for her 'secret' motives, like pearls of wisdom for committing homicide, she has already given to us without even opening her mouth or putting pen to paper. Over my years of interviewing serial killers I have come to realise it is not what these people say, or write, it is what they refuse to say, or have a convenient memory loss about, that is equally important in understanding their psychopathology.

During my time working with the serial killer Kenneth Bianchi, I constantly asked for the five missing pages from his interview sessions with police that he'd sent to me. Bianchi claimed to have lost them. He told me he couldn't understand where they had gone and apologised for this error. However, I arranged for his cell to be given a shakedown. Lo and behold, he had these five documents all along, and they proved crucial to my research into understanding his warped mind.

Dennehy says she murdered Lukasz Slaboszewski because he flirted with her, and nothing else. Then she told Julie Gibbons in a 2014 letter that had she killed all three men out of vengeance.

She says she murdered Kevin Lee because he was not paying her for redecorating some of his properties, or that she knew that he had told his wife about Lukasz's death, or more likely is the case that she thought that Kevin would call the police on learning that a second man had been killed in another of his bedsits. A highly unlikely scenario as Lee was up to his neck in trouble, anyway.

Dennehy says she murdered John Chapman because he had momentarily spotted her having a bath – the case more likely being she was to be paid by Kevin Lee for Chapman's eviction, which she would do 'by any means'. Then she changed her story and attributed the murder to Leslie Layton. 'Les killed John in a pathetic bid to impress me,' she wrote in a letter to Julie Gibbons.

She attempted to murder Robin Bereza and John Rogers solely because she wanted to steal their dogs, allegedly.

Perhaps the real motive was that she was simply a sadist who loved the sight of blood. When I put all of this to her eventually she replied in a letter dated 8 June 2014: 'My motive is mine alone just as is my punishment is mine and mine alone. You have a knack of winding me up. You are getting my back up.'

During her trial a consultant forensic psychiatrist gave evidence that Dennehy had been diagnosed as suffering from paraphilia sadomasochism, where sexual excitement is derived from inflicting pain, humiliation or bondage on another. She herself has admitted this, going further by confirming that she enjoys receiving the same. Like all perversions this condition tends to become increasingly extreme and violent over time as it is repeatedly re-enacted. Dennehy became hooked on causing pain and suffering. As psychoanalyst Coline Covington eloquently puts it: 'At the heart of violent crimes there is a powerful unconscious fantasy that is being played out in reality by the perpetrator. The fact that the fantasy is deeply rooted in the killer's psyche also means that its enactment is unlikely to be ultimately satisfying. The reality of the past remains unchanged in the unconscious. This is what often leads to crimes being repeated.'

Covington suggests that for Dennehy the scenario acted out 'was seduction followed by brutal stabbing to death. The victims were specifically men and, as the prosecution pointed out, humiliation was an important factor.' She adds, 'It is a scenario that suggests that Dennehy may have wanted to hurt – destroy – these men in the way she may have felt hurt herself in the past, i.e. at first made to feel wanted and desired and then cruelly attacked and humiliated.' As Joanne herself explained: 'They shouldn't have flirted with me, here was the danger.' But this in no way explains away the brutal, almost lethal, attacks on the two Hereford men she had never seen before and they most certainly had not flirted with her.

The question then arises, could or would Dennehy have murdered Gary Stretch, Leslie Layton or even Robert Moore? To help us find the answer, let's rewind to her early teens, where we will find our first clue.

Even as young as fourteen Joanne Dennehy was a

manipulator of people, which suited her own needs and selfish ends, and when anyone, including her own parents, were of no further use to her, or impeded her wants and wishes, she dumped them.

John Treanor was convenient to her because he enabled her to find lodgings wherever they ended up. Dennehy could shoplift with him and she had two daughters with him merely so that she could draw child benefit. This money she spent on alcohol and drugs. However, the children, like Treanor, soon became a burden to her and that is why she treated her former lover and their daughters in the repetitive and dismissive manner that she did. She exhibited all of the typical behavioural patterns of a sociopath/psychopath for they have no conscience at all. They know the difference between right and wrong, but they simply don't care.

Clearly, towards the end of the relationship with Treanor Dennehy was becoming increasingly mentally unbalanced, progressively more violent and now murder had entered her mind. She met up with Stretch, who was also a tool she could use to good effect. Apart from his intimidating size, she knew that he was a simpleton, he'd become besotted with her and when she whistled, he would come running like an obedient dog. However, to give him some credit, it is fair to say he can just about read comics, but he does have a disability when it comes to connecting his brain to a pen, confirmed by the letters he wrote to Gibbons and Dennehy while on remand. When checking out his handwriting I noted several of these letters were almost certainly written on Stretch's behalf by another inmate.

MOTIVE

Without doubt, Joanne Dennehy had been itching to kill someone for years, ever since she plunged a dagger into the carpet shortly before John Treanor hightailed it to Glossop, leaving no forwarding address.

Sadly, her first victim, Lukasz Slaboszewski, was her induction to homicide. Having set a perfectly laid trap, she was cunning as a fox. This was a trial run for she was about to dip her toe into bloody waters. I am convinced in my own mind that she would not have taken on such a powerfully built man without hedging her bets. Whether or not Stretch actually participated, according to his own words he was very close by - perhaps in case things got out of hand. He would do anything for Dennehy, anything at all. As Julie Gibbons has suggested in a newspaper article: 'She must have had him under her spell.'

Dennehy could not have disposed of Lukasz without Stretch's help in getting the corpse into the wheelie bin, insuring and driving the Vauxhall Astra, and finding a remote location to dump the body. This, I believe, was a sacrificial murder, for she later told a psychiatrist that she had killed Slaboszewski to see if she could actually murder a man and she told him that she liked doing it. Therefore, she treated Lukasz as an item to be used, abused and disposed of. For Dennehy, Gary Stretch was an extremely valuable, no-questions-asked asset indeed, as proven by his helping her dispose of the body.

With regard to Kevin Lee, it would reasonable to suggest that he and Dennehy used each other, with Joanne coming out on top. She soon realised that like her, he had the morals of an alley cat. It is also true to say that while she appeared to enjoy sex with both sexes, this wasn't actually the case. It was just something she did when it suited her and for no other reason. She simply went through the motions, using her sex and flirty, teasing allure to manipulate men.

Kevin Lee fell hook, line and sinker for her charms. So strong was the attraction that he would, like Stretch, do anything for Dennehy, even if that entailed risking his marriage, giving Joanne money to buy a car to dispose of a dead body, even putting on one of her dresses. He knew that she enjoyed inflicting pain and receiving it, so presumably he admired this sadistic streak in her and was even turned on by it. And, when she whistled with promises of more kinky sex, just like Slaboszewski, he came running. Kevin Lee gave her grace-and-favour lodgings in return for her tenant enforcement and eviction talents, acts in which Stretch participated by doing exactly as he was told. However, unbeknown to Lee he was rapidly reaching his own sell-by-date; he simply did not have a clue.

If one can give any credit to Dennehy, she could certainly multi-task by scheming and luring other men into her homicidal orbit with promises of sex. She had shown Lee the dreadful contents of the wheelie bin at 11 Rolleston Garth. Then, having met Robert Moore earlier via Leslie Layton, and having 'come on strong' to both these hapless individuals, she opened the bin to Moore's daughter, a fourteen-year-old whose name is subject to a s.39 Children and Young Persons Act 1933 order which protects her identity until she is eighteen. Dennehy knew that Moore would not grass her up to the police because he was in love with her. His genitalia now ruling his brain, Moore was now truly out of his depth and, like Kevin Lee, he didn't have a clue either – nor, for that matter, did Layton.

MOTIVE

We now turn to the luckless John Chapman, who incidentally not only shared 31 Bifield with Layton, they were drinking buddies as well. Both of these men were in the same boat. Kevin Lee had served eviction notices on them but they refused to budge and so on his instructions Joanne Dennehy moved in. Soon realising that Layton could become another tool, she started flirting with him too. Within a few days he was crazy about her, to the extent that he would turn a blind eye to anything and everything that was going on, while hovering on the sidelines was the towering Stretch to ensure that he did just that.

Having watched and studied Chapman's behaviour for several days, Dennehy knew that he always went to bed very drunk. Indeed, during the afternoon before the morning of his murder, Dennehy had visited the Virams store, where she had generously bought John a lot more alcohol to help send him on his way. Once asleep, he was helpless. However, she was seething with anger. Kevin Lee allegedly still owed her money for cleaning up 11 Rolleston Garth.

If Lee wanted Chapman evicted then she would do just that. So, during the early hours of Good Friday, 29 March 2013, Joanne stabbed John Chapman to death, enjoying every second of the frenzied attack. Following this she bumped into Layton as she came out of the bathroom. In a pathetic effort to impress her, and Gary Stretch, Layton took a photo of the dead man's blood-spattered body. Soon he would be helping them dump the corpse in a ditch.

Now it was Kevin Lee's turn to get his comeuppance. For a while he had proved to be an invaluable asset to Dennehy but now he had become a liability – and very dangerous one at that. Already he knew too much for he had confessed his affair to Cristina; he had seen the body of Lukasz in the wheelie bin, allegedly told his wife about it, and had given money to Dennehy to purchase car to be used to dump the corpse in a ditch. Added to this was the fact that he apparently owed Dennehy money and perhaps thought that he could avoid paying by buying her a couple of CDs and pandering to her deviant sexual needs. To Dennehy's Jekyll and Hyde nature this would have been a slap across the face. She would lure him round to Rolleston Garth, kill him and then dump his body in manner, which to her mind, he deserved, leaving it for all the world to see.

But was Stretch present when Kevin Lee was murdered? Was it because, to ensure the killing went off without too much fuss, no risks could be taken, even if it was only Dennehy who did the stabbing in much the same way as the couple participated in the Lukasz Slaboszewski murder? According to Dennehy's reasoning it worked then, so why should it not work again?

We know that when Stretch, Dennehy and Layton met up shortly after Chapman's murder, Layton was effectively told to make himself scarce so he went shopping with Robert Moore, while Joanne and Gary did a little conspiring alone. By then, Stretch already knew that Dennehy wanted to kill Kevin Lee because he owed her money and because allegedly he was sexually harassing her. He even told Gary Stretch who knew exactly where to dump the bodies. They would have two corpses at two different locations, along with Kevin's car to dispose of, so they would need another driver and they couldn't afford to hang about.

When Layton arrived back at 38 Bifield, he soon learned that he was about to be pressed into grim service for Stretch and Dennehy would have told him that he was now an accomplice in murder. With the pair not giving him any option, he had to go along with whatever he was told. Plans had been made and with Chapman's corpse starting to decompose, there could be no turning back. If Leslie desisted they would kill him too, or certainly pin John Chapman's murder on him, as Dennehy later tried to do by claiming at one time that Layton had murdered Chapman in an attempt to impress her. If anything, the only reason why Layton had not as yet become another victim was because he was still of use. One didn't say 'no' to people like Dennehy and Stretch, simple as that. For Leslie Layton there was no way out and he didn't possess the morality, or the guts, even less the intelligence to contact the police.

Therefore, perhaps the scenario surrounding Kevin Lee's demise went something like this. Without doubt, Dennehy lured him to 11 Rolleston Garth with the promise of sex but all the while with premeditated murder in mind. Was Stretch on hand just in case something went wrong? Layton was waiting nearby, ready to assist where he could. He brought along the tarpaulin previously supplied by his mate, Moore.

With Kevin Lee now dressed to kill in a black sequined dress and also stone dead, we know through witness statements that the group – with Layton driving Kevin's Mondeo, the body in the back, and Dennehy and Stretch leading in the Vauxhall – left Rolleston Garth and drove out to the ditch at Newborough, where his body was found the following morning. We also know that it was Layton who was driving the Mondeo before it was set on fire, after which the group returned to 38 Bifield in the Vauxhall, collected John Chapman's body and then dumped that off, too.

Effectively, Leslie Layton was now surplus to requirements. With Dennehy's bloodlust temporarily sated, Gary Stretch – just as he was soon to do to Georgina Page at her King's Lynn flat – threatened Layton with his life should he give any information to the police, if and when they came calling. Layton knew that Joanne had killed three men, and he had seen what she had done to his former pal, John Chapman. He had watched from the sidelines as Lee and Chapman's bodies had been thrown into ditches. By now he would have surely reckoned that he was lucky not to be lying there with them.

Layton was caught between a rock and a hard place. No wonder he was 'wracked with guilt', as Mr Justice Spencer remarked, over that Easter holiday weekend, but not so upset that he frequently updated Dennehy after the police twice interviewed him. As any homicide cop will confirm, Layton almost certainly did this to keep her sweet and to reassure the pair that he had no intention of grassing them up. Weak-willed Layton would save his own skin at any cost.

The final person Dennehy used in her killing spree was Robert Moore, who, like Lee, Layton and Stretch, was besotted with her. As previously mentioned Moore's daughter had seen Slaboszewski's body in the wheelie bin and she had told her dad, so when Layton asked him if he could have the use of a tarpaulin, like a fool he agreed to loan it. He, too, was aware that another two murders had been committed because Layton and Dennehy had already texted him. He also allowed

Dennehy and Stretch to stay the night at his place after Lee was murdered, and the following evening he fed the couple as yet another sweetener before they went on the run.

So, what did Moore get out of this? Not much, not even a peck on the cheek from Joanne, who had almost certainly promised him more in one of her raunchy text messages, but he did earn himself four years behind bars. Well done, Robert, but this still leaves us with Gary Stretch. Could Joanne have killed him too? In a heartbeat, of course, yes!

At Stretch's trial, his counsel, Mr Karim Khalil QC, likened his client to being Dennehy's 'Nodding Dog', and how appropriate is that? From the moment she and 'Gaz' met, she knew that he would be invaluable to her. Indeed she soon came to the realisation that although he was none too bright, like a loyal pet he would come running, should she whistle. If she asked him to lie down, he did. If she asked him to snarl and bark, he would, and like any mean hound she needed a kennel in which to keep him. Kevin Lee provided such a kennel for Stretch at number 2 Riseholme, which inside, and out, was in fact so disgusting that any right-minded person wouldn't dream of keeping a dog there.

Unfortunately space in this book for the inclusion of many police photographs is limited. Therefore, as much as I would have wanted, I cannot show you even the exterior of the property but let me just paint a word picture for you of the front aspect, if I may.

Number 2 Riseholme is relatively new in construction. It is not, as one might expect, a comfy thatched cottage with hanging baskets full of well-tended pretty flowers hanging from the porch, or enjoying a luxuriant front lawn with a pixie sitting here and there. You will not see this address featured in *Country Life*. The porch roof of this pink/red brick and white, double-glazed windowed dwelling has several slates missing, seemingly most appropriate because Mr Stretch, as is now obvious, has many slates missing from his own roof, too. There is a grey slab path leading to the front gate and either side of what purports to be garden, grass fights gallantly in an ever-losing battle to see sunlight.

Now, close your eyes and imagine this: collect several large builders' skips of rubbish and delicately scatter the contents into the front garden of 2 Riseholme. Add to this a few bulging black plastic sacks of household refuse that the dustmen would never in a million years handle owing to health and safety regulations, throw in some timber, sawdust, a rolled-up urine- and excrement-stained carpet and overlay with well-thumbed porn material. Yes, that's about it, I believe. Job done! And this is before you even step through the front door. The stench is terrible. Oh, and the taxpayer is handing out good money to people like Gary Stretch to treat what could be a perfectly decent place to live in like this.

Having done away with Slaboszewski, Chapman and Lee, and after threatening to kill Layton, Moore and Georgina Page if they spilled the beans, Dennehy used Stretch in an attempt to escape justice by fleeing west to Herefordshire. To his credit, he did have a valid driving licence and insurance – she didn't, so Joanne could not have gone far from Peterborough without Gaz's help, despite the fact that steering the Vauxhall car must have proved difficult for him – with his knees up to his chin!

MOTIVE

Would they have gone their separate ways, had they not been arrested in Hereford? Maybe, maybe not, however I am inclined to believe that if at any time Stretch had posed a threat to Dennehy, or insulted or abused her, she would have stabbed him to death without a second thought. She would have bided her time and while he slept, punched knife stabs into his throat and heart until he was dead. As her previous record has adequately proven, her 3-inch lock knife, combined with demonic strength, was an 'equaliser', one no man caught off-guard could withstand.

25

GARY STRETCH - 'A LOSER FROM DAY ONE'

According to psychoanalyst Coline Covington writing in *The Week UK*, as few as one in six serial killers are women. Whether she is referring to only British killers or she has empirical evidence to show this is a multi-national statistic, I am unsure. Nevertheless, she says, 'The number of known female serial killers has increased significantly since the 1950s.' Covington adds, 'What has also changed, in line with the changes in women's social roles, is the profile for women serial killers. These women are now wielding guns and knives whereas in the past they tended to use poison and other covert means of killing. The method of killing has become markedly more phallic and less associated with women's roles as nurturers.'

'Women killers are also less likely now to have had a prior relationship with their victims,' says Covington, 'and their motives have changed. "The Black Widow" female serial killer of Victorian times, who murdered one husband after another for their money, no longer predominates. Women serial killers, like many of their male counterparts, murder for power and attention, and often as a way of creating an illusion of control as a reaction to a history of serious abuse. Murder may also promise a final triumph over abusive relationships from the past.'

Females acting alone are extremely rare. Indeed, several times during my research for this book, I was asked whether or not Joanne Dennehy would have turned to committing serial homicide had she not had someone like Gary Stretch to perhaps support her and help her dispose of the bodies?

To help answer this question we might seek out case histories in an attempt to find a female who, solely and without any assistance, killed more than three times with a cooling-off period between events. Somewhat remarkably, to find the first female who fits the criteria here in the UK we must turn back the calendar 143 years at the time of writing to 1871. Her name was Mary Ann Cotton and she was suspected of killing over 20 victims in the small north-of-England village of West Auckland.

Mary Ann Cotton (ne Robson) was born on 31 October 1832 to a County Durham mining family. She was a pretty girl with plenty of admirers. In 1852, at the age of twenty, she married her first husband, a twenty-six-year-old miner called William Mowbray. Three children died mysteriously during the couple's first four years of marriage. In 1860, and then in 1864, a son and daughter perished of what was diagnosed as scarlet fever.

In January 1865 Mowbray injured his foot. The injury turned, inexplicably, into diarrhoea, which, even more inexplicably, proved fatal. With the death of her husband, Mary Ann was left with a life insurance legacy of 35 and three offspring. By the middle of the year one of those children succumbed to gastric fever. And then the others would start to go the same way.

Now in Sunderland, Mary Ann was working at an isolation hospital for contagious diseases. On 28 August 1865 she married one of her former patients, an engineer called George Ward. By December of that year, Ward had become ill with a number of puzzling symptoms that doctors put down to a liver complaint. On 21 October 1866, he died of what was tersely recorded as 'fever'.

His widow did not stay lonely for long. The next month Mary Ann found a position as housekeeper to a Sunderland shipwright by the name of Robinson. Death came quickly to the house. On 23 December 1866, Robinson's ten-month-old son was buried. In the spring of 1866, he was joined by his six-year-old brother and eight-year-old sister – and Mary Ann's own eldest daughter too.

In each case the cause of death was given as gastric fever. Nor was the 'fever' limited to the Robinson household. Mary Ann went to stay with her mother in March 1867 and a mere nine days later the old woman was in her grave.

Mary Ann became pregnant by Robinson and on 11 August 1867, the couple married. Their daughter was born on 29 November, only to die four months later of gastric fever.

Robinson then discovered that Mary Ann had been stealing his mortgage money and the pair had a showdown. Mary Ann fled, taking their newborn child with her. She left the baby with a friend, who returned it to Robinson on New Year's Day, 1870.

Meanwhile, Mary Ann wasted no time. In January 1871, a friend – Margaret Cotton – introduced her to her brother, Frederick. He and Mary Ann became lovers, with the inevitable consequences: Cotton's daughter died on 28 January 1871 and the diagnosis was typhus. Frederick's sister Margaret then died on 25 March 1871 after suffering severe stomach pains.

In the September Frederick and Mary Ann were married. But Mary Ann was making a bigamous marriage, and so she entered the name of Mowbray on the register. A few weeks later she took out a life insurance policy on Frederick's two sons. The following January, she and Frederick had a son of their own. However, Mary Ann did not endear herself to her neighbours. She was cagey about her former life and folk noted that she had given birth only seven months after the wedding. And when, after an argument, a neighbour's pigs died of a mysterious illness, it was assumed that, in a fit of revenge, Mary Ann had poisoned the creatures.

That spring, the Cottons moved to the Durham village of West Auckland. They now numbered five: Frederick, Mary Ann, their baby boy, and Frederick's two boys. Before the year was out, 'gastric fever' claimed Frederick and two of the children. However, Mary Ann and her stepson, Charles, survived.

Mary Ann then allowed a lover, Joseph Nattrass, to move in. Gastric fever killed him. A fellow called Quick-Manning took his place, and Mary Ann fell pregnant by him. This baby died in March 1872, just a few months old, but Mary Ann was soon pregnant again. But when Charles, who had been cruelly treated by his stepmother, died in July 1872, a doctor tested the little corpse for arsenic. Mary Ann was duly arrested and found guilty of poisoning the boy. Traces of arsenic were also found in the exhumed bodies of all those who had died of 'gastric fever' while in her deadly care.

She pleaded not guilty at her trial at Durham Assizes in March 1873. The defence line was that the dead boy had been accidentally poisoned by arsenic contained in green floral wallpaper used in the home. But Mary's purchase of soft and arsenic (ostensibly for cleaning bedsteads and destroying bedbugs) proved ominous. She was sentenced to death.

The then Home Secretary, The Right Hon Henry. A. Bruce, 1st Baron of Aberdare, refused to commute the sentence, despite a mounting wave of sympathy and demands for a reprieve, and, the hangman, William Calcraft, botched the 24 March 1973 hanging because the drop was too short. In fact it was three minutes before Mary Ann's body ceased convulsing at the rope's end. It was suggested by Sir Charles Russell, who led the prosecution, that her motive was either to gain insurance money or to pave the way for a new marriage.

Hot on the heels of Mary Ann Cotton's execution was fifty-seven-year-old Amelia Elizabeth Dyer, a serial murderess known as the Reading Baby Farmer.

Onetime member of the Salvation Army, Mrs Dyer, who was separated from her husband, took in children at her Bristol home. In 1895 she moved to Reading, advertising that she would board and adopt children. In March 1895, a bargeman on the River Thames fished out of the water a child's corpse with a tape around its neck, wrapped in a parcel bearing a Reading address. But Amelia, who used several aliases, had already moved to another house in Reading. Meanwhile, two more infants were found dead in the river.

Dyer was arrested in April 1896, but tried to commit suicide by hanging herself. By the end of that month the bodies of seven children had been found; all had been strangled with a tape and wrapped in parcels. Charged together with her son-in-law, Mrs Dyer made a brief statement absolving her alleged accomplice and accepting full blame.

At her trial in May 1896, the defence sought to prove that she was insane. It was not known how many babies she had killed, but as she had been farming children for fifteen years it was likely that the total was more than the seven known victims. She herself said, 'You'll know all mine by the tape around their necks.' Dyer's motive was one of greed – she accumulated fictitious boarding fees by quickly disposing of the infants placed in her care.

She was executed on 10 June 1896 at Newgate, where her ghost was said to have haunted the chief warder.

A far more recent case is that of Beverley Gail Allitt. Born Sunday, 4 October 1968, she was convicted of murdering four children, attempting to kill another three and causing grievous bodily harm to six more. Allitt certainly qualifies for the 'Serial Killer' title because her crimes were committed over a period of 59 days with short cooling-off periods in between.

LOVE OF BLOOD

Between 21 February and 22 April 1991, while working as a State Enrolled Nurse in the children's ward at Grantham and Kesteven Hospital, she administered large doses of insulin to at least two of her victims and an embolus (a large air bubble) was found in the body of another girl.

It was only after fifteen-month-old Claire Peck, who had been admitted to the ward following an asthma attack on 22 April 1991 that Allitt's crimes were discovered. After being placed on a ventilator, she was left alone in her care for a short while, during which time the child went into cardiac arrest. She was resuscitated but died after a second episode of cardiac arrest, again following a period when she was left alone with Nurse Allitt.

Staff became suspicious about the number of cardiac arrests on the children's ward and the police were called in. After a thorough search through her employment records they found that Allitt was the only nurse on duty when all of the attacks on the children occurred and she also had access to the drugs.

Allitt was charged with 4 counts of murder, 11 counts of attempted murder and 11 counts of causing grievous bodily harm. She entered pleas of not guilty to all of them. On Friday, 28 May 1993, she was sentenced to life imprisonment, which she is currently serving at Rampton Secure Hospital, Nottinghamshire.

Allitt's trial judge recommended she serve a minimum term of 30 years, meaning she would not be released until at least 2022. By then she would be fifty-four, and then only if she was considered not to be a risk to the public. Up until Joanne Dennehy was sentenced, this represented one of the longest sentences given to a woman in Britain.

Allitt's motives have never fully been explained. According to one theory, she exhibited signs of factitious disorder, also known as Munchausen's syndrome or Munchhausen's syndrome by proxy, which may explain her actions. This controversial disorder is described as involving a pattern of abuse in which a perpetrator ascribes to, or physically falsifies illness in someone under his or her care to attract attention. The name 'Munchhausen' originates from the Baron of the same name, the subject of a series of exaggerated adventure tales written in English by R. E. Raspe (1737–94).

Therefore, going back as far as 143 years I can only find three British female serial murderers who acted alone. One used arsenic – in France dubbed *poudre de succession*, or 'inheritance powder' – while another strangled babies with a ligature. In the more recent case concerning Beverley Allitt, insulin was used to commit murder. All of the other British women who have been involved in serial murder had a male accomplice and it was usually the man who did the actual killing – we can count Fred with Rosemary West, and Ian Brady with Myra Hindley, amongst them.

This, of course, brings Gary Stretch into the picture, for just like the Wests, Hindley and Brady, he and knife-wielding Dennehy formed a team'. It is not believed by anyone that Rose West and Myra Hindley would have become serial murderers had they not had male accomplices, therefore I suggest the same applies to Joanne Dennehy. However, I do believe that she was primed to kill a man at some time in her life, but acting alone she would never have crossed the threshold into serial homicide. She would have been caught soon afterwards because she was not sophisticated enough to evade justice.

The previous chapter explains how Stretch may have assisted Dennehy and, if this was the case I would say without hesitation that Gary Stretch was a borderline serial killer.

With regard to 'accomplices' the law is specific with no elbow room for argument. The person who directly and immediately causes the *Actus Reus* (the guilty act) of a crime is not necessarily the only one who is criminally liable for it. By the Accessories and Abettors Act 1861, s. 8 as amended by the Criminal Law Act 1977:

Whosoever shall aid, abet, counsel or procure the commission of any indictable offence whether the same be an offence at common law or by virtue of any act passed or to be passed, shall be liable to be tried, indicted and punished as a principal offender.

The effect of s. 1 of the Criminal Law Act 1967 is that this provision is now applicable to *all* offences whether former felonies or misdemeanors. Those who aid, abet, counsel or procure the commission of an offence are conveniently designated 'secondary parties'. The common law of felonies designated the actual perpetrator 'the first degree' and designated secondary parties into principals in the second degree – those individuals who participated at the time when the felony was actually perpetrated – and accessories before the fact – those who participated at an earlier time. As we have seen by his own belated admission to Julie Gibbons and confirmed by Dennehy, Gary Stretch was most certainly a 'secondary party' to the murder of Lukasz Slaboszewski and very likely, Kevin Lee.

Refreshingly, the abolition of felonies has made no change of substance. No one who was not previously so became liable to conviction as a result of this reform. The modes of participation in crime, which the law recognises, are unchanged.

Where there are several participants in a crime the principal in the first degree is the one whose act is the most immediate cause of *Actus Reus*. In Dennehy's case she wielded the knife. With regard to secondary participation, if this man aided and abetted her in the actual *Actus Reus* of the killing of Lukasz Slaboszewski and Kevin Lee, then without his being present when these men were killed, they may well have still been alive today.

Acting on legal advice I am bound to say that I must conclude with the fact that there was no evidence to charge Stretch and the 'two exculpatory letters while on remand are not evidence upon which there would be a realistic prospect of conviction.'

It has been established that Gary Stretch is, like Dennehy, a pathological liar. A man who when finally arrested would lie and cheat, in fact do anything to save his own skin. We remember the observation made by DS Mark Jinks, who interviewed Stretch: That he was 'frugal with the truth'; that although he was the driver of the Vauxhall in Hereford, Stretch claimed that he had no idea that Dennehy intended to stab Robin Bereza. And he went on to claim that he had no inkling that she had stabbed either man, only becoming aware that she had attacked John Rogers when she returned to the car. But this cock-and-bull story was a non-starter after Mark Lloyd, Robin Bereza and John Rogers gave their evidence at trial.

Mr Justice Spencer also referred to this issue in the matter of Leslie Layton, who stood by and watched the disposal of two bodies without protest and failed to inform the police. The same applies to Stretch: he was close by when Dennehy stabbed to death Lukasz Slaboszewski. He says he was. It is highly probably that he was in attendance when Kevin Lee was killed. Voluntary presence at such events, then, is some evidence on which a jury – had they been told – might have found that the accused Stretch was there with the intention of encouraging the murders. He was certainly encouraging, aiding and abetting Dennehy in the attempted murders of Robin Bereza and John Rogers, so his *modus operandi* is now well established.

Another, perhaps easier way of determining Stretch's possible culpability is the legal principle of 'Joint Enterprise'. Created more than 300 years ago it was originally created to help authorities discourage illegal dueling by prosecuting the duellers and any witnesses. Today it is often used to help convict gang members involved in serious crime. Several people can be charged with the same offence although their involvement in the crime may be different.

Under the joint enterprise law a person can be found guilty if they knew that a crime might occur or if they encouraged the person who actually committed the offence, even if they were not present at the scene of the crime. It falls to prove that the defendants agreed to act together. The agreement can be made without being spoken and it does not need to be planned.

According to research by the Bureau of Investigative

Journalism, between 2005 and 2013, 1,853 people were prosecuted using joint enterprise for murders that involved four or more defendants. However, the law is controversial because a person can be held criminally for another's actions. Lord Phillips, former Lord Chief Justice, said that joint enterprise needed reform as it was 'capable of producing injustice,' adding, 'you have to rely on juries and on the judge to say who was involved and how. There is a huge discretion on how it is used by prosecutors.'

On the advice from her legal team and for still unidentified 'legal reasons', Joanne Dennehy refused to enter a plea until her trial. Then out of the blue she claimed full and total responsibility for the three murders. As her sister, Maria, later said, 'I think Joanne did that to control the situation. She likes people to know she's the boss,' which is a typical sociopathic trait.

Dennehy was also manipulating Gary Stretch while he was on remand by initially sending him fawning letters. She wanted the world to know that she was a heinous serial killer and she would not give him any of the credit for being an accomplice. It is possible that this carefully constructed façade fell apart when Julie Gibbons wrote to her, enclosing Stretch's correspondence. Joanne then spilled the beans to Julie, saying that Gary was actually present when Lukasz Slaboszewski was killed. Stretch then wrote to Gibbons and confirmed it.

In a Friday, 21 March 2014 *Daily Mirror* article written by Louie Smith, Gibbons claims 'I used to feel responsible for Gary but not any more – I am going to cut off all contact.' However, I rather get the impression that she is still fearful of him today. Remember that he was served with an indefinite restraining order in 2004 for threatening to murder her, should she cooperate with the police. We know that he threatened Georgina Page with death if she grassed him up. Most likely he did the same with Leslie Layton and Robert Moore and almost certainly he threatened Mark Lloyd with a pistol in Kington, Herefordshire.

When Julie Gibbons sugarcoats Stretch, saying: 'I don't think he could see that she [Dennehy] was bad. The Gary I know would have run a 1,000 miles in the opposite direction because he hates trouble,' she is keeping him sweet. Either that or she is utterly misguided, because Gaz wasn't running 1,000 miles in any direction when he tipped Lukasz Slaboszewski's bloodied corpse into the wheelie bin. Indeed, after Dennehy had attacked Robin Bereza he drove her in the direction to a place where he knew she would find another suitable dog-walking victim.

26

INSIDE JOANNE DENNEHY'S HEAD

If you treat me as an animal, I'll treat you as an animal. I do
what I want to do, cos I might not be in the right mood that day.
Treat me like a dog, I'll bite you like a dog. Do you understand?
I demand respect. Give me that respect and I can be okay.
Treat me like an ass and I can be an ass. Understand?
JOANNE DENNEHY, TO A PRISON OFFICER IN 2014

While working in the United States during the nineties I enjoyed the company of US Marshals Parnell and Mike McNamara, out of Waco, Texas. One of our many conversations turned to the subject of 'surveillance', with Parnell piping up over a slab of steak, ranch fries and gravy: 'The trouble with surveillance is that most times you don't see anything.' This also seems to me to apply to the study of the psychopathic mind and the likes of Joanne Dennehy, for one can observe such an individual for decades and never come close to what makes them tick. Moreover, there is a very good reason for concluding this: the killers, themselves, have not really got a clue, either!

If we are to even begin to try and understand why Dennehy became a serial killer we should return to her early years. Indeed let's take a few tentative baby steps ourselves towards the edge of the abyss and take a cautious peek in while asking, first of all, was she psychologically damaged some time during her formative years through until she went off the rails, aged fourteen?

'Where do we come from? Who are we? Where are we going?' These three great questions from Gauguin's triptych we can apply to the life and crimes of Joanne Dennehy while sifting through the chronology of her early life in an attempt to find the seed of her evil.

If a child's bonding with his/her parents is satisfactory, and he/she is brought up in a healthy environment, then the child goes through a healthy development process. That much is obvious but there is far more to it, for if the opposite occurs then a child may be psychologically damaged beyond repair. On the face of it, Joanne had a stable home life, with hard-working and loving parents who wanted only the best for her and her sister Maria, who recently implied in a *Daily Mail* article dated Saturday, 15 February 2014 article, that her father could sometimes be a bit strict – but what caring parent is not?

As a tree grows, the young tree that it once was never disappears; rather, layer upon layer comes to be superimposed on its core. Deep inside, the baby tree that it once was is still alive. The way in which the young tree first took shape, the forces that acted on it, the twists, turns, bends and breaks caused by wind, rain, humans or disease all determine the shape the tree assumes as it matures and ages. No matter how well it is cared for, it will never completely outgrow any neglect when it was just a sapling. If we were to cut it down and examine its innermost core, we would discover that the young tree that it once was continues to exist at its central core. Still alive, it forever retains its original form. What it was becomes the foundation for what it will be. Just as the living tree retains its early core, within the core of each of us is the child we once were. That child constitutes the foundation of what we have become, who we are and what we will be, serial killer or not.

In the late 1970s under the umbrella of the FBI, interviews with convicted killers became the core of the Criminal Personality Research Project, partially funded by the US Justice Department and involving Dr Ann Wolbert Burgess of Boston University and other academics, with the then FBI Supervisory Special Agent Robert K. Ressler as principal investigator. Using a research protocol of some 57 pages, the team interviewed 36 individual incarcerated murderers, concentrating on their histories, motives and fantasies; also their specific actions. Eventually, the team was able to discern important patterns in their lives and to learn something about their developing motivation.

In his book *Whoever Fights Monsters*, author Robert Ressler (who was the consultant in the 1991 movie, *The Silence of the Lambs*) writes: 'In the opinion of a number of experts, our study was the largest, most rigorous, and most complete investigation of multiple murderers ever undertaken, one that included the greatest percentage of the living, incarcerated multiple murderers.'

In a 1968 article, forensic psychiatrists Doctors Katie Bush and James L. Cavanaugh Jr. of Chicago's Isaac Ray Center called the research 'exemplary' because of its breadth and said that: 'its conclusions warrant evaluation in great detail.'

One of the most valuable conclusions resulting from this study was that there is no such thing as the person who suddenly changes from being perfectly normal and erupts into totally evil, disruptive, murderous behaviour.

Most of the male serial killers I have interviewed over some 20 years graduated from committing petty crime in their juvenile years to fantasising about bondage in their early twenties, then became Peeping Toms, moving on to sexual assault through to rape and serial rape before crossing the threshold into sexually motivated homicide and then on to committing serial murder. Therefore, the behaviours that are precursors to murder have been present and developing in that person's life for a long, long time – often since childhood.

For example, I corresponded with the sexual sadistic serial killer Kenneth Bianchi, aka 'The Hillside Strangler', for several years before I interviewed him at the Washington State Penitentiary, Walla Walla. I had been through his history with a toothcomb; I had exclusive access to his adoptive mother, Frances Piccione, his former girlfriends, all of his medical history, psychiatric evaluations, schooling and employment records. The City of Rochester Police, LAPD Homicide, the FBI and the Bellingham PD all gave me copies of every document and scene-of-crime photograph they had. And I personally visited every location and spoke to scores of people with first-hand knowledge of Bianchi.

This sexual deviant had been petty thieving before he was seven years old and was already fantasising about sex with ten- and eleven-year-old girls – 'women', as he later called them. Below is how this sick monster described his first encounter. You may find it shocking because the girl in question was just nine years old and there were many more children he abused afterwards, going on to kill two of them:

While my hormones increased, it was not until my sophomore year when I had my first experience with a partner. It was when I was about eleven years old when I had my first solo experience. My first love was blonde, thin build, and easy to speak with. She had a cute way of flirting, head tipped a bit. A beautiful smile across her face. She smelled divine, as women do.

Our first sexual encounter was at her home, with her parents and sister away. It was brief and I was so nervous my hands shook. I tried my best to be patient and gentle as I assumed a man would be. I'm certain I was hurried and, with a touch of experience, I wore no protection, which she had insisted on. When we finished, I just held her there. It was the most beautiful and memorable experience I'd had up to that point in my life.

Bianchi's full story is included in my book, *Talking with Serial Killers 2*, also published by John Blake.

Of the female serial murderesses I have interviewed, all of them – with the exception of Aileen Wuornos – refused to discuss their early years, but some of Aileen's history has been outlined earlier in this book. And, like Joanne Dennehy, all of them were bisexual, heavy drinkers and drug users.

Another conclusion reached by the Criminal Personality Research Project destroyed the common myth that all murderers come from broken, impoverished homes. The team's sample showed that this wasn't really true. Many of the murderers started life in a family that was not desperately poor, where the income was stable, as in the case of Joanne Dennehy. More than half lived initially in a family that appeared to be intact, where the mother and father lived together with a child or children. These were on the whole intelligent offspring, as were Joanne and her sister Maria. Though 7 of the 36 subjects had IQ scores below 90, most were in the normal range, and 11 had scores in the superior range – above 120.

Robert Ressler is also at pains to point out, somewhat ominously perhaps: 'Nonetheless, though the homes seemed to outward appearances to be normal, they were in fact dysfunctional.' Half of the subjects had mental illness in their immediate family; half had parents who had been involved in criminal activities. Nearly 70 per cent had a familial history of alcohol or drug abuse. *All the murderers, every single one of them, were subjected to serious emotional abuse during their childhoods. And all of them developed into what psychiatrists label as sexually dysfunctional adults, unable to sustain a mature consensual relationship with another adult, as witnessed in Dennehy's 12-year on-and-off relationship with John Treanor* [author's italics]. However, apart from Joanne's dysfunctional periods spent with Treanor, there is no evidence that there was anything dysfunctional in Dennehy's parents – quite the opposite seems true with the following proviso.

In her internationally acclaimed book, *The Drama of Being a Child*, world-respected psychoanalyst Alice Miller has written that parents need not necessarily be physically abusive to the child for the passively cruel parent, who imposes a rigid set of conflicting beliefs upon a child, can in so doing create a monster.

From birth to age six or seven, studies have shown that the most important adult figure in a child's life is the mother, and it is in this time period that the child learns what love is. Every child has a need to be noticed, understood, taken seriously and respected by his/her mother. As Dr Alice Miller says: 'In the first few weeks and months of its life, the child needs to have its mother at its disposal, must be able to use her, and to be mirrored by her.'

The research carried out by Robert Ressler and his colleagues found that the relationships between their subjects and their mothers were uniformly cool, distant, unloving, neglectful. There was little touching, emotional warmth or training in the ways in which normal human beings cherish one another and demonstrate their affection and interdependence. Ressler adds: 'These children were deprived of something more important than money – love,' and this sadly resonates with the way Joanne Dennehy later treated her own two daughters [names removed to protect their identities].

While there cannot be any suggestion that Kevin and Kathleen Dennehy did not love Joanne, *all* of Ressler's subjects ended up paying for such deprivation throughout the remainder of their lives and society suffered, too, because their crimes removed many people from the world and their assaultive behaviour left alive equally as many victims who remain permanently scarred, as Dennehy herself has done.

Writing in *The Week UK*, psychoanalyst Coline Covington says this about Joanne Dennehy: 'Our first love relationship and the most powerful person at the start of our lives is our mother. It is possible that Dennehy's violence was directed at her loving mother who had betrayed her in having another child with her husband.' She adds, 'This situation is often experienced as a painful rejection and betrayal by the older child, particularly so when that child has been idolized. This "special" treatment can be immensely narcissistically damaging as it places huge emotional expectations on the child and ignores the child's basic needs and limitations. The child becomes a god without limits and, because of this, without security.'

However, Maria Dennehy says that she and her sister were treated as equals by both parents and Joanne was doing just fine until she turned fourteen. She was, by all accounts, just a normal, well-balanced adolescent. This, of course, is Maria's perception; Joanna may have held an entirely different view and this could be why she turned out to be the only rotten apple in a small basket of otherwise good fruit.

The now-executed Connecticut sexual sadist and serial killer, Michael Bruce Ross, had three siblings. Their mother, Patricia, was a borderline schizophrenic who had spent time in the state mental hospital. She would twice abandon her husband and children only to return home and she never hid the fact that she was forced to get married by her parents because she was pregnant with Michael. From the outset he was an unwanted child. Nevertheless, the Rosses went on to have more children, who were regularly beaten and psychologically abused by both parents.

Michael remembered his mother's mood swings, which all the children feared, and I can confirm this to be true after speaking with one of Michael's siblings. They couldn't understand how she could laugh after making them ill by feeding them bad meat. Or why she would ruin her daughters' clothes with a box of dye. Patricia tried to trick young Michael into shooting his pet dog, after convincing him that it was suffering after a short illness. So, by all accounts, Patricia was simply 'The Mother from Hell'.

Yet, all four kids loved their mother, simply because she was their 'mom'. They grew to accept her mood swings, and learned to keep out of the way when she was angry. Like unwanted pets returning even meagre scraps of affection with devotion and loyalty, the three children had to love her just to survive. Yet, Michael turned out to be the only rotten apple for his sisters went on to live healthy and rewarding lives. But despite his horrendous childhood Ross continued to love his mother and father until the end of his days.

Psychoanalyst Coline Covington makes the suggestion in *The Week UK*, that following on from this dynamic, 'Dennehy may have been trying to kill two birds – or parents – with one stone,' adding, 'She was enacting revenge on her mother who betrayed her and destroying her rival, her father, so that in fantasy she could regain her position as ruler-child, able to control the world around her.' However, Joanne Dennehy has not blamed her mother for anything, but she has accused her father of sexually assaulting her around the ages of six and seven to anyone who would listen, to include Kevin Lee – as substantiated by Kevin Lee's business partner Paul Creed - and Gary Stretch.

'I was abused as a child' is therefore one of the many excuses amongst serial killers when they later attempt to mitigate their crimes, hoping for a more lenient sentence, a reduction in sentence or, in the US, to appeal against a death sentence. One look on the Internet at any Death Row inmate's appeal papers illustrates not only are these convicted felons inventive, their attorneys are even more so. Here you will find bad potty training, no potty training, fell off a playground swing, or tripped down some stairs and banged my head; bed-wetting until I was twelve; forced to wear my sister's dress at school and the other boys laughed at me, or the more inane: 'The Lord ordered me to kill. He came into my bedroom in a ray of light. I hid under my bed cos I was scared, so I did as I was told'. And if the appellate cannot come up with something different, the lawyers will. There is always Satan so we must not forget him either, and what follows is a case where a lawyer went completely over the top and earned himself millions of US dollars into the bargain.

If it were not for a sensational bestselling book and subsequent motion picture, *The Amityville Horror* (1979), along with several sequels and scores of books and thousands of newspaper and magazine articles, the village of Amityville, Long Island,

and the story of the slaughter at the DeFeo's home 'High Hopes' on Ocean Avenue in 1974 would have evoked hardly any interest. As it is, 'Amityville' – which suggests peace and contentment – has become identified with what was marketed as an outstanding true horror story but which, in the final analysis, is only a well-publicised, run-of-the-mill haunted house tale with overtones of mass murder.

You can order the first movie (forget the sequels) via Amazon, but did the evil spirit of a dead Indian chief truly haunt the house? Was the property really built on the site of an ancient Indian burial ground? Did green slime ooze from the walls and blood pour from the taps? Did a pink pig fly around in the garden and did flies plague the place during the murders of the entire family of six as they slept in their beds? Absolute hogwash!

With a plea bargain agreement in one hand, a movie and book contract in the other, DeFeo's attorney William Weber had started his case by arguing that Ronald DeFeo was insane and mitigating this haunted house yarn before a pinched-faced, no-nonsense Judge Thomas M. Stark. I interviewed Judge Stark at his home, at Riverhead, Long Island, and realised that he was the type of man who would lynch a Mormon if he knocked on his front door more than once, and whose great grandfather probably shot every Indian – friendly or not – that came within musket range. However, it then came to light that over a few bottles of wine during the evening after 'Butch' DeFeo was sentenced on 4 December 1974, Weber and the new owners of 'High Hopes', George and Kathleen Lutz, had had high hopes for themselves. They cooked up a story that would shock the world and so 'The Amityville Horror' was born.

Although Weber was severely disciplined for breaking his canons and ethics, he made a small fortune in the process, taking money from anyone he could exploit. He teamed up with Professor Hans Holzer, a ghost-hunter born in England. Together they wrote a book called *Murder in Amityville*, which subsequently became the 1982 motion picture, *Amityville II – The Possession*.

During the 1990s, as one of a 12-part series called 'The Serial Killers' we made an investigative TV documentary on the case, interviewing all of the principal characters, to include DeFeo and Mr Weber. At his Central Park apartment in New York City I met Hans Holzer. He was then a dear old chap, full of bonhomie, although very suspicious of the film crew around him. But I got the distinct impression if I had said I'd been visited by an angry Indian chief while researching my project, he would believe that too. Then, as I was about to leave, this tall, stooped man stopped me in my tracks and pointed to the grandfather clock, ticking away in his living room. 'Do you hear that?' he whispered, 'Tick, tick, tick, tick,' before adding, 'The clock always ticks. One day, just one day, when the clock strikes midnight the Indian chief will rise again at "High Hopes". Dead Indians do not like to be insulted.'

Make of that what you will. However my advice, based on not a little experience, is: never trust a word an ambulance-chasing lawyer says in mitigation for a client, and if you meet a professor in ghosts, run a mile! But I have to leave DeFeo on a lighter note.

During my investigation into the Amityville slayings I met Detective Dennis Rafferty and Lt. Robert Dunn at the Suffolk

County Police HQ, Yaphank, NY. These two hard-nosed cops had gained a confession from DeFeo, and they had a remarkable 'prosecution involving verbal confession rate' of 94 per cent – a rate that far exceeded the 55 to 73 per cent in almost any other jurisdiction in the US.

'Is it true,' I asked them, 'Did you really hit Ronnie with a telephone book?' 'Nah, we didn't hit him,' came the reply. 'We beat the living shit outa him with one, cos he was a fuckin' dumb prick! Chris, have you seen the size of the Long Island directory – it's a big mother, we can tell ya!'

They then got down to business and showed me the murder weapon, the victims' bloodstained clothing, cartridge cases and the scene-of-crime photos; also the pictures of DeFeo's siblings, Dawn (eighteen) – her head imploded on one side, Allison (thirteen) – face destroyed, Mark (twelve) and John (seven) – both shot in the back. The parents too were shot in the back. Then, having seen all of this, the cops took me out for a cold beer.

It goes without saying that Ronald DeFeo also claimed that he had been sexually and psychologically abused as a youngster. I have interviewed many murderers who have made such claims, which for the most part are untrue. While we are all too aware that during the last four decades child abuse has become exposed as a social blight, there is not a scintilla of evidence that so many serial killers were abused on the scale they assert. I include Joanne Dennehy in this summing up as well.

Christopher is an unassuming, bearded Englishman with a heart of gold and he gets results.

As an interrogator, he is as cold as ice.
Russell J. Kruger, Chief Investigator, Minneapolis PD

Harvey Louis Carignan, aka 'Harv' the Hammer, is responsible for the killings of 30 or more young girls and women. Presently, 'Harv' is incarcerated at the Minnesota Correctional Facility, Faribault. He told me in a letter dated 14 April 1993:

Even now, it seems my childhood was short, only a few days long. There is nothing about it I cling to and nothing to look fondly backwards toward. From where I sat then, and sit now, it was, and is, truly a pit of despair.

In later correspondence he claimed that he never knew his genetic father and his mother was too sickly to look after him. This much is true, but he then said that he was sexually abused by a babysitter and humiliated in front of his class, then by a female teacher while at reform school. There is not a shred of evidence to support any of it. According to the FBI, his Mandan, North Dakota school records show that a female teacher was constantly reprimanding him and he had abused younger boys. On one occasion he took his penis out in class and masturbated in front of everyone. Oh, and I almost forgot this. In mitigation for at least three of his murders he walked into court dressed in a white robe and Jesus-type sandals. He said that God had ordered him to kill women. Naturally the jury didn't buy it and he was given several life sentences. Prior to him appearing again on charges of kidnapping, rape and multiple murder, his attorney told Harvey: 'God didn't help you out last time so I doubt he'll change his mind this time around.'

When I interviewed 'The Hammer' face to face, he merely blamed all of his victims for getting themselves killed: 'I murdered them to stop them making false allegations of rape against me,' he said. What – *all* of them?

The now-deceased serial killer Arthur 'Art' John Shawcross, aka 'The Monster of the Rivers', told me during an interview on 19 September 1994 that his mother and an aunt had sexually abused him as a young child. There is no evidence of that either. But then again, he claimed it was the Army who taught him to kill but didn't tell how *not* to kill when he was discharged. He boasted that he was like an army-type Rambo who slaughtered 50 VC, including women and babies, then single-handedly burned their villages when his service record proves that he was a mere storeman, who worked 200 miles from where the action was. Then, like Carignan, God came up on Art's excuse list. 'It was The Lord who ordered me to kill prostitutes, who all had AIDS,' he told me which didn't entirely explain why he had unprotected sex with them before they were murdered, or why he had killed two very young schoolchildren.

In fact, I would be extremely hard pushed to find a single killer who I have studied in-depth, who didn't falsely blame their parents somewhere along the line for the way they turned out: John Wayne Gacy, Kenneth Alessio Bianchi or the now-executed English serial killer John Martin Scripps, who blamed his behaviour on his deceased father, who, in 1968, had committed suicide by placing his head in a gas oven. Also,

Theodore 'Ted' Robert Bundy, Henry Lee Lucas, Englishman John David Guise Cannan and Keith Hunter Jesperson. All of them have blamed someone else for being the root of their problems rather than taking the responsibility upon themselves.

Maybe a father was strict, maybe a drunk. So what if mother had another child? I could go on and on, but when I learned that Joanne Dennehy was blaming her father for sexually abusing her, or that she may have been narcissistically damaged by her mother because she gave birth to Maria, I took it all with a pinch of salt. Next, Dennehy will be telling us that it was her mum's fault that she dressed Kevin Lee up in a black, sequined dress. That it was her dad's fault that Lukasz Slaboszewski popped around for a bit of fun and games. And it was both their faults that John Chapman was butchered in his bed. Lord only knows who she will eventually blame for her attempting to stab to death Robin Bereza and John Rogers!

Dr Elliott Leyton has taught anthropology at the Queen's University of Belfast, the University of Toronto, the Hebrew University of Jerusalem and at Memorial University of Newfoundland, where, in 2001, he was professor of Anthropology. He has worked with police forces around the world, notably the FBI; is the author of 11-plus books and is past president of the Canadian Sociology and Anthropology Association. Elliott may also be considered something of a renegade and I can imagine him saying to me now in his usual, matter-of-fact way: 'Millions upon millions of children every year have problems in their earlier years and have younger siblings but they don't all turn into serial killers, do they? Show me some empirical evidence that just one single individual has graduated into serial homicide just because he, or she, has a younger brother, or sister, and I would be amazed.'

To help us understand the true possible causes of Joanne Dennehy's downward spiral into homicidal violence a little better, perhaps we might refer to a study entitled 'From Violent Juvenile Offenders to Dangerous Violent Offenders', published in *Sociology of Crime, Law and Deviance Volume 4*, 2003. The authors are G. Roger Jarjoura (School of Public and Environmental Affairs, Indiana-Purdue University, USA) and Ruth Triplett (Department of Sociology, Old Dominion University, USA). Their classification of predictors of violence very much echoes the research protocol used by Robert Ressler and his team of experts and lies at the root of these questions: Where did Joanne Dennehy come from? Who was she and where was she going?

The following list of predictors show that Dennehy's difficulties started to manifest themselves with family problems in her early teens.

Predictors of Future Serious Antisocial Behaviour
[Joanne Dennehy indented where applicable]

Predictors of Future Serious Antisocial behaviour are broken down into four levels: Community-level; Family-level; School-level and Individual-level.

Community-level
• High rates of poverty/unemployment

- High rates of mobility
- Access to firearms
- Media portrayals of violence

Family-level

- Poor supervision
- Poor discipline
- Family conflict
- Parental support of violence

School-level

- Antisocial behaviour during schooling (starting in her early teens)
- Poor school performance (starting in her early teens)

Individual-level

- Early onset of delinquent activities
- Association with delinquent peers
- Use of alcohol to the point of intoxication
- Use of illegal drugs/substances
- Brain damage
- Complications during parental care
- Delinquent attitudes
- Rebelliousness
- Pathological lying
- Physical and verbal abuse towards parents and teachers
- Propensity towards sensation seeking
- Low impulse control

Certainly there is no evidence of parental alcoholism or drug abuse in the Dennehy household. Nor is there evidence of physical or psychological abuse and up to the age of late thirteen, Joanne appeared to have been an emotionally healthy, well-educated, well-adjusted, well-spoken teenager, who excelled in her studies, enjoyed music and sports. Indeed, she was almost ready to be hotwired into a university, where she would study law.

It is true to say that most children who come from healthy or dysfunctional childhoods don't go on to murder people, or to commit violent antisocial acts, as Professor Elliott Leyton might agree. The reason for this is that when they start to cross the line, they are rescued by strong hands in the next phase of childhood, that of preadolescence. But all of Ressler's subjects were certainly not saved from drowning – instead they were pushed further under during this phase of their lives. From the ages of eight to twelve, all of the negative tendencies present in their early childhoods were exacerbated and reinforced. It is assumed that there are always points of intervention and Joanne's parents and her teachers frequently did try and intervene in an effort to reverse the offending behaviour of a girl who was becoming a potentially dangerous individual. However psychological counselling, which may have got to the heart of the problem and moved the girl away from the path towards deviant behaviour, was a missed opportunity.

But there is an important aspect to note here. Where there is some intervention at this stage, the child who has been 'rescued' may go on to disappoint the family, become a truant, not respond overtly; but as an adult may never offend, at least to the extent of committing abductions, sadistic acts and murders. However, a person on the track towards antisocial behaviour can be re-booted only so far; the chances, as evidenced by Dennehy's behaviour, are that he/she will become a largely dysfunctional adult. For Joanne to have been reshaped and to return completely to a normal life after she absconded from home and became hooked on drugs was unlikely so she is quite unique: this angelic little girl from a well-adjusted home developed into a psychopath, going on to graduate in serial homicide.

In his contribution to the 1986 anthology, *Unmasking the Psychopath*, leading psychologist Robert D. Hare proposed a 20-item checklist for the psychopathic personality, and how many of these can we tick with regard to Joanne Dennehy?

- Glibness/superficial charm
- Grandiose sense of self-worth
- Need for stimulation/proneness to boredom
- Pathological lying
- Cunning/manipulative
- Lack of remorse or guilt
- Shallow effect
- Callous/lack of empathy
- Parasitic lifestyle
- Poor behavioural controls
- Promiscuous sexual behaviour
- Early behavioural problems
- Lack of realistic, long-term plans
- Impulsivity
- Irresponsibility
- Failure to accept responsibility for own actions

- Many short-term marital relationships
- Juvenile delinquency
- Revocation of conditional release
- Criminal versatility.

The un-ticked boxes are correct because Dennehy has finally accepted responsibility for her actions, which rather contradicts her earlier claim that she was sexually and psychologically damaged by her father as a young child. It also blows out of the water any notion that it was her mother's fault because she gave birth to Maria, too. Besides, Maria Dennehy is at pains to point out that Joanne was a loving sister to her. They more or less got on like the proverbial house on fire. And although she never married Joanne did 'enjoy' scores of short-term relationships, so these are two grey areas for us.

Psychopathy and its causes have been a source of study and mystery for years. Even the name of the disorder has changed three times: Psychopath. Sociopath. Antisocial Personality. Some practitioners have simply written off the disorder as the embodiment of evil. A psychopath is often defined as a person who lacks the ordinary social feelings of conscience, regret and empathy. Often charming, witty and intelligent, these are superficial people whose shallow nature is only evident to those close to them. Often their charm leads friends and loved ones to expect great things, as did Dennehy's parents, and such people are frequently let down. Self-gratification is all-important for the psychopath. If Joanne wanted something, she set out to obtain that something with scant regard for the consequences. During her journey along 'Murder Road', she ran every red light stoplight, come what may.

A decade ago I met with Judge Stuart Namm, a former Suffolk County judge, Long Island, New York, while I was making the aforementioned TV documentary on Ronald 'Butch' DeFeo Jr, and I interviewed Mr DeFeo several times at the Green Haven Correctional Facility, Stormville, New York, New York State. Stuart and I went on to work together on many projects and he once said this to me:

> Society has rules which we are all obliged to live by otherwise there would be anarchy. The accused persons I deal with every week know of the consequences, and the punishment tariffs for living outside the law. They make their decisions, not me. Neither police, nor me are babysitters. These criminals simply do not care.

Although fully aware of society's rules, they mattered little to Joanne Dennehy and Gary Stretch, as did the effects of their actions inflicted on their victims and their intended victims, those closest to them and the people around them. Simply put, they did not give a damn.

Unfortunately, psychiatric treatment is of little help to psychopaths as they are often too manipulative to allow themselves to be helped. All psychopaths are diagnosed as having an antisocial personality disorder – a disorder that means they periodically violate the rights of others. This violation can manifest itself as stealing, lying and drug and alcohol abuse. As with all psychopaths, Joanne Dennehy has shown no remorse for her crimes. Under interrogation she remained calm and matter-of-fact, if she said anything at all. As DS Martin Jinks remembers: 'Despite being generally cooperative and attentive throughout my time with her, she simply answered "No comment" to all questions.' Therefore, Dennehy exhibits a genuine lack of feeling for what she has done. She gave no thought to her daughters' welfare or to the victims themselves or their families. Her only concern was, and is, for herself. For she *had* the ultimate power – control over life and death.

Two people, the late John Chapman and Moore's daughter described Joanne as a 'Man-Woman' who revelled in describing herself as 'gay', one who presented herself as being vulnerable to those she intended to exploit. Some observers say that she actually wanted to be a man, others that she wanted to be more powerful than any man.

All of the above-ticked boxes form the very kernel of a sociopath's psychopathology. They are the foundation stones upon which this disorder is built. However, while psychiatric treatment and the prison system cannot remove Dennehy's inherent psychopathy, it can and will exercise ultimate power over the offender – the carrot-and-stick behavioural modification techniques, as described previously, until the subject in question is powerless and comes to heel. And, it is appropriate to say, just like vicious dogs that snarl and bite they are either put down or collared tied to a very tight leash indeed.

The manner in which we were treated as children and how our parents treated each other, good or bad, we observed and responded to emotionally then stored away in our memories.

If we were neglected, teased or ridiculed and made to feel bad, insignificant or incompetent by our parents or other children, such feelings, hurts and fears not only define us, they are stored away and become part of us. These feelings become familiar, and to a child who has little with which to compare them, they seem 'normal'. Fortunately, good feelings, happy memories and impressions of love and warmth are also present. Accomplishments that made us feel proud, the knowledge of what we are best at, and all the little rewards we received contribute to our formation as well.

Children, like adults, define themselves according to how they were treated and then attempt to live up, or down, to the labels and expectations others apply. It is on these emotional building blocks that our entire self-concept is erected. We never outgrow our foundations, rather we build on them; and foundations do not disappear or go away, they tend to get buried. Nevertheless, our entire future rests on such foundations.

Children do not analyse or process their experiences in the manner an adult would process similar information. They do not have well-developed language skills and are more greatly ruled by the immediacy of emotion. Hence, a great deal of this early experience, including their initial self-concept and all attendant joys, triumphs, traumas and bad feelings, is internalised and stored away in the portion of the psyche that is not controlled by the language-dependent conscious mind, that is the unconscious. This is why it is so difficult to remember events, be they good or bad, that occurred when we were young.

With all of the above considered it seems that Joanne Dennehy enjoyed a perfect childhood, therefore, we must look elsewhere for clues as to the reasons why she eventually turned into a serial killer and this is why I say that drink and drugs played such a crucial part in her downfall.

27

THE CHILDREN

Mum's voice should never be far away.
Dr Alice Miller

At the outset of this book I mentioned that I always strive to find something good on any journey I take along 'Murder Road'. This, I penned:

During my frequent journeys along 'Murder Road' I am always desperately seeking some form of redeeming factor that might come from any of the cases I am investigating. I have found not a single one yet – not even a snippet, not a micro-speck of decency is anywhere to be found. *Love of Blood* has proven to be no exception.

But, as I draw towards the end of this particular journey, maybe with the benefit of hindsight while looking back over these pages, something has come to mind, a little something that may educate and encourage us all. Maybe, in some kind of lateral way, if you will, Joanne Christine Dennehy, at the expense of her children, and the way she lived her life while destroying the lives of others, can give us something back after all.

If the murders of Lukasz Slaboszewski, John Chapman and Kevin Lee and the attempted killings of Robin Bereza and John Rogers were cold-blooded acts of premeditated violence in extremis, one day, although the grief of the deceased's next-of-kin will take decades – if ever – to heal, and Bereza and Rogers slowly come to terms with the trauma they suffered at the evil hand of Dennehy – if ever – there are two other innocent victims in this tragic case whom we may be inclined to forget: Dennehy's two daughters. Perhaps a tragedy, indeed.

As a legacy to skunk, other types of toxic drug addiction and heavy alcohol ingestion, the last thing on any user's mind should be to have children until they have kicked their habits. If a parent has a drug problem then it affects the child at every stage of the pregnancy. Almost all drugs pass through the placenta to reach foetus, and even more problems may arise later on during the pregnancy, affecting how the placenta actually works. There is also a risk of the placenta coming away from the uterus, which can be life-threatening, and heavy drug use can reduce the amount of oxygen that reaches the baby, which may not grow as expected.

Taking cannabis or even worse, skunk, during pregnancy may make the baby more unsettled and more easily startled after birth. In the long term it can cause behavioural and learning problems. There is also a possibility of a low birth weight and a higher risk of cot death. Added to this was Dennehy's heavy consumption of alcohol, especially whisky.

All alcohol is a toxin and heavy drinkers often miscarry, have a premature birth or a stillborn. Their children can become panicky, anxious, suspicious or paranoid and later develop a psychotic illness. Despite this, Joanne Dennehy drank large amounts of whisky and doped herself insensible with skunk so her behaviour bordered on psychotic. A user of cocaine, with no decent place to live, she was forced to shoplift to put junk food into her mouth but she and John Treanor sailed on regardless, with Dennehy first falling pregnant when she was just sixteen.

All of this toxicity would travel into the foetus, but neither Treanor nor Dennehy thought twice about it. Had Treanor any intellect at all, hopefully learning from past experience, then thinking about taking this evil woman back time and again, getting her pregnant for a second time around should have been the last thing on his mind. But it wasn't – and it gets worse.

A newborn relies heavily on its mother during those initial precious years to develop physically and mentally into a healthy adult. Some believe depriving a young child of fundamental sensory input, especially tactile stimulation, is tantamount to condemning the newborn to a life of psychological pain and violence. Experiments on monkeys and other primates show that in the absence of maternal sensory stimulation the creatures become destructive and violent, eventually attempting a form of suicide by repeatedly banging their heads against the sides of their cages.

Although many children are not actually planned – which was certainly the case with Dennehy's children – and a significant number may not be wanted in the first place, most parents-to-be accept the fact that they are going to have a child and do not deliberately inflict the inconvenience of the child upon it. When that does occur, the child will grow up to be a scarred adult but again, most healthy people can live with those scars and not become emotionally disabled. However, children in this category are invariably at a high risk of confrontation with the criminal justice system at some point before they reach adulthood. Their socioeconomic status, the quality of their home life, the amount of physical or emotional abuse they receive, and the violence present in their environment will, in large measure, determine the extent of that risk.

The late US Senator Patrick Moynihan suggested a lack of sex education amongst young people (and contraception appears to have been the last thing on Dennehy and Treanor's minds), especially parents who have existed for long periods on welfare or below the poverty level, which Dennehy and Treanor certainly had, is creating an entire generation of children who will also become almost permanent wards of society.

We witness this every day – families in social housing, living on benefits with ten kids or more, who tax the liabilities of the social services system to provide for them and ultimately many will enter the criminal justice system, where they will create an additional burden. 'These are unwanted children,' as Senator Moynihan said, 'Children whose very existence serves only to feather the nests of their irresponsible parents at the cost of the state. Whose very existence is perceived by their parents as a form of retribution.' There is much empirical evidence, indeed we are overloaded with so much of this evidence it cannot be denied that as many of these children reach childbearing age, they, too, will spawn another generation who are unplanned and unwanted.

Indeed, cold-as-ice Dennehy despised her daughters and all that came with motherhood, to include the father. She hated weakness yet thrived on it and she exploited weakness. A user and an abuser, she had treated her teachers and parents with utter contempt and Treanor knew this. She treated her daughters likewise. To her, they were like aluminium takeaway meal containers – fit for purpose then thrown away – in Dennehy's case to gain social housing and child benefits to support her deviant lifestyle. According to one neighbour she frequently beat Treanor black and blue, too. Yet for his part, John Treanor still loved Joanne to bits, so much so that he took her back no less than three times to repeatedly subject himself, and his daughters, to the same physical and psychological abuse – it is as blunt and tragically banal as that.

Now, I hope, you are truly getting inside Joanne Dennehy's head and also the minds of the moronic fools who surrounded her.

I would never hurt a child.
Joanne Dennehy to various people

During infancy physical, social and emotional interaction are all crucially important in the neurological, social and emotional development of a child. In order to thrive and prosper, and to withstand emotional stress and other negative onslaughts, children need all the love and physical stroking they can get. In this regard youngsters are so needy that they are biologically driven by their limbic systems to seek out loving contact.

'Every child has a need to be noticed, understood, taken seriously and respected by its mother,' says Dr Alice Miller in her groundbreaking book, *The Drama of Being a Child.* Miller adds: 'and in the first few weeks and months of its life, the child needs to have its mother at its disposal, must be able to use her, and to be mirrored by her. Mum's voice should never be far away.'

Therefore, it would correct to say that during this crucial period neither of Dennehy's daughters enjoyed the benefits of having a mother. Yes, John Treanor was to some extent on hand, but like so many children born into dysfunctional families these two girls must have surely been emotionally deprived and damaged. If not, then it is a miracle, and although this author has no knowledge of their present circumstances at least they are in safe hands now.

Being the lawless, renegade, free-spirited person that she was, then why did Dennehy have a child in the first place when she didn't plan for one, or want one cluttering up her life and had no intention of caring for it? To be blunt, having sex with John Treanor certainly did not light her fire or her maternal fuse because she was sleeping with scores of men, and women, throughout the 12-year relationship. For either of them to have considered bringing a child into this world under these circumstances defies belief.

It is likely that being in love with Dennehy, as he claims he was, Treanor wanted Joanne and himself to be a real family, for he has said this much. However, now knowing Dennehy for who she truly is, one gets the impression that she may well have been thinking, 'Well, if you want a child so much, let's do it and you can take care of the consequences because I don't give a fuck. I will still come and go as I please. No one tells me what to do.'

That Treanor took her back time and again, then brought another child into the world with this woman from Hell, suggests that in order to survive emotionally, he was capable of 'splitting off' from his weaker self. To do this he used denial and repression, which broadly means when one is unhappy with a situation, one puts any conscious thought of it out of one's mind. This may have been his mental defence mechanism, a vital requirement for him to survive, even to save his children. And when it became all too much, he scooted back to his mother to recuperate and give himself breathing space before returning to Joanne, for him and his kids to be abused again.

But the fact that John loved Joanne so much allows us a look at another aspect of their relationship for some people are reluctant to break off relationships with abusive partners because they view the little love they occasionally receive (and the occasional sex, which seems, paradoxically, to go hand in hand with abusive interactions, at least during the initial stages) as a privilege that only this person can grant. In addition, many individuals perceive the 'love' they receive from their abusive, critical partner as a reward for the abuse recently suffered. When abuse is eventually followed by 'love' the love makes the abuse even more tolerable. In Dennehy's case, what 'love' she gave to John Treanor was, in fact, her way of controlling him.

Take, for example, the principles of reinforcement as they

are applied in gambling situations and overlay this onto the relationship between Dennehy and Treanor. You put your pound coin in the slot machine and you lose. So you do this again, and again you lose. This is followed by a third and fourth try at which point you are about to give up and move on to the next slot machine – losing is not fun. However, on the fifth try you win 5,000. You are now willing to put up with three or four losses because they pale in insignificance to the possible reward you might receive. Indeed, the tension and excitement of knowing a winner may be coming up drives you to continually put money in this machine until finally at some point you rationally realise that your losses now far exceed your winnings. Unless you are addicted to gambling and the pain of losing, you walk away.

The same thing happens in relationships and it most certainly applied to Joanne Dennehy and John Treanor. His anticipation of being loved, of being a 'proper family' as he put it, was a wonderful high that only Dennehy could provide and drove him to try, try again since he was positive, in his own mind, that he would win some day.

Unfortunately, Treanor was, like Joanne's parents, dealing with a narcissistic sociopath and therefore to her what logic he had appeared delusional. To her he was weak and she had power over him. She could push him to such an extent, knowing he would run back to his mother but come back to her on the promise of another win. And this happens frequently when, regrettably, sometimes the strength of the emotional attachment and the dependency win out, and the individual – in this case, John Treanor – is drawn back to the abusive relationship.

Because the individual is addicted and has occasionally received a 'loving' reward, they do not walk away.

This confused package of mental and financial instability spilled into the girls' home on a daily basis. The screaming, and the fighting and the loud music; curious strange faces going in and out of the place; 'guests' who wanted sex with their mum, who treated the children as a nuisance. And the consequences? Without doubt the parents' joint paranoia was soon rubbing off on their daughters.

Children can have parents who burn them with cigarettes and break their bones but they will still cling to those parents in search of love. Their parents are their world, the *only* world they have. Children need love and are biologically predisposed to seek association and physical contact, most especially with the mother, and once these bonds have been established they are extremely difficult to break. So intense is the need for stimulation that sometimes a bad parent is better than none at all. If mothering and the stimulation of physical contact are not provided regularly, this may even result in the child's death.

> We [John and I] *don't allow anyone into our house when our girls are here.*
> Mrs Treanor, to the author, July 2014

However, if contact and interaction with the mother is restricted during the early phases of infant development, through their teens, the ability to interact successfully with others at a later stage of life may be retarded. In other words, if a child is not firmly attached to its mother figure and has been neglected by her early in life, his or her ability to form loving attachments increasingly narrows and then disappears, possibly forever. The child becomes attached to no one, and his or her ability to form loving attachments later in life will be abnormal if drastic countermeasures, such as counseling, are not taken.

In all of this, apart from murdering three people and attempting to kill two more, Joanne Dennehy has much to answer for. However, having given John Treanor a hard time in this book, one should give him some credit. In the absence of mothering by Dennehy, Treanor managed to compensate because he clung onto his daughters. After all is said and done he is still their dad.

Lee Wuornos's baby son was taken away from her by Social Services straight after the birth. He has grown up to become a strapping fellow, full of promise, with a professional career in front of him. Yet, despite his mother's stigmatic reputation, he still uses her surname. He knows all about his mom and he misses her greatly.

Blood is thicker than water, and in his case I would totally agree with that. John Treanor, and his wife, might just achieve what Joanne Dennehy could not do – give the two girls, as her parents did for Joanne, a reasonable start in life and ensure their dreams really do come true.

Now that would be a truly wonderful thing.

28

SUMMARY

I am going to marry a serial killer
JAMES BUDD, *THE SUN*, 7 SEPTEMBER 2014

We are almost at the end of our journey into the mind of sadomasochistic serial killer Joanne Christine Dennehy but before we finally arrive at our destination perhaps now is the time to reflect on our trip thus far along this particular 'Murder Road'.

We have established that female serial killers working alone are very rare individuals. In the UK there have been less than a handful of such women since Victorian times, the last being Beverley Allitt. Two of these women used toxic substances to kill by stealth, another used a ligature to strangle babies.

In the US female serial killers acting alone without assistance are also few and far between. However, aside from Aileen 'Lee' Wuornos – who used a firearm – they have all poisoned their victims for various motives in one form or another. Therefore, unless I am proven wrong, Joanne Dennehy would have become the first female serial killer in UK and US criminal history to stab three men to death without an accomplice at hand. And remember the statement made by prison inmate Anna Chambers, who said: 'She [Dennehy] didn't like it when people said she killed three people. She liked to boast she had killed five and did not like it when people said she had failed.'

However, examples of females working with men to commit serial homicide are all too frequent occurrences around the world. Criminal history is littered with them. Female serial murderesses usually have an accomplice, frequently a male partner in crime – Ian Brady and Myra Hindley, Frederick and Rosemary West, for example – although female serial killing couples are not unknown, as we have seen with Cathy Wood and Gwendoline Graham in the United States.

This draws me to the inevitable conclusion that although Joanne wants to take the credit for becoming one of the first female serial murderers working as a single entity in UK history, she most certainly is not. And the police have discredited the claim, made by Dennehy, that she has killed more than three men. Therefore, in serial homicide terms as far as her self-proclaimed exclusivity is concerned we can take this with a pinch of salt for, as I have previously suggested in this book, might Dennehy not have become a serial killer without perhaps Gary Stretch aiding and abetting her? In the eyes of the law this might have made him an accomplice in two homicides and, therefore, was he technically as guilty as she?

With what sparse information available to us concerning Joanne's formative years up to early adolescence we can only rely on her sister's few words published in the national press to provide some sort of picture. Throughout Mr and Mrs Dennehy have remained resolutely silent. Obviously protective of her parents, Maria allows us a glimpse of Joanne enjoying a happy childhood, sitting in a back garden tree singing songs to Maria – a chocolate-box formative years scenario, and probably true. But then Joanne flipped. Why? Prior to this event there is nothing in Joanne's nor indeed the Dennehy family's history that could be construed as indicators or predictors red-flagging any tendency towards antisocial behaviour just over the horizon. Here, it appears, was a perfectly normal young girl who, like a train running smoothly along its tracks, suddenly derails with no warning.

In 1996, aged fourteen, Joanne Dennehy ran off with a fairground worker who was four years her senior, and it was at this point in her life that she was introduced to sex, skunk and hard liquor. In her *Daily Mail* article of 15 February 2014 Maria admits, 'Our parents were very protective. Perhaps they were a little too strict,' and no doubt when Joanne was eventually brought home there was hell to pay. Skunk, as we now know, has been linked to the causation of mental illness and there can be no doubt that having used it frequently along with alcohol, this may have seriously affected Joanne's still-developing brain and impacted on her problem-solving skills for the drugs and drink started to control her. The more she was reprimanded, the more she rebelled against her teachers' authority and she also developed a spiteful, vicious streak towards her parents. This was the perfect storm and it carried on until finally she walked out of the parental home to be with John Treanor.

At this point in her life there could be no going back. Not

only was she running away from home, her family, schooling and a promising career in law, she was also fleeing from her responsibilities and from herself. From that day on, every time she held up a mirror she would see the once respectable teenager much loved by her family, who had thrown everything away. This, I believe, was the beginning of the terrible rage that would continually boil inside her, eventually culminating in brutal serial homicide. Subconsciously she hated herself for what she had become and she would exact her revenge, not only through self-harming but by hurting society as a whole.

Quite frankly, in absconding with Joanne Dennehy, twenty-one-year-old John Treanor really should have known better but he had no job, no money nor commonsense. He had known that she had run away from home several times before but there he was, effectively abducting an underage girl and moving her into a property owned by a drug dealer and infested with addicts, a place where cheap booze and drugs were readily available. Had he had possessed any moral backbone he would have contacted the Dennehys and explained that their daughter was in dire straits, but he didn't. Instead he shoplifted with her to put food in their mouths and to pay the rent. He then got her pregnant, with all the toxic substances she introduced into her body affecting the foetus throughout the term.

Knowing Joanne Dennehy as we now do, one gets the impression that having a baby would have been the last thing on her mind. Self-centered and selfish, she valued her freedom too much.

While Treanor insists that he loved Joanne very much, in no way did she reciprocate his feelings. Indeed, secretly she despised him for being so weak. He became her first lapdog and she could do what she liked, when she liked and come and go as she pleased. She could, and did, treat him like dirt – sleeping with other men, and women, sometimes while he was present without fear of any real protest. Then, when their first daughter was born, she withdrew all maternal love and subjected the child to a home where bedlam reigned supreme. There were days, even weeks, when she would run off with someone else and then when it suited her, she would return to Treanor. When things got completely out-of-hand he would run back to his mother with the child in tow, only for Dennehy to whistle and back he would go again.

Aged twenty-two, Dennehy now had the bit firmly between her teeth. At this point in her life she was in trouble with the police for assault and had also been sectioned under the Mental Health Act. She was diagnosed as having a psychotic disorder, being 'emotionally unstable and prone to unpredictable behavioural explosions'. All predictors pointing towards further antisocial behaviour and the beginnings of fully emerged psychopathy.

Yet, armed with all of this knowledge including the fact that the highly-manipulative Dennehy went back to her parents as part of her parole conditions and had messed that up by destroying their new conservatory, Treanor took her back and got her pregnant a second time around, knowing, or at least he should have known, that she'd treat their next child with the same contempt as she did the first, and himself likewise. It was only when she plunged a dagger into the floor of their home and screamed, 'I wish I could fuckin' kill someone!' that the penny finally dropped and he left for good. She was now twenty-seven and he was thirty-three.

Details of the period between 2009 when Treanor finally dumped Dennehy to when she resurfaced with Gary Stretch in early 2013 are rare. We know that she served several prison sentences, at least one of them for assault occasioning actual bodily harm, but considering what would soon follow these amounted to 'minor crimes', as Mr Justice Spencer and the police have pointed out. We don't know when or where she met Gary Stretch in the town of March, Cambridgeshire, but they were both out on parole at the time. It is thought they met either in 2010 or 2011, and they kept in touch until late 2012 or early 2013, when they joined forces and came to Peterborough, seeking lodgings through Quicklet.

What we do know as fact is that Stretch fell in love easily. Physically a car wreck, he had the mental age of a teenager – and not a bright one at that. It would also be fair to say owing to the size of his body combined with the small size of his brain and a mouth full of rotten teeth, women were not queuing up to throw themselves at his feet. Therefore, any attention Dennehy gave him was akin to rewarding a dog with a pat on the head and giving it a bone. Little wonder the much younger, quite pretty and well-spoken Joanne was able to manipulate him so easily because he wanted, indeed he had to believe, every single word she said to stay within her orbit.

Joanne told him that her parents had kicked her out of the family home when she was just fourteen years old. She said her father had sexually abused her when she was just a kid and explained that John Treanor had taken her daughters away from her. As Julie Gibbons has said, this would have resonated with her with Stretch. He would have believed every single word that passed her lips.

Like Treanor, Stretch was besotted with the manipulative sociopath. He would do anything she asked of him. Stretch effectively became her minder on the promise of a future consensual sexual relationship with Joanne, all the while knowing this would never happen. To her, he was just another tool in her box and not a sharp one at that.

There came a time – and again we may never know precisely when – that Kevin Lee and Joanne Dennehy hit it off sexually, also becoming partners in dodgy eviction deals. Both arrangements went hand in hand, it seems to me, but Joanne had already tuned into Lee's roaming eye from the outset. Here was a married man of property, with money in the bank. Someone she could exploit and use for her own ends. If she played him right, he would become, like Treanor and Stretch, yet another nodding dog. Dennehy was sure about it, and she was certainly correct for she had sensed that Lee was ego-driven from the day she first walked into his office.

To begin with, Lee had gone against the wishes of his office manager, Paul Creed, in giving Dennehy and Stretch lodgings. Lee actually believed Joanne when she told him that she had served a considerable prison term for murdering her father because he had abused her as a young child. In overruling Creed, Lee was keen to prove his machismo; effectively, if he gave Dennehy accommodation then she would be required to return the favour. She did this in spades to eventually kill him.

I say that Lee was ego-driven because behind his wife's back he had bragged to several of his mates that he had a bit on the side; that she was kinky and every man's dream when it came to sex, to the degree that he boasted that he would wear one of Joanne's dresses because it turned them on so much. What he didn't know, because his ego forbade it, was that the very act of sex was of no consequence to her at all. It was just something she needed to do to achieve whatever ends she needed. In fact sex left her stone cold.

Psychopaths/sociopaths are control freaks. Subtle and cunning, their true nature is concealed beneath a mask of normalcy. I suggest that Joanne wanted the now-besotted Kevin Lee completely under her thumb, with the added bonus that with Stretch she could fulfill her terrible goal of killing someone, as she had told John Treanor while in a drunken rage. She has admitted this much to psychiatrist Dr Farnham; she enjoyed doing the murder. With the brutal stabbing of Lukasz Slaboszewski she realised this nightmarish dream and now she had taken the first step towards becoming a serial killer. Then, to finally have Kevin Lee under her complete control, the ever-confident psychopath that she now was knew that he would do anything to help her cover up the murder.

For his part Gary Stretch was himself no stranger to murder. He had witnessed the killing of thirty-three-year-old prisoner Brian Haynes several years earlier in Peterborough Prison, and certainly I do not think that Dennehy could have murdered Lukasz Slaboszewski and Kevin Lee then disposed of the bodies without, perhaps, the cooperation of Stretch acting as her accomplice when the murders were committed. He was, indeed, the enabler and was present when she attempted stabbing to death the two Herefordshire men. I would suggest that his modus operandi was, therefore, established.

But I would also hazard a guess that Lee didn't owe Dennehy a penny, and this submission of mine is supported by the fact that had he been sexually harassing her, she must have been a willing party to his attentions in this regard. Lee sent her an Easter card, bought her two CDs and about an hour before his untimely death boasted to his pal, David Church, that he was going to pop round to 11 Rolleston Garth, put on one of her dresses and have kinky sex with her.

To Stretch, the words from our manipulative Dennehy telling him: 'Kevin owes me money and he is sexually harassing me,' would have struck a nerve. He would have recalled Joanne's tale that her father had sexually molested her as a youngster. Being the doting, though totally irresponsible father to their children, as Julie Gibbons has claimed, Kevin Lee – much in the way that Treanor allegedly previously used and abused her – was now pestering *his* Joanne. To this simple-minded, love struck man, these were all complete truths despite the fact that they were lies. To keep Dennehy, Stretch had to believe in her; he had to comply.

Stretch's *modus operandi* is now well established. This is evidenced by the attempted murders of Robin Bereza and John Rogers, for not only did he convey Dennehy in a motor vehicle knowing she had another murder in mind, when the attack on Bereza was thwarted by the arrival of another car he drove her to another place where he knew dog walkers could be found. This amounted to conspiracy to murder for which he was given two concurrent life sentences amounting to 19 years.

SUMMARY

Just as with Slaboszewski, Dennehy would again use the irresistible bait of kinky sex to get Kevin Lee through the front door. Could Stretch have been waiting, hiding in another room, while Lee slipped on the black sequined dress? Then Joanne produced the lock knife and started the killing. The non-passive Lee had put up a fierce struggle. Could Stretch have restrained him until the man died? Sitting outside in the green Vauxhall Astra was Leslie Layton. Dennehy and Stretch quickly rolled the corpse into Moore's tarpaulin and the trio humped the grim bundle into the rear of Lee's car, after which they drove off in the two vehicles to dispose of their latest victim.

As for John Chapman, he was passive because he had been in a deep, drunken sleep. It was a killing easily accomplished by the cowardly Dennehy acting alone, but she still needed Stretch and Layton to get rid of the body.

While writing this book I sent a second letter to Gary Stretch. In it I asked if he would confirm, or deny, being present when Kevin Lee was killed. I did not receive a reply.

But why, in Hereford, was Dennehy suddenly so insistent about targeting men out walking their dogs? I think that we can rule out her ridiculous explanation of simply wanting a dog as a pet because she could have picked one up anywhere. Therefore, what was so special for her about a man who had a dog with him, and what was the link between man and dog? She claims to love dogs with a passion, yet there she was, trying to steal one such creature from the very person who fed and cared for it – its master. What follows is, of course, open to debate, but looking deep inside Dennehy's mind I see her first meeting with John Treanor, who was out walking his Alsatian resonating here. We know how quickly she grew to despise this man because of the shocking way she treated him over a period of 12 years. So, perhaps the act of trying to murder a man walking his dog was, to her dysfunctional mind, a way of trying to kill off Treanor, too?

During my research for this book I came across several people who observed that Joanne Dennehy must have been an extremely angry person but this is an understatement although it did strike a chord, as it will, no doubt, to the reader. In fact Joanne hated herself for what she had become and she projected this hatred onto others as punishment in the same way as she had previously stuck pins into herself and slashed her abdomen with a razor blade, later to project this self-harming onto the stabbing and slashing of others. And it is interesting to note how this rage manifested itself and developed with each killing and the subsequent attacks. It has been argued that she enjoyed the killing for the sake of it. Maybe she did, maybe not, but it is still worthy of some consideration.

The murder of Lukasz Slaboszewski consisted of a single stab to the heart. It was Dennehy's way of fulfilling the statement she made to John Treanor – that she wanted to, 'Fuckin' kill someone.' She murdered Lukasz just to see if she could do it, and she says that she enjoyed it. 'After that it became kind of more-ish,' she later told Dr Farnham. However, looking back at this first murder, it is clear that it brought her no long-term satisfaction at all. Instead it proved a short-lived catharsis for the hatred boiling within her was not sated with this first bloodletting, far from it.

The murder of John Chapman, who was fast asleep, allowed

full rein to her fury. She stabbed the helpless man once in the neck, severing the carotid artery, and then plunged the knife into him five more times with such force that one blow went straight through his breastbone. However, this still did not satisfy her because she had fallen short of causing him to 'suffer'. The next time around she would really come down hard and Kevin Lee bore the brunt of it, for her rage was still there and it refused to go away.

Lee was almost a by-product of Dennehy's desire to punish others for what she herself had become. And I think that it would not be unreasonable to suggest that he literally took it upon himself to walk into Joanne's killing ground. The murders of Slaboszewski and Chapman had failed to assuage her inner turmoil in any way. Indeed Slaboszewski had gone down in a heartbeat, while Chapman put up no fight at all. Dennehy now knew that she could kill without a second thought or a moment's loss of sleep (and maybe, if Stretch's correspondence to his former partner is to be believed, with Stretch on hand to back her up), with Kevin Lee she could launch an almost 'Jack-the-Ripper' style attack on a man, who, to her mind, was weak, unfaithful to his wife and due whatever came his way.

I use the term 'by-product' somewhat clinically and without emotion, for if one studies serial killers at any length, one must leave one's own revulsion for their dreadful deeds to one side. I have interviewed face to face so many serial killers and mass murderers – men and women – who have sat an arm's length away from me and who have gleefully boasted, and tried to control and manipulate me with accounts of their awful killings, just to get a response that suits their warped psychopathology.

That's what they do, you see – they manipulate because that is their sociopathic calling. And when it suits me I will sympathise, agree with them; allow them to think they control me because I am now their best friend. I will convince them that they are more intelligent than I will ever be, stroke them like a cat. It is the oldest trick in any interrogator's book, but the subject's over-inflated ego will not permit him, or her, to see it coming.

I will offer up any bait that I think my subject will like, and then, when I have them on my hook, like any good fisherman I'll give the line a strong tug, with a 'So what?' When this happens, they finally realise that they have been conned. Then and only then does the true nature of the beast reveal itself.

With all of this in mind, regarding Kevin Lee I will also use the clinical description of 'sell-by-date', for in the general scheme of things he had served his purpose and was no longer required by Joanne Dennehy. Indeed, considering everything, he was now a liability to them.

Serial killers use, and abuse, victims for their own selfish ends. When they have finished with their prey, they dump the bodies like so much trash in much the same way as one would handle a late-night takeaway kebab. They'll consume the meal and then toss the carton away. Remorse is never on any psychopath's menu, they are as cold-blooded as that.

And kill Kevin Lee she certainly did. Dennehy vented on him all the frustrations of not having been satisfied with her two previous murders, going into overkill mode. A single stab to the man's heart could never be good enough, she stabbed him five times in the chest. Post-mortem examination of the body showed defensive wounds, indicating that he had fought for his life, during which time she enjoyed watching him 'suffer' – so much so that she writes to a penfriend, if we are to believe her – that she filmed the murder being committed, which again may suggest that Stretch was present, because if she was doing the killing, who held the camera? Nonetheless, police could find no evidence of this so-called claim.

So, was the murder of Kevin Lee enough to exorcise the demon raging within Joanne Dennehy? No, it was not, for she went even further by displaying, in a ditch, his black sequined-dressed body, buttocks exposed, with an object inserted into his rectum for all to see in the ultimate humiliation. This was Dennehy sticking two fingers up to society and, in doing so, she had rewarded Kevin with an unequivocal, 'Don't fuck with me' message; one to be passed on to Cristina Lee about the true, underlying nature of her cheating husband.

But did this murder satisfy Joanne Dennehy. Not at all for she went on to Hereford, where her first attack on Robin Bereza failed because by the Grace of God, she inflicted just two wounds although any one of them could have proved lethal. When Stretch then pointed out John Rogers, she went berserk in broad daylight. Thirty stabs in all – deep wounds to his chest, abdomen and back. Two collapsed lungs. A perforated and exposed bowel, seven ribs fractured; defensive injuries to his hands and arms, and a grievous psychological legacy from which he will never completely recover. Dennehy was effectively butchering the man in the street and had she had achieved this aim, she would have made Jack the Ripper appear a lightweight – that's how evil Joanne Christine Dennehy really is.

Our road map has been lacking in precise detail simply because at this present time there are no real details to include. Law enforcement from two jurisdictions and the judiciary agree with this.

Earlier in this book we went through the accumulative effect of forensic intelligence gathering: CCTV, ANPR and telephonic data. Then there were the DNA, blood groupings, fingerprints and witness statements – all of which, when put together, gave the police a watertight case against Dennehy, Stretch, Layton and Moore. However, let's go one step further and use their own words: what they have written down in ink, what they have told each other and anyone else to include the police and me, for these utterances have much the same value as the telephonic data that ensnared them. Their written words are not 'circumstantial evidence', they are physical evidence because they exist as a matter of record and cannot be deleted.

And I will leave you with this final thought. If ever you are invited into a prison and asked to pay to watch a version of *Sister Act*, remember that amongst the cast could be the drug smugglers, peddlers, robbers and killers who are intent on ruining so many peoples' lives.

DCI Martin Brunning did not reveal his views about the *Sister Act* performance when I told him about it. I would not have expected him to do so, but I most certainly can:

It's an insult to all those who have suffered at the hands of these evil women. It is a damned disgrace, but James Budd, a love struck builder from Worthing, West Sussex, thinks otherwise –

he is engaged to marry Joanne Dennehy, so you might wish to reach for the valium right now!

In a Sunday, 7 September 2014 *Sun* article written by Rob Pattinson and Shaun Wooller, halfwit Budd boasts that he and Dennehy fell for each other through letters about dogs. However, she has warned him: 'You are declaring yourself to be the soulmate of a notorious serial killing psychopath. Lol. Not exactly the girl next door.'

But heavily tattooed Budd, who has never met or spoken to Dennehy, told the *Sun* that he is not afraid of her and loves her. 'We all need someone we can lean on,' he said.

Smitten 48-year-old Budd, who has a 16-year-old daughter, charmed Dennehy with pictures of his Staffordshire bull terrier in April 2014. 'My best crony is my dog, a goofy Staffy, rescue dog,' he explained in a letter, adding, 'who thinks what's cave is hers including my bed (*sic*).'

Lovestruck Dennehy replied with fond tales of her German shepherd called 'Hitler' – a dog she has never owned. James asked her for her hand when the relationship became serious in July. She wrote, 'I would marry you in a heartbeat,' and suggested: 'You dress as Elvis and I'll wear the canary suit. I'll walk down the aisle to Jailhouse Rock.' Indeed, she is already signing her letters 'Joanne Budd-Dennehy'.

According to Mr Budd, who was convicted of GBH at Guildford Crown Court in 1990 and sentenced to a reduced term after he apologised to his victim, they plan to apply to the Prison Service for permission to wed behind bars at HMP Bronzefield in 2015. He says: 'We've both been through a lot. We understand each other.' For her part, Dennehy has told him in her love letters that she will be a 'nagging wife.' And, she is obviously worried about his health, for she says: 'You need a lot of greens. If we are working on the timescale of 30 years, we need you in tip-top health,' adding, 'you are the one man who has breathed life into me.'

Sodexo Justice Services, which manages HMP Bronzefield for the Ministry of Justice, told the *Sun* that they do not comment on individual prisoners, but I can assure fiancBudd one small thing. This ex-con will never be allowed anywhere near the prison, let alone marry Dennehy within the prison's walls.